James Sterling

NEWMAN AND THE MODERN WORLD

Christopher Hollis

NEWMAN
AND THE
MODERN WORLD

DOUBLEDAY & COMPANY, INC.

GARDEN CITY, NEW YORK

1968

Library of Congress Catalog Card Number 67-11182
© Christopher Hollis 1967
All Rights Reserved
Printed in the United States of America
First Edition in the United States of America

Contents

Introduction

WHATEVER DISPUTES there may have been over the last century about Newman's orthodoxy or his standing as a Catholic teacher, they have been, we can say, now finally resolved. Few, if any, influences from the past have been more potent over the deliberations of the Second Vatican Council than his and there is the testimony of Pope Paul VI himself to the power of Newman's influence. In the ceremony of the beatification of Blessed Dominic Barberi on October 27, 1963, the Pope linked together Blessed Dominic and Newman as 'the two saintly figures'.[1] There were indeed other men of the nineteenth century who prepared in their various fashions the way for the modern developments. There is in itself no purpose to be served in appointing a table of precedence among them, but their names are not alive today to the extent that Newman's name is alive and, if we are tempted to select the Catholic of the nineteenth century who more than any other prepared the way for the Church of the twentieth century, we have at any rate, it seems, the Pope's authority for choosing Newman.

The Times in a review of Miss Meriol Trevor's Life of Newman[2] wrote a little oddly that 'his was not a lasting force like Fox or Wesley.' It seems a peculiarly insular judgement, for it is a curiosity of Newman that, though he himself was in his personal habits the most home-bound and narrowly English of men, his posthumous influence has been world-wide. Indeed it has sometimes appeared that he has been more widely honoured in other countries than in his own. The influence of Fox and Wesley has been geographically far more narrow. But beyond that, the influence of Wesley has been of a different kind from that of Newman. Wesley became—in spite, it is true, of himself —the founder of a denomination, as did Fox, and the founder of a denomination gives, as it were, posterity a vested interest in his name. There are many who call themselves Wesleyans today whose interest does not especially lie in those doctrines of salvation which Wesley was concerned to preach. It would be hard to say of Wesley, as of any other founder of a movement or of a denomination which has endured, to what extent the movement today owes its teaching to its founder

[1] Herder Correspondenz, January 1964, etc.
[2] The Pillar of the Cloud. Light in Winter. Macmillan.

7

and to what extent his followers use his name as a title while the movement goes on its way of its own momentum. There are Marxists today, but who would say how far the original teaching of Marx was responsible for what they were saying or doing? There are Christians. Are the lives of all of them entirely dominated by the teaching of Christ? Newman is of a different kind. There are no Newmanians in the sense that there are Wesleyans or Marxists. He did not make himself the founder of a formal movement. Therefore any influence that he exercises over the modern world he exercises as a direct result of his own teaching and for no other reason.

There have been plenty of biographies of Newman, and, in particular since the appearance of Miss Meriol Trevor's work, there is certainly no call for another. Father Dessain's collection of Newman's letters keeps us in perpetual debt to him. No attempt is made in this book to estimate in any detail those personal influences within and outside his family that played so large a part in Newman's life, nor to delve into the quarrels by which, during at least two periods of his life, he was so sadly beset. Such matters, fascinating in themselves and essential for a biography, will only be referred to in passing and in so far as they are necessary to throw light on the inquiry with which this book is concerned. Nor is this a scholar's re-estimate of the value of Newman's writings. That task too has been frequently attempted and, as time goes on, is attempted with increasing frequency, alike in England and in other countries. All the great Continental scholars—Bouyer, Congar, Fransen, Kung—have confessed their debt to Newman. This book is solely concerned with trying to discover what was the quality in Newman's teaching that makes it so especially pertinent to the modern world and is likely to make it increasingly pertinent to the world of the coming generation. Mr. Coulson, Mr. Alchin and Miss Trevor in *A Portrait Restored*[1] have, it may be said, in a measure already performed this task, and indeed my debt to that excellent work is self-evident and most freely acknowledged. Yet it is not merely a question of restoring a portrait. It is to some extent rather a matter of recognising that a situation has come into existence which Newman foresaw and which few others of his day were able to foresee.

[1] Sheed and Ward, Stagbook Series.

I

The Secularised Church

THE RELIGIOUS WORLD of today is a very different place from the world of a century and a quarter ago. Then it was generally held desirable, whether in Catholic or Protestant countries, that there should be an intimate alliance of Church and State. The business of the Established Church was to defend the established social order. Demands for political reform or for a redistribution of property fell unhesitatingly under ecclesiastical condemnation. As vigorous was the condemnation of any intellectual movement which challenged accepted methods of argument or laid claim to new discoveries. With the growth of education among the laity clergymen could no longer command the monopoly of secular jobs that they were able to command in the Middle Ages but they still kept to themselves the monopoly of educational posts. They claimed and exercised the weapon of repression against all dangerous thoughts. All the denominations—each in its various ways—laid claim to a total possession of revealed truth, which had, as they alleged, been entrusted to them once and for all, to which nothing could be added and from which nothing could be subtracted.

In a century and a quarter all has changed, and few have had more to do with the change than Newman. Today in most countries, even in Europe, the notion of the State Church has vanished. Even where it survives it is no longer considered of supreme importance. In such a country as England membership of the Church of England no longer carries with it any of the privileges which it carried when Newman was a young man. In Catholic countries the faithful, far from being encouraged to claim privileges for themselves and their Church, have specifically been commanded by the Second Vatican Council to respect the religious liberty of all men. Outside Europe there have grown up into power new countries to whom the separation of Church and State is a cardinal principle of policy. In the intellectual sphere the Churches no longer see any sense in fighting a losing battle against all new thought. They have recognised that on many points modern man does not find the traditional arguments for religion cogent, have seen the folly of merely repeating that propositions are proved when those who hear them are not able to accept them and are seeking in freedom to discover new methods by which to state and demonstrate their faith.

As John XXIII put it, in calling for the *aggiornamento*, 'The deposit of faith itself, that is to say the truths contained in our ancient doctrine, is one thing, but the form in which those truths are announced is another.' The Church which in the early years of the last century saw in democracy an almost inevitable ally of atheism now recognises it through the mouths of Pius XII and John XXIII as the best and most natural form of government. It is now held that not only is the Christian religion the religion that Christ founded but it is also the religion which the Holy Spirit guides and its Church, far from being automatically suspicious of all novelty, claims that its doctrine must inevitably develop as new needs call for new definitions. In education the clergy have wholly lost their monopoly in Protestant countries. Clerical headmasters and clerical Heads of Colleges are today almost unknown, and even among Catholics an increasing number of responsible posts are being given to laymen. The progress over the years indeed has by no means been a steady one. As always happens when old habits are changed there are suspicious conservatives who grumble impartially against all novelty and hot-headed enthusiasts who in their anxiety for change threaten to destroy the very fabric of things. Newman in his career was to have plenty of difficulties from men of the first sort; and in the early years of this century the so-called Modernist movement was both to produce iconoclasts, who in the name of progress would have destroyed all traditional religion, and heavy-handed repression of them which would have destroyed all progress and freedom. Yet in the end we can say that with Pope John XXIII's call for *aggiornamento* and with the summoning of the Vatican Council to implement his policy the Catholic Church was finally committed to the policy of change, and of these changes, to which it has committed itself, every one, as Cardinal Gracias bore witness, found among its first advocates Cardinal Newman, the apostle of development and of the flight from clericalism.

Newman did not, it is true, set out on the pilgrimage of his life in any way foreseeing all the causes to which he would be committed.

Just as all his writings were by his own confession pieces of occasion, so it was largely through circumstances that he came to advocate much that he did advocate. It was very largely because, long before he had come to consider the claims of the Catholic Church, he had thought out for himself his beliefs from first principles that he was very well aware of the sceptical alternative; because he had first learnt to think as a Protestant and an Evangelical, that he was shocked by the complacent self-sufficiency of the Roman clerical stereotyped text-books of the 1840's; and because he understood the different points of view from personal experience, that he was able to establish himself as the first of ecumenists. He came to see from experience that there was no chance of getting the Christian religion accepted in the modern world unless it freed itself from the dry formulae, abandoned its reliance on repression and stepped down into the market place ready to exchange idea against idea with the man in the street. He saw that the Church lost rather than gained through too close an alliance with secular politicians who were generally only interested to use it. He saw that it must make reason and science and learning its allies rather than its enemies and that the Church was the whole people of God and must not be allowed to become the mere machine of what he was later to call 'a clerical camarilla'[1]: that the Christian gospel was a gospel offered to all men and one which must be preached to all men—not something to be preserved in secret by men hiding in catacombs.

Professor Novak in his *Open Church* has spoken of the necessity, as indeed has Pope John XXIII, of expressing the Christian truths in terms suitable to each existing age. Professor Novak has criticised what he calls 'non-historical' Christians who think they have found a timeless language and that all that is required is to go on repeating the unchanging formulae, irrespective of whether they any longer carry any significance to their hearers or not; and he has made the point—which is evidently just—that those who talk of such an unchanging Christianity are in fact usually using language which is not really so much the language of eternal principles as of the historical situation of a yesterday that has passed away.

The Christian story was in the first generations of the Christian era of its nature a challenge. The Christian apologists, if we may judge from the *Acts* and the *Epistles* of St. Paul, were of course concerned to propagate Christ's ethical teaching, to bid men to love one another,

[1] *Irish Papers*, 1872.

to direct attention to the Sermon on the Mount, to praise the overriding virtue of charity. But this was not their primary concern. The duties of charity were indeed important but they were important as consequences of the acceptance of Christ's claims, a result of which was to give him the right to teach with authority. The challenge with which the Christian apologist faced the world was the challenge of the fact that Christ rose again from the dead. 'Unless Christ be risen again, then is your faith vain'; and that claim was of its nature surprising—to first hearing, indeed, almost self-evidently absurd. It had, if it was to be accepted, to be demonstrated before a sceptical world.

Now move on some twelve hundred years or so and we have moved into an entirely different society. The Christian then lived in a Christian society—in a society where every institution claimed, sometimes truly and sometimes falsely, to have a Christian foundation. The ordinary man in the mediaeval street never met anyone who was not a Christian. He knew in a vague sort of way that there were men outside the boundaries of Christendom—Mohammedans and the like—who were not Christians. For what mysterious purpose God had seen fit to withhold from them the gift of faith, what final fate might be awaiting them, he certainly did not know and probably never stopped to speculate. Christendom was at warfare with the non-Christian world outside itself. It was a city under siege. Heretics within Christendom were therefore traitors within the gates. As such they were to be suppressed. The learned might trouble themselves with asking what were the evidences for the Christian claims. The man in the street certainly did not bother his head with such inquiries. He accepted the Christian claims. He had grown up with them. He took their truth for granted. They no longer seemed to him surprising or a challenge. They seemed to him self-evident.

The logical consequence of such an acceptance perhaps should have been that such a man ought to have argued that the Christian promises, if true at all, are of their nature incomparably more important than any of the passing benefits which this world can offer. He should perhaps, like John Wesley, have unhesitatingly preferred 'the Heavenly Crown to the earthly half-crown' and gladly have given up everything for Christ. The rare saint and mystic of course did so. *L'homme moyen sensuel* by no means did so. In some cases it may be that the worldly life was a consequence of a covert scepticism. It was wiser not publicly to confess to doubts about the Christian promises but at the same time the chances of their truth were not sufficient to make it sensible to regulate one's life on the basis of confidence in them. But it is probable that only a minority was as consciously calculating as this. The majority was frankly double-minded. The earthly rewards might be less enduring but they were more immediate. Let us seize them, even if afterwards we regret them. *Video meliora proboque; deteriora sequor.*[1] By and large, and with every allowance made for heretics and sceptics and infidels, this was a society of persons who believed—who, whether they obeyed its precepts or not, thought that there was no doubt what the Christian faith was.

The challenges of the sixteenth century created a new situation. Europe was divided between Catholics and Protestants. Few openly denied the basic Christian story. None dared to do so publicly, but half Europe did openly deny that the Pope had authority to interpret it. For a hundred years Europe was torn with bloody war between Catholic and Protestant, each seeking to impose upon the other its interpretation of Christianity. It proved that neither was strong enough to do so. As a result after a time moderate and sceptical men, wearying of the unending blood bath, began to say, 'It is clear that we can never have unity. Let us at any rate have peace and, as for religious truth, there are learned men on the one side and learned men on the other. Does not their contention prove that we do not know nearly as much about these ultimate matters as either side pretends?' So the victory in the long-drawn-out battle between Catholics and Protestants went to the *tertius gaudens* of the *politiques*. In every country of Europe in one form or another, for a polity whose first duty was to sustain religious truth as the rulers saw that truth, was substituted a polity whose first business was thought to be the preservation of domestic peace.

On the political plane these *politiques* who came to power in the second half of the seventeenth century were of course by no means professed atheists. Every country in Europe had an official established religion, Catholic or Protestant as the case might be, and every country imposed disabilities on those who rejected the official religion—treated them in one way or another as second-class citizens. Yet the formula of *cuius regio eius religio*[2] carried within itself and of its nature a covert scepticism. If the Frenchman was expected to be a Catholic and the Englishman expected to be a Protestant and if it was to be taken for

[1] I see and approve the better, but hold to the worse.
[2] Religion established according to the religion of the ruler of the State.

granted that propositions about the nature of things which must essentially be either true everywhere or not at all, were to be decided by an accident of geography, it clearly meant that those who were the architects of such policies did not really believe that ultimate truth was attainable or that it greatly mattered what version of it a man professed.

The practice of the established religion was of course encouraged. Indeed, as time went on, even the practice of the nonconformist religions was tolerated in a restricted fashion, but the word 'practice' was interpreted in a very much narrower sense than it had been in previous centuries. In previous centuries all Christians, whether Catholic or Protestant, had believed that the Christian religion was of its nature concerned with the affairs of this world as well as with those of the next. It was its business to decide what economic practices were legitimate and when a war could properly be called a just war. In the eighteenth century organised religion ceased to concern itself with such matters. It did not in any formal sense abdicate its pretensions, but the State, alike in Catholic and in Protestant countries, had got into its own hands a complete power of patronage to all high ecclesiastical posts. Therefore, as a result, no one was appointed to such posts if he was at all likely to protest against any of the policies of the State. The chief ecclesiastics were on the other hand left in possession of very large incomes and very great wealth, and the main concern of a high proportion of them appeared to be to protect that wealth. By a strange perversion of values they took the Church's cautious admission that the possession of private property was not in itself necessarily to be condemned and turned it into an assertion that the prime business of the Christian religion was to ensure that private property—and their own private property in particular—was absolute and sacrosanct.

A natural consequence of this development was that all those who were in protest against the inequalities of the times thought of the Church, Catholic or Anglican as the case might be, as their enemy, as a powerful organisation devoted to the prevention of reform and the redistribution of wealth. In France, from the fact that ecclesiastics themselves forbade the Church from raising its voice about what seemed to them the most urgent problems of the day, such thinkers as the Encyclopaedists deduced the conclusion that God did not exist; or if, as deists, they admitted that in some metaphysical, ultimate fashion

He did exist, at any rate He could not and did not interfere in the affairs of men, and therefore men had no reason to concern themselves with Him. Writers like Voltaire, who did not go so far as to proclaim atheism, denounced a persecuting orthodoxy which used its powers not to teach Christian doctrine but to protect itself in its economic and political privileges. He raised the cry of *Écrasez l'Infâme* and was for ever proclaiming in France that they managed things better in England.

In England, in fact, the Church of England of the eighteenth century was at least as destitute of social protest as the Catholic Church in France, and sincere religious feeling flourished most vigorously among the Methodists, who were eventually driven outside the Established Church altogether. But, though critics might well complain of the insufficiency of eighteenth-century English religion, there was not there the overt repudiation of religion that was common at the time in France. A Bolingbroke or a Hume were exceptions, but most of the rulers of Church and State in eighteenth-century England continued publicly to profess religious belief of a sort and probably in the overwhelming majority of cases really believed that they believed. But they accepted from the climate of opinion around them the conclusion that Christianity imposed upon them no inconvenient social duties.

The French Revolution attacked and abolished the economic privileges of the higher clergy along with its attack on all economic privileges. To the general surprise it was discovered that religion was much more vigorously alive among the underprivileged, lay and clerical, than had been generally understood. Pius VI and Pius VII fought for the essential, as opposed to the merely economic, rights of the Church against the revolutionaries and against Napoleon and enhanced the prestige of the Papacy by the dignity with which they did so. But the attacks of the revolutionaries caused Consalvi after 1815 to set the Papacy firmly on the side of the absolute monarchs as the enemies of all revolution and indeed of all reform. Christianity had been accepted by the early Christians as a challenge. In the Middle Ages it was a part of the air that a man breathed. In the eighteenth century it was looked on as the purveyor of privilege by those who were lucky enough to receive its privileges, without bothering too much whether it was true or false. In the first half of the nineteenth century the ecclesiastics themselves enjoyed far less in the way of economic privilege than had their predecessors of the *ancien régime* but the Church was looked on as the defender of secular order and that order's economic privileges. Its doctrines, as they were understood, were sincerely believed. There was much less cynicism than in the previous century, but the most important of its doctrines was thought to be the defence of the absolute rights of property. De Maistre,[1] the prophet of that age, saw the executioner as the supreme symbol of Christian authority.

In England also after 1815 religion was regarded primarily as the defender of order and the rights of property and the unqualified opponent of all reform. Only the religion there was of course a different religion. The Gordon Riots shortly before had adequately shown that the British public was imbued with a hatred of Catholicism, that, when whipped up, came to little short of madness. The persecutions of the Church in France at the time of the Revolution, the hospitality given to French *emigré* priests, did perhaps a little to moderate bigotry but only a very little. In the first quarter of the century one of the main political issues of the day was Catholic Emancipation. Responsible politicians had generally come to see that emancipation was, if not desirable, at any rate inevitable, but public opinion certainly agreed with George III in opposing it. The Catholics in England (as opposed to Ireland) were so inconsiderable a minority that they did not play, and could not have played, whatever concessions were granted to them, any part of importance in shaping the minds of Englishmen. To the ordinary English family—to such a family for instance as that of Newman—Catholicism was indeed an alien and evil creed but it was no more considered that there was danger or possibility of an Englishman embracing it than there was of his becoming a werewolf.

The vigour of sincere religious feeling was at that date found in the Methodists who, excluded as they were from positions of responsibility by Test Acts, had no reason to love the Establishment, whether it be of Church or State; nevertheless, under Wesley's leadership, they were resolutely opposed to revolution. The majority of the population called itself Anglican and adhered to the Church of England but without great enthusiasm. So long as they still lived in their villages they lived in a pattern of life which involved a regular attendance at Sunday's church. When they drifted into the new industrial towns where houses and factories had been built more rapidly than churches, the old.

[1] The leading protagonist of the post-1815 Catholic reaction. Author of *Du Pape*, *Soirées de St. Petersbourg*, etc.

pattern of their life disintegrated and to a large extent they fell away from religious practice.

The higher clergy of course, as in pre-revolutionary France, enjoyed enormous wealth and privileges and, since they were appointed to their positions by the politicians, there was little chance of a clergyman receiving promotion if he was not prepared to use his influence to support the established order. Yet the great majority of those who called themselves Anglicans derived no direct personal benefit from the Anglican system. Hostile critics might assert that the masters of society upheld the Established order simply because that order was to their financial advantage. But the contention was clearly in fact an over-simplification. There were doubtless in the England of that day a very few confessed unbelievers. There were of course many people who retained a simple faith. There were doubtless some who harboured secret doubts but who preferred not to publish them—whether out of a merely cynical self-interest or because they genuinely thought that the spread of doubt would be an encouragement to disorder. The great majority sincerely believed that there was a God, that Christ was God, that there was a future life. They broke the sexual rules, but they thought that they sinned when they did so. They thought that marriage both was and ought to be indissoluble, and the most incontinent would have been genuinely shocked by proposals to regularise divorce. They thought that religion had no business to interfere with the workings of the so-called economic laws. Its business was to act as a subsidiary policeman—to use its influence to prevent attacks on the order of society. There were rewards and punishments beyond the grave and it could be confidently believed that at the Last Judgement Conservatives would be properly rewarded and Radicals as properly punished.

It was into such a society that Newman was born—a society in which religion was supported by its friends as the upholder of order and attacked by its critics as the enemy of freedom. To Newman from his very earliest days religion simply was not primarily about that at all. What mattered to him was the personal relationship between himself and God. Religion indeed had a social content. It bound man to his fellow man but only because it first bound him to God. He came in later years to quarrel with the Church of England largely because it accepted too great a dependence on the authorities of the secular world and to join the Church of Rome, with what good fortune we shall see, in the hope that it would be free of that dependence.

It was not possible that this half-faith of religion for order's sake should for long endure without challenge. It was inevitable that the unprivileged, seeing that the privileged invoked the sanctions of religion against others but did not much allow them to regulate their own conduct, should ask whether the privileged really believed and whether their Christian faith was really true. Either they revolted from official religion to embrace some more sincere but less official body such as the Methodists, or they turned against religion altogether as a hypocrisy. The value of the Church as a mere policeman, if it was not thought to be more than a policeman, was small. 'Religion,' thought Newman's father, 'when carried too far, induces a softness of mind.' It was the general view of moderate men of moderate means that Christianity after a fashion was true, that it should be spoken of with respect, that the privileges of the Church should be upheld but that one should not be fanatical about it. But, if it was not necessary to obey its precepts in this world, what need was there to believe its promises about another? Laymen, privileged or unprivileged, Lord Melbourne or the village atheist, were not much prepared to allow ecclesiastics to retain their privileges once they became doubtful whether their claims were valid. The wiser religious leaders saw this and saw the need for the Church to produce adequate title deeds and the fruits of good conduct. Even though outspoken unbelief might not be common, yet the age was not one where the existence of God could any longer be taken for granted as it could be in the Middle Ages. In St. Thomas' time it was perhaps possible to advance proofs for the existence of God to some extent as a logical formality, conscious that whether the proofs carried conviction or not, in fact people would believe in God's existence. Newman was born into a world where such acceptance could by no means be taken for granted. It was essential to find for it a firm and irrefutable foundation.

Newman was one of the great autobiographers. We know therefore the various stages of his mind, as we know that of St. Augustine and of Pascal but of no others. We know from the confession of the *Apologia* that as a youth he was not what he afterwards would have considered as religious. He was naturally meditative, disinclined to take anything for granted, as prepared as a Montaigne or a Descartes to ask the ultimate questions such as *Que sais-je?* and to be content only with the ultimate answer of *Cogito, ergo sum* (I think, therefore I am). He was not at that time acquainted with Berkeley and records in the *Apologia* that, oddly enough, even in later life he never studied Berkeley's works. Professor Cameron, in his essay on *Newman and Empiricism* in his *Night Battle*,[1] finds Newman to be following rather in the footsteps of the yet more sceptical Hume. It was a curiosity of the classical education of the nineteenth century that the philosophic student knew his Plato and his Aristotle backwards but had no encouragement to read any later philosophical author. Yet, acquainted with him or not, Newman, like Bishop Berkeley, early concluded that he could not in the nature of things know anything but his own ideas. *Esse est percipi* (The test that a thing is is that it is perceived). There was, and could be, no certainty that those ideas corresponded to any reality outside themselves. 'I thought life might be a dream, or I an angel,' he writes in his *Apologia* of those early years,[2] 'and all this world a deception, my fellow angels by a playful device concealing themselves from me and deceiving me with the substance of a material world.' If the only thing that he knew was his own ideas, in what way could he still exist when he was no longer capable of perceiving and what reason was there to think that he would continue to exist after the present life was ended? Indeed, if anything survived the grave, in what sense could that personality be said to be he, since everything that now made him what he was would manifestly be altered? As early, he records, as the age of five, he was already asking himself the questions, 'Who am I? What am I? What am I doing?' About ten years later he remembered copying out some verses by Voltaire which denied the immortality of the soul and muttering to himself, 'How dreadful, but how plausible.'[3]

It was a little more than a year after he had transcribed these verses that he experienced his conversion. As he described it long after, in 1859:[4] 'Thy wonderful grace turned me right round when I was more like a devil than a wicked boy,' and thenceforward for the rest of his life his belief in God was unwavering. What did he mean by this confession? Was his experience that of the partaker in a revivalist meeting, when in a moment of high excitement the patient makes professions of devotion which—so the unsympathetic sometimes say —often do not outlast the moment and leave him at the end little better

[1] Chapter 12, 'Newman and Empiricism', p. 219, Burns and Oates edition.
[2] Part Three, p. 96, Collins Fontana edition.
[3] P. 97.
[4] *Private Journal.*

than he was at the beginning? Newman has left us no hint that it was in any excited assembly that his conversion took place; but, what is more important, although of course at that time there was no question of his conversion being in any way a conversion to the Catholic Church, even a conversion in that direction, and although he still remained and was to remain for many years an Evangelical convinced that Rome was the Church of anti-Christ, yet never in his later Catholic days did he waver in his belief that this conversion was a genuine conversion. The explanation certainly is that, whatever the exact nature of his experience, he remained throughout life an intensely logical man, who thought that propositions must be taken in their proper order. It was first necessary to establish that there was a God. This was the first and, as he confessed in the *Apologia*, the most difficult step. 'Of all points of faith,' he there wrote, 'the being of a God is to my own apprehension encompassed with most difficulty and yet born in on our minds with most power.' Only when the existence of God was established was it logical to go on to consider whether Christ was God. Only when that was established was it logical to go on and ask where the Church of Christ was to be found. If there was not a God or if Christ was not God, what could it matter where His Church was to be found? Newman was therefore grateful for this first experience which settled for him once and for all the first of the three great questions, even though there was still much ahead before he could come to an answer to the other two.

This early conversion did not at all cause Newman to abandon his idealistic approach—in the metaphysical sense of the word 'idealist'. The world around him which men called real still seemed to him insubstantial. There were, he thought, 'two luminous beings, myself and God', of whose existence alone could he be certain. Why could he be certain of the existence of God? It is indeed a sufficient answer to the claims of solipsism to say that no man can believe that he is the whole of reality. He cannot help but believe that there is existence outside himself. But, though this may prove that there is some sort of external totality of reality, it cannot of itself prove that that totality of reality is God, as the word is usually used.

Why did Newman believe in God? What was God as he understood it? The traditional view says of the relationship between God and conscience, 'Somebody must have made the universe. New discoveries about the history or the antiquity of the planets do not affect the argument that there must have been a beginning of things. Reason tells me that there is a God Who created me. Therefore since I am His creature I owe Him a duty.' Kant shortly before Newman had reversed that argument[1]. Aroused by Hume from his 'dogmatic slumbers', he had found that the traditional proofs of the existence of God, onto-logical, chronological or physico-theological, were unsatisfying. They only reached their conclusion, he argued, by begging the question. We are told that everything must have a cause. But such a proposition, even if accepted, cannot prove the existence of God. For, if everything was made by something else, then who made God? As Newman was to write in the *Grammar of Assent*, 'It is to me a perplexity that grave authors seem to enunciate as an intuitive truth that everything must have a cause. If this were so, the voice of nature would tell false; for why in that case stop short at One who is Himself without cause?'[2] If it be pleaded that the chain of causation must start somewhere, why should it not just as well start with the universe as start with a God who made the universe? Why should not the universe itself have always existed and had no beginning? Why should there be a *Primum Mobile*? Is it not as little difficult to all comprehension to say that things were always in motion? Either way all things inevitably go out into eventual mystery. What happened in the phenomenal world happened for a cause. But could there be cause where there was not time and limitation? Did cause and effect apply in the transcendental world of absolutes? God may be a condition for our thinking, but that does not in itself prove that He actually exists any more than proposi-tions about the properties of infinity or a triangle prove that there is such a place as infinity or that any absolute triangle anywhere exists. It may be that without a God things do not make sense. But what reason is there for certainty that they do make sense? May not all be a nonsense? The argument from design may prove that Paley's watch had a watchmaker who arranged its parts. But he did not create these parts. It is important not to evade issues with question-begging phrases.

The theologians appeal to the natural law. But the natural law cannot from its own terms of reference resolve a controversy. It can tell us that certain habits—let us say, cannibalism—are so universally repug-nant that those who indulge in them may fairly be called sub-human. But it is idle to appeal to the natural law in condemnation of practices

[1] *Critique of Pure Reason.*
[2] *Grammar of Assent*, 'Presumption', p. 63, Burns and Oates, 1870.

in which many healthy people habitually indulge with no sense of wrongdoing. So it is to no purpose to point to the so-called proofs of the existence of God if there are many people of intellectual competence who do not find those proofs convincing.

But, argued Kant, though we cannot deduce conscience from the existence of God, we can legitimately deduce God from the existence of conscience. The voice of conscience within tells us that we ought to perform certain actions. Thus conscience means that we are somehow identified with the scheme of things. How can one owe a debt unless there is Somebody to whom it is owed, 'a cause of nature as a whole,' as Kant put it, 'which is distinct from nature'? 'There is,' he thought, 'therefore implied in the idea of the highest good a Being who is the Supreme cause of nature, or author of nature through his intelligence and will, which is God.'

Newman throughout his life took a point of view that was not very different from that of Kant. Many years later he was to write in his *Grammar of Assent*;[1] 'As we have our initial knowledge of the universe through sense, so do we in the first instance begin to learn about its Lord and God from conscience; and as from particular acts of that instinct which makes experience, mere images (as they ultimately are) upon the retina, the means of our perceiving something real beyond them we go on to draw the general conclusion that there is a vast external world, so from the recurring instances in which conscience acts, forcing upon us importunately the mandate of a Superior, we have fresh and fresh evidence of the existence of a Sovereign Ruler, from whom those particular dictates which we experience proceed.' And again,[2] 'Conscience does not repose on itself, but vaguely reaches forward to something beyond itself and dimly discerns a sanction higher than self for its decisions, as is evidenced in that keen sense of obligation and responsibility which informs them.'

The difficulty—or at any rate apparent difficulty—about basing belief in God on the word of conscience is to know what to say of the man who has no conscience and recognises no obligation—to a Richard III, boasting he is 'myself alone'. It may be that there are not many of whom this can be said. Conscience almost always peeps out somewhere even in the most unprincipled of men. There is something which they draw the line at doing. Yet it would be hard to deny that there are any who

[1] *Grammar of Assent*, 'Presumption', p. 60, 61.
[2] *Ibid*, p. 107.

are utterly unprincipled and, if such exist, there is perhaps little that one can say of them save that, like the cannibals, they are not fully men. They are deprived of one of the essential qualities of a man even more completely than is the colour-blind or the stone deaf. The argument, as an argument, is perhaps somewhat question-begging since the question whether a man does owe such an obligation is the very question under discussion. But what else can one say? How can these matters be settled in the last resort except by an appeal to general experience?

In any event it must have been some such ideas that Newman had in mind when he said that before his conversion he was 'more like a devil than a wicked boy'—though it must be confessed that the phrase is not as clear in meaning as was Newman's general habit. Certainly we know a good deal from the *Apologia* about Newman's boyhood habits. He was, if his confessions are frank, as we cannot doubt that they are, not what one would ordinarily call 'a wicked boy'. He wrote later in 1861 with some understanding and sympathy of those who in youth had the temptations of sexual desire and succumbed to them. But he specifically tells us that he himself never had such an experience. He says, discussing such stories in Thackeray's novels, 'It has been my own happiness not to have known them experimentally, but I easily understand there must be an ecstatic sweetness in the first unlawful kiss given, which to the very end of life will carry with it its own (seeming) evidence of its innocence and allowableness.' He can hardly have been what the general world would have called 'a wicked boy'. But, if he said that he was a devil rather than a wicked boy, one presumes that he meant that even if he did not break regulations he lived a careless life, indifferent to God. Most people would not hold this in a young boy to be a fault as grave as it appeared to the later religious Newman, and in any event the word 'devil' seems a somewhat curious word to choose for the description of it. For the devils are not atheists or creatures indifferent to God. They are creatures deliberately defying Him with their 'I Will Not Serve'. It is hard to believe that the shy, well behaved young Newman was ever of such a sort, ever deliberately striving to destroy the faith of others. Nor indeed does he leave us any evidence of any action which bears the mark of such a characteristic. Yet it seems that that is what he must have meant when he called himself a devil.

Such was Newman's adolescent position. Of course at that time he had no sort of Catholic apologetic purpose in basing his belief in God on these 'personalist' grounds rather than on the traditional Thomist intellectualism. At the time when in his adolescence he first wrestled with these arguments, he had hardly heard of the Catholic Church and very likely had never heard of St. Thomas at all. It is arguable that, if he had been brought up otherwise—if he had from first learning become acquainted with these arguments in the persuasive form in which St. Thomas put them rather than in the debased form in which Paley put them, if in his early reading he had not been made familiar with the empiricist case which found its culmination in Hume, he would have argued differently. Who shall say? Such hypothetical questions are of little meaning. The fact is that Newman did start to think thus about the most fundamental problems in early youth and continued to think thus throughout his lifetime, and that fact has been of enormous practical importance because his approach corresponds much more nearly to that of the modern man than does that of the Thomists.

The Catholic Church in the early nineteenth century, frightened by the horrors of the French Revolution, believed almost without qualification in a policy of repression and censorship. Whatever may be desirable on the political field, the possibilities of repression on the intellectual field are comparatively limited. Authority can suppress a book. It can bid men when they write or when they speak in public to use such and such arguments. But it is not within a man's power, however anxious he may be to try, to be persuaded by arguments that he does not find cogent, and the fact remained that after Hume and Kant the traditional arguments for the existence of God were simply not believable. It was possible to repeat them in words. It was possible, when they were refuted, for authority to invoke anathemas on those who refuted them, but the only result of such policy was to produce a generation which refrained from thinking because thinking was too dangerous. Thinking is only possible in an atmosphere of freedom. Mere obedient repetition is not thinking. It was this absence of thinking which Newman was to discover in Rome when he went there as a Catholic immediately after his reception in the late 1840's—men repeating tags of St. Thomas but without any real systematic statement of the position. The First Vatican Council repeated obstinately its traditional assertion that the existence of God could be demonstrated, and called on the faithful to accept it. 'God, the beginning and end of all things,' it said, 'can certainly be known from created things by the light of human reason.' But, though the faithful might try with their lips, it was a question what they were able to accept in their hearts.

After Pius IX's death in 1878 Leo XIII attempted to sponsor an intellectual revival of genuine Thomism. This was a worthy task, for no one could deny that Thomism was one of the great philosophies of the world and the world's culture was the richer for its deeper understanding. But at the same time Leo put no obstacle in the way of Newman's restatement of his own radically different position in his *Grammar of Assent*. Pius X, Leo's successor, as a part of his very necessary campaign against Modernism, attempted to impose Thomism as a compulsory discipline, to insist that all seminary teaching should be in its terms. The effect of this was to create a divorce between the language of the seminary and the language of the world. The seminarian found that the teaching which he received was of no use in helping him to talk to men of the world. The Catholic culture was in danger of becoming a mere irrelevance to the problems of the world. Seminarians often learnt their formulae by heart, and as rapidly as possible, in order to pass their necessary examinations, anxious to get out into the world and talk about the things that really mattered.

For this reason the question of Catholic education was one of the main questions that the Second Vatican Council found itself called upon to answer. In the decree on the Formation of Priests the existing seminary system came under severe criticism, and many innovations have been ordered for the near future. Among them is the abandonment of the notion that the Thomistic system should be considered as a hallmark of orthodoxy and that only scholastic philosophy must there be studied. 'While basing themselves on that perennially valid philosophy, of which they are heirs,' said the decree on the Formation of Priests, 'they should pay attention to the later developments of philosophical inquiry, particularly those which are most influential in their own country.' Cardinal Léger of Montreal, in blunt criticism that would have seemed strange to Pius X, went further and said that the expression '*philosophia perennis*' was absurd and should never be used. 'There was no philosophy which was not the product of its own time and new times demanded new methods of expression.' Now it is clear that the habits of linguistic analysis which Wittgenstein has introduced into modern philosophy in the *Tractatus Logico-Philosophicus* are much more sympathetic to Newman's habit of language than to the rigid

Thomistic phraseology, and Bergson's '*Elan vital*' much more akin to Newman's 'The whole man thinks'.

Newman never made any claim to establish a new orthodoxy which was to displace the old orthodoxy; but the admission of his approach —of the approach to those problems which he followed from earliest youth and long before he became a Catholic—as a legitimate approach has provided a language in which the secular and religious man of today can at the least converse together; and it has made religion palatable to many who in its more rigid form would have found it unacceptable.

2

A Work for me to Do

WHATEVER THE STRENGTH of the Kantian argument which derives
the existence of God from the existence of conscience, it clearly
furnishes no reason for the acceptance of the Divinity of Christ, nor
did Kant in any way accept that Divinity. There was a very large gap
to be bridged between the belief in God to which Newman's thinking
had brought him and the full Christian position. Perhaps the gap was
less evident a hundred and forty years ago than it is today. Today the
world is full of men who assert that there is a God but are not able to
accept the Divinity of Christ. In the early years of the last century men
were more ready to think that the battle was between atheism and
belief. People had lost their sense of the surprise and challenge of the
Christian claims. However that may be, Newman was naturally
enough in maturer years to become fully aware of the surprise of the
claim and to show himself well alive to the necessity of supplying
reasons for his acceptance. He was to supply such reasons very fully in
his *Grammar of Assent*. But at sixteen it does not appear—naturally
enough—that he was aware of the gap. It was so much in the air of the
times that religion was the Christian religion that a young man, once
he accepted the existence of God, easily assumed the Divinity of Christ
without noticing how gigantically more he was accepting than his
argument in any way justified.

Throughout his early years at Oxford Newman had accepted of
course the Divinity of Christ, had practised regularly as an Anglican,
had, when required to do so, signed the Thirty-nine Articles, but it had
never occurred to him to ask himself questions about the nature of the
Church or the proper relations between Church and State. When he
went to Oriel as a Fellow, one of the former Fellows, Whately, who
still resided in Oxford, and who was afterwards to be the Archbishop

of Dublin and Newman's antagonist, took a kindly interest in the young man and enlisted his help in some literary work. Newman wrote for Whately's *Encyclopaedia Metropolitana* articles on Cicero, on Miracles and on Apollonius of Tyana. It was, by Newman's confession in the *Apologia*, Whately who first aroused his interest in the problem of Church and State.

Whately's conception was not then, any more than it was to be later, in any way what Newman would have considered a Catholic conception. His point was what would seem to many a point of common sense but of a somewhat superficial and philistine nature. The Elizabethan conception, argued Whately, was of a society of which all the members were comprised for secular purposes in the State and for religious purposes in the Church. In such a society with the Sovereign as Head of the Church it was not illogical that the practices of the Church should be regulated by a Parliament, all of whose members were by definition members of the Church of England. It may not have been an ideal arrangement since it was notorious from the first that a number of persons swore the oaths and received the sacraments of the Church of England solely in order to qualify themselves for secular promotion and with hardly a pretence of sincere belief, but at least the arrangement was not on the face of it self-evidently ridiculous. But after a time it appeared that, in spite of the Cecilian desire, it was not possible to persuade the whole population to accept the Church of England. There were Catholics who rejected it on the one hand and Nonconformists who rejected it on the other. As long as Parliament was the authority that rules the Church of England, it was reasonable that these dissidents, if they were to be tolerated at all, were at least to be treated as second-class citizens and barred out from such posts as might give them an effective say in the affairs of the Church of England. That was the policy and—as Whately argued—a very logical policy of the eighteenth century. But in Whately's day Nonconformists had already been admitted to Parliament and it was fairly clear that before long Catholics and—who knows?—perhaps even Jews and total disbelievers would be admitted. This changed the whole nature of the arrangement. It was reasonable that the Church of England should be ruled by a wholly Anglican Parliament. It was intolerable that it should be subjected to a Parliament whose members might be of any or of no religion. A special and wholly Anglican commission must be set up to control the affairs of the Church of England.

What Whately said was, as far as it went, sensible enough, but it was, to the student of Newman and indeed to the student of all subsequent religious history, more interesting for the questions that he neglected to ask than for the questions that he did ask. Whately never asked what constituted a Church the true Church or a branch of the true Church. He never asked whether Christ himself had established any special order of authority in his Church. He thought that it was intolerable that the Church of England should be subordinated to the control of non-Anglicans. It never occurred to him that there could be any objection to bishops being subordinated to laymen so long as the laymen were Anglicans. His ideal constitution was in fact a completely Erastian constitution. The Church was to his mind a body to be ordered about. He never thought of it as a body which had itself a right to order. Yet Newman at least learnt from Whately that there was a further problem to be considered.

The other Oriel colleague from whom he learnt an important lesson was also a man with whom he was destined afterwards to be in serious conflict—Hawkins, the future Provost of Oriel. Newman, having been ordained a deacon, worked as a curate in the parish of St. Clement's of which Hawkins was the vicar. The Calvinist belief was that men were saved by faith; that there was no half-way house of purgatory between heaven and hell; that, if a man was converted and gave all his faith to Christ, he was saved and that, if he was not converted, then, whatever his works, they availed him nothing and he was inevitably damned. Newman had been brought up as an Evangelical. Whatever else he may have meant by his confession that before his conversion he was 'a devil', he presumably meant that he was then in a state in which, had death found him, he would be damned. After his conversion he was in a state ready for salvation.

A Calvinist who carried Calvinism to a wholly inhuman length could perhaps argue that human beings were elected for salvation or damnation, irrespective of whether they were virtuous or vicious, as the world normally reckons virtue and vice. But no man of the smallest psychological insight could believe that human beings were in fact clearly divided into the absolutely good and the absolutely bad. Therefore, since Newman was a man of great psychological insight, it was inevitable that, as soon as he had had any experience of human nature, he would abandon this crude division of the sheep and the goats. The experience, as it happened, that led him to abandon it was the experience of parish visiting in St. Clement's parish, and the instructor who opened his eyes was Hawkins. Visiting in the parish, Newman discovered, as was to be expected, that it would be absurd to call the great majority of his parishioners saints. They all had their defects and committed their sins. They did not by any means live in the conscious company of God, but at the same time it would be equally absurd to deny that they were at times capable of acts of great generosity and kindness and even love, which it was reasonable to believe must be pleasing in the eyes of God.

It was Hawkins who in conversation with Newman during the Long Vacation laid before him what, in contradiction to that which he had previously been taught to hold, he now recognised to be common sense. 'Men,' said Hawkins, 'are not saints or sinners. They are not as good as they should be but better than they might be.' They were, concluded Newman, 'in the condition as if they had some spiritual feelings but weak and uncertain'.[1] But, if that was the psychological truth, what was the theological conclusion that one should draw? If men were not 'either saints or sinners', was it reasonable to believe that God treated them as if they were to be either admitted immediately into heaven or consigned irrevocably to hell? Could the Last Judgement be a sort of Public Examination in which, say, 50% was the Pass mark, and those who just got 51% were at once admitted to eternal bliss and those with 49% went howling? Whatever Protestant formularies might say, was it not inevitable that there must be some place or state of purgatory where the stained but not wholly irredeemable soul can be prepared for its beatitude?

Neither the influence of Whately nor the influence of Hawkins of course in any way brought Newman nearer to the Catholic position. But it has often been said of Newman that in his lifetime he changed both the nature of the Anglican and the nature of the Catholic Church. 'He has left an indelible mark on two great religious bodies. He has stirred movements which still agitate the Church of England and the Church of Rome,' has written Dean Inge. It is certainly true. Sometimes the charge is made by critics who accuse him of having been a disruptive influence unable wholly to absorb the spirit of any body which he joined. Sometimes it is made by admirers. Whether a matter for praise or for criticism it is certainly a fact and a remarkable fact. No one else has in modern times played such a double role as his. Monsignor

[1] *Autobiographical Writings*, p. 77; 'Autobiographical Memoir III.'

Ronald Knox is perhaps the nearest competitor and Monsignor Knox, remarkable man as he was, would have been the last to claim that his rank approached that of Newman whether in the Anglican or in the Roman Church. Still it is curious as we look at Anglicanism today to notice how these two early positions which Newman occupied in Anglican thought have today been both entirely successful. The Anglican *Guardian* at his death called him 'the founder, we might almost say, of the Church of England as it is'.

Whately's position was within its own limits impregnable. Whatever the High-and-Dry's, interested only to defend their own privileges, might expect, the claims of the Church of England at a time when it was the Church of all Englishmen were at least deserving of consideration; but, when the Anglicans had become only one among a number of denominations to be found in England, their privileges were neither defensible nor tolerable, and the position in the nineteenth century was of course far more absurd than it had been in Elizabeth's time. For in Elizabeth's time the Church of England was subject to a Parliament that was merely an English Parliament. By the nineteenth century it was subject to a Parliament of the United Kingdom and members from Scotland, Wales and Ireland could sit and vote on this purely English matter. The erosion of the Church of England's privileges which was to be the steady process over the nineteenth century was even in these early years inevitable and a man of prescience in the 1820's could have foreseen it. But such a man at that date, looking forward to the future, would probably have foretold that sooner or later the Church of England would be disestablished. Disestablishment seemed in the logic of things and of course in the second half of the century was always one of the most prominent demands in every radical programme. One of the most remarkable developments of modern English politics is the total abandonment of any demand for disestablishment even by the most extreme politicians of the left.

Unkind critics will say that the disestablishment of the Church of England is no longer demanded because the Church is so feeble that her disestablishment is no longer worth calling for. It is not wholly true. The truth is rather that the Church of England survives because she has been reformed very much along the lines that Whately and Newman suggested. In the nineteenth century the Church of England was still really ruled by Parliament. Clergymen who used allegedly illegal ornaments were really brought up before the courts and sent to prison.

The proceedings were too odious and too ridiculous and as a result in modern times the Enabling Act has vested in purely Anglican bodies —Convocation and the Church Assembly—a virtually total power of legislative control over the Church of England—exactly what Whately and Newman advocated. It is true that, as is perhaps inevitable if the fiction of a State Church is to be maintained, Parliament has still kept to itself a final power of veto, and this power was of course really exercised on one notable occasion when in 1926 the House of Commons rejected the Deposited Prayer Book which the bishops were asking it to legalise. But that strange episode did not in fact prove the reality of Parliament's authority over the Church of England. It proved the reverse. For, though the bishops were rebuffed, in fact Anglican clergymen continued to use the Deposited Book exactly as if it had been legalised.

As total and as curious has been the victory of Hawkins's theories within the Church of England. Hawkins, when he pointed out to Newman that most people were neither very good nor very bad but of a middle sort, did not imagine that he was enunciating a theological principle. He thought that he was merely pointing out to a young man a fact of common observation which he ought to know, and one wonders at first thought why Newman required to be taught so obvious a lesson. But there is a wealth of historical background to the story. If one believes in a future life and a judgement, it would seem at first sight but common sense to believe that most people at any rate must go first to some sort of purgatory. They are neither good enough for an immediate heaven nor bad enough for hell, and so the mediaeval Christian took the existence of purgatory for granted. It was only in the late Middle Ages that vigorous opposition to purgatory grew up. That opposition based itself on the ground that the references to future fate in the New Testament speak of heaven and hell and of a clear division of mankind into the saved and the damned but that references to purgatory are at any rate much less explicit. But such reasoning in itself would hardly have been found compulsive. Men turned against purgatory of course because of their very just indignation at the corrupt practices and the sale of indulgences associated with it. The result was that Protestant Englishmen and Protestants elsewhere believed in this absolute division of mankind at death into the saved and the damned and Newman, brought up of course in the evangelical tradition, grew up with such a belief.

Newman accepted it but it could only be fitted into a theological scheme by the acceptance of purgatory. Such an acceptance was to the society of the 1820's, where men either believed in nothing or else believed in hell-fire, an eccentricity. Today opinion in the Anglican Church has come round entirely to Newman's view. A man who believed in hell-fire in the sort of way in which believers believed in it in the 1820's would be considered mildly cracked. Even the defenders of the theoretical possibility are today careful to explain that they do not believe that anyone necessarily goes there. The belief in purgatory, whether or not the exact word is used, would on the other hand be generally accepted as reasonable. Newman himself did not at that time or at any later time repudiate the belief in hell. As he explained in the *Grammar of Assent*, he did not think that the tradition of the Church permitted such a total repudiation, but the belief, though necessary, was always painful to him. He clearly could not bring himself to think of any individual in hell and, as the *Dream of Gerontius* shows, his mind turned more naturally to the picture of purgatory. He had no Dantean relish for hell, but his influence, whether he altogether wished it or not, has clearly been in the direction of weakening the belief in absolute badness. Even among Calvinists the full Calvinist belief is not today very widely held.

Yet for all the debt that he owed him, Newman soon quarrelled with Hawkins when Hawkins became Provost of Oriel. The quarrel was in the first instance about Newman's interpretation of his duties as a College Tutor. Hawkins as a liberal was inclined to think that Oxford was a place where the young men had best be left to learn from untrammelled experience and to discover for themselves the opinions which they were going to embrace. Newman took a much stricter view and thought that a tutor ought to act as a moral director of his pupils. Indeed it is fair to say that the young Newman was much more ready to think that virtue could be directly taught and vice prevented by measures of suppression than was the later, wiser Newman who was to write the *Idea of a University* thirty years afterwards. As a result of this quarrel with Hawkins Newman was compelled in 1830 to give up his Oriel tutorship, and from that date held no teaching office in the University—a fact which had its importance in the development of events.

But before his resignation of the tutorship Newman had had another quarrel with Hawkins which, in view of his later history, has its amusing side. In 1829, frightened by the Clare election and the threat of civil war, the Government of Peel and Wellington, which had been put in office to oppose Catholic Emancipation, reversed its policy and decided to bring in an Emancipation measure. Sir Robert Peel was the Member for Oxford University. He had been elected at the previous election as an anti-emancipation candidate. He now offered himself again as a supporter of emancipation. Hawkins as a liberal was delighted and offered Sir Robert the support of the Oriel Common Room. Newman took the line that Hawkins had no right to make such an offer and that in view of his total reversal of policy it would be a scandal should Peel be re-elected. Newman was of course at that date not even vaguely inclined towards Roman Catholicism and indeed still thought of the Pope as Anti-Christ. But it was not wholly out of hostility to Catholicism as such that he opposed Peel, and of the problems of Ireland which had been mainly responsible for the Government's reversal of policy he was at that time entirely ignorant. In truth he did not so much object to Peel bringing in Catholic Emancipation as to what seemed to him the cavalier insolence of his treatment of the University, expecting it to support one year a policy exactly the opposite of that which it had returned him to support the year before. He thought that, if Peel was going to bring in Catholic Emancipation, decency required that he should be ejected from his University seat and compelled to find another constituency—and this is what happened. Peel was defeated at Oxford and had to find a seat at Westbury.

Yet, though Newman's cause was thus victorious, he was a little shaken to discover some of the allies with whom he found himself yoked. A high proportion of the Oxford Fellows of that time were merely blind reactionaries, who cast their votes without question against any detail of reform in the affairs of either State or Church or University—'Z's' as Newman and his friends called them. As Newman was coming increasingly to feel that the evils of the times were fundamentally caused by the faults in the constitutions of Church and State and University as they were then interpreted, he could not feel very comfortable with such allies.

Hawkins played, then, this strange double role in Newman's life. On the one hand he taught him to look to the real experience of life rather than to accept arbitrary and unproven theories. On the other hand by causing his resignation of the tutorship he gave him unwittingly the opportunity to practise his precepts and to announce them to the world. Freed from College ties, he set to work on the first of his books —*The History of the Arians in the Fourth Century*—which he began in the early 1830's, though it was not to be published until 1834. It was of course a common Protestant contention that the Christianity of the early centuries was a simple and uncorrupted faith and that in later years power-loving priests had introduced corruptions and complications into the faith and perverted its original simplicity. The Reformation had been a movement of protest against those corruptions, which looked back to the purity of the original gospel. Newman, of course, at that time and for many years afterwards did still believe that the mediaeval Church had added to the original faith such accretions as mariolatry, the invocation of saints, transubstantiation and the like, against which the Church of England did right to protest. But Hawkins's lessons or his experience at St. Clement's had taught him that it was at least not one party alone which had been guilty of corrupting the original faith by its accretions. The Calvinist doctrine of justification by faith alone was, he had come to believe, at least as unscriptural and as accretionist as any of the beliefs of the Roman Church. Therefore, if the argument was to have any value and not simply to consist of empty assertion against assertion, it was necessary, before one appealed to the primitive tradition, to go back and study the history of those early times and to discover what did actually happen then.

It was a task that was little undertaken in the English world of that date, and Newman discovered that the picture of a world of simple faith uncorrupted by the sophistications of later theologians was a picture that was wholly false. The truth was rather that from the first —from the days even of the *Acts of the Apostles*—there were disputes about the exact content of the faith. 'I am of Paul and I of Apollos,' and from the first there was a voice of authority which was accorded the power to settle these disputes and to define the doctrine. 'It has seemed good to the Holy Ghost and to us.' In particular in the fourth century there was the gigantic heresy of Arius. For a time it seemed from a mere comparison of power and influence that it was likely that the Arians would capture the Catholic Church. Their arguments seemed to first appearance at least as plausible as those of Athanasius. Athanasius was by no means able to champion the Catholic cause, secure that he had the backing of the world behind him. On the contrary it was rather as fighting *contra mundum* that he had to take his

35

stand. If the Son was begotten of the Father, must He not have been begotten in time? Must He not have been created? Is not any other opinion self-contradictory nonsense? So said the Arians. Their argument seemed a strong one. Yet in the end the Athanasians conquered and the Arians were defeated and the Christians of subsequent centuries —the Christians of Newman's own day, whether Catholic or Protestant—were found simply taking it for granted that Christian doctrine was the Athanasian doctrine, and that it was and always had been self-evident that Arius was wrong. The Church was from the first a deciding body with a power of authority, and the Christian religion did not grow and could not have grown except under the support of such a body.

The study of the fourth-century Arians, important as it may be, was not in itself of such a nature as to make Newman a great figure in the public eye. But before the book appeared Newman did become such a figure for quite a different reason. In 1833 he set out in company with his friend, Hurrell Froude, and Froude's father, a Devonshire archdeacon, on his first foreign journey. The story of that journey is well known and need not here detain us. He travelled through the Mediterranean. He visited Rome which he found cleaner and less disedifying than he had expected. 'What can I say of Rome,' he writes, 'but that it is the first of cities and that all I ever saw are but as dust (even dear Oxford inclusive) compared with its majesty and glory? Is it possible that so serene and lofty a place is the cage of unclean creatures?' At St. Peter's he found 'everything bright and clean and the Sunday kept so decorously.' But 'as to the Roman Catholic system I have ever detested it so much that I cannot detest it more by seeing it; but to the Catholic system I am more attached than ever and quite love the little monks of Rome; they look so innocent and bright, poor boys.'[1]

The three travellers called on Wiseman, then still the Rector of the English College in Rome—the first Catholic priest whom Newman ever met. Then the Froudes returned to England but Newman insisted on making alone a second visit to Sicily. Why he wished to make this visit he could not, as he confessed, himself explain. It was not that he thought that Sicily was an edifying place. He thought very much the reverse—that it was a place from which he felt Christ to be absent in a unique and horrifying manner. It was not that he wished to study Roman Catholic practices—even supposing Sicily to be a good place

[1] Letter to his Mother.

for such studies—for at that time, as he confessed, he did not even know that Catholics believed that the Blessed Sacrament was present in their churches. Sicily was at that time a wild and dangerous and inhospitable land. Newman fell ill there and almost died. His Italian servant thought that he indubitably would die, but Newman obstinately maintained that he would not die, because, as he said to his servant, naturally to the servant's complete incomprehension, 'I was sure that God had some great work for me to do in England.'[1]

He recovered. He returned to England. On the way he wrote his famous hymn 'Lead, kindly light,' inspired by the Straits of Bonifacio off the coast of Sardinia. But the kindly light for whose leadership he was calling had of course no sort of connections with the authority of the Church of Rome, nor, lying on his sick-bed in Sicily, did he doubt that the great work to which he was called was work for the Church of England.

Returning to England, he soon discovered what was, as he thought, this work. On July 9, 1833, he reached Oxford. The following Sunday, his colleague in Fellowship at Oriel, John Keble, preaching the Assize Sermon in St. Mary's Church at Oxford, denounced what he called National Apostasy. As this sermon is commonly thought of as the inaugurator of the Oxford Movement, it is worth stopping to analyse in some detail what it was that Keble said and why he said it.

The occasion of Keble's complaint might seem to many a strangely small storm in a teacup. The Whig Government was proposing to amalgamate a number of the Irish dioceses and thus to reduce the total of bishops. The Church of Ireland—then and for nearly forty years afterwards an Established Church—was what few could today hesitate to call an anomaly and a scandal. It was supported by tithes wrung out of the Irish Catholic tenants who had thus to support a religion which they detested and which, in so far as it devoted itself to any task at all, devoted itself to the task of fighting the tenants' own Church. Its high dignitaries were frequently absentee, frequently English, whose only interest in Irish affairs was to ensure the maintenance of the Protestant ascendancy and of the Act of Union which had been passed a little more than thirty years before by means of blackmail and broken faith. Many of them had hardly any genuine members of their flock at all. That some money should be saved by at any rate reducing the number of these bishops might seem to be the plainest common sense and that the

[1] *Apologia*, p. 121, Part III.

Catholic tenants should at least be freed from the obligation of maintaining a Church which they detested the plainest justice.

Keble denounced National Apostasy, but the Irish might well ask which nation was supposed to be apostatising. An occasion when the English were a little abating from their attempts to rob the Irish of their religion was an odd occasion to choose as an example of national apostasy. But Keble, to do him justice, was not particularly concerned to deny that the affairs of the Church of Ireland needed to be put in order. He was only concerned to deny that the State had any right to put them in order—that the secular State had any right to impose itself upon the divinely founded Church. Keble's claim for the independence of the Church of England from the State was quite different from the claim which Whately had made some years before. All that Whately had been concerned to claim was that the affairs of the Church of England should not be regulated by people who were not Anglicans. Keble was concerned to claim that the Church was an institution founded by Christ with a divinely ordered constitution; that authority over it had been entrusted to bishops and that it was a blasphemy if secular politicians—it mattered not whether they were in personal profession Anglicans or not—should presume to regulate the Church's affairs.

The theory, however attractive it might be in the broad, bristled with difficulties on any detailed examination. To begin with, whatever ought to be the constitution of the Church of England, it seemed manifest that it was not in fact anything in the least like what Keble wanted it to be. The Sovereign, who had no apostolic succession, was the legal Head of the Church. If new bishops were to be created they had to be created by Act of Parliament, and it was not at once apparent why, if an Act of Parliament could make bishoprics, it could not also unmake them. Secondly, to many people it would have seemed plausible enough to maintain that the Church should be autonomous in matters of doctrine. To argue that its property was sacrosanct was quite a different matter. The temporalities of religion were surely a matter properly under the control of the Secular Power. After all, it was in virtue of an Act of Parliament that the Church had the right to exact tithes. Why should not an Act of Parliament have the right to revoke what it had a right to grant? It might perhaps be argued that the State had a right to cancel or modify the tithes, but it was for the Church to decide for itself what were the details of economy which it was to impose upon itself to meet this diminished income. But Keble did not condescend to such distinctions. He denounced the whole arrangement without qualification.

It was, it must be confessed, singularly inept to choose an Irish target for the first shot of this campaign and, had Keble been a man of greater sense of tactics, he would have reserved his fire until he could shoot at something whose destruction could more easily arouse popular applause. Whatever the arguments with which Catholics and Non-conformists might assail the position, it was at any rate not self-evidently absurd to say that the Church of England was the Church of the English people—the Church of Christ—in England. It was self-evidently absurd to say that the Church of Ireland was the Church of the Irish people—the Church of Christ—in Ireland. It was a body that only existed—it could only claim the title of Church of Ireland—as a fiction of secular law. It was of all bodies that existed that which was least qualified to question the authority of the law of the State. A man might argue—however powerful the arguments that might be brought against him—that the Church of England was the Catholic Church in England. He could hardly escape ridicule if he chose to argue that the Church of Ireland was the Catholic Church in Ireland, for that was a contention which every Irishman, Catholic or Protestant, was agreed in denying. They who agreed with one another on nothing else agreed solely on that point. And indeed it was only by calling in the most unprepossessing of allies that Keble was able to fight his battle at all.

Just as Newman, in his fight against Catholic Emancipation in Oxford, found himself standing cheek by jowl with the 'Z's', the extreme and most high-and-dry of the defenders of privilege, so with Keble and the question of Irish tithes. The sceptical, cultured, un-enthusiastic Prime Minister, Lord Melbourne, looking at the problem with an eye that was indifferent to all denominations, saw the question of Irish tithes as absurd. He would have liked to have abolished them altogether. He saw that there was no possibility of content in Ireland so long as they persisted. His able and intelligent Under-secretary, Drummond, agreed with him. But landlords who drew their rents from Irish lands were powerful in the House of Lords. They wanted no tinkering with the Irish land system at any point for fear that, if once touched, the whole iniquity of the system would entirely collapse; and a less simple-minded man than Keble would have understood that the greater part of the outcry of protest about 'the Church in danger' came from men who cared very little whether the Church was in danger or not, but were much more concerned with their own rents.

When we speak of the Irish question we usually think of the political demand of the Irish people for self-government and independence. That was a question in which Newman took little interest. Indeed, at this early date he was deeply and unfairly suspicious of O'Connell whom he thought of, quite absurdly, as a dangerous revolutionary, and later, as we shall see at the time of the Irish University controversy, he was to show himself somewhat insensitive to the effect on the Irish mind of the fearful Famine of the '40's. The particular issue which Keble raised was soon abandoned by intelligent men even among faithful High Churchmen. It came to be seen that the Establishment in Ireland was indefensible, and in the second half of the century it was the High Church Anglican Gladstone who abolished it; and Newman's colleagues in the Tractarian movement, like Church, who had remained within the Church of England, supported Gladstone in his abolition.

Yet Ireland has had a unique importance in the development of modern Catholicism as a result of this strange history—quite apart from the self-evident importance of the steadfastness and loyalty to the Church of Irishmen. Ireland was the only country in Western Europe which was Catholic without ever having been a part of the Roman Empire. As a result, the Irish never had the feudal landed system which reigned in the rest of Europe. At the Reformation the territories that remained Catholic corresponded for the most part and with surprising fidelity to the old boundaries of the Roman Empire. Ireland and Poland were the only countries which had not been Roman but remained Catholic. In the nineteenth century the normal ambition of a country in Europe was to have a State Church. The State recognised and gave its privileges—Catholic or Protestant as the case might be— to the dominant national religion. Even by the closing years of the century a Pope as enlightened as Leo XIII ruled that the ideal condition for the Church was that it should be recognised and guaranteed by a Concordat with the State. The Catholic who lived in a neutral or a non-Catholic State, according to this theory, lived under a certain disability and could not expect quite to enjoy the full Catholic life. Now in Ireland alone was there a State religion which was not the religion of the people—a very gross anomaly.

By our time State support of the Church has become much less important. In Italy, it is true, as a result of the settlement of the conflict between the Vatican and the Italian State Catholicism, for better or for worse, has been recognised as the official religion, and since Italian examples bulk so large in Vatican minds, this has given a certain continuing respectability to the idea of a Concordat. But in the more important Catholic country of France the State broke its relations with the Church in the early years of the century and by general agreement, in spite of many disadvantages, financial and otherwise, the Church has on the whole been the gainer from the breach. Pope John XXIII was much more like Newman in his suspicion of men in high places and in his awareness of the corrupting force of power than his predecessors had shown themselves to be. He found even among Catholics 'people who belong to Jesus Christ and by right to the Catholic Church but who have nothing of the sense of Christ and even less of the *sensus ecclesiae*,' and recorded that 'I am always in contact with the so-called great of this world but distressed by the pettiness of their minds in regard to the supernatural.'[1] So far from desiring political support for the Church he stated in his Inaugural Address to the Vatican Council that 'the princes of this world sometimes in all sincerity intended thus to protect the Church but more frequently this occurred not without spiritual damage and danger,' and the Vatican Council in its decree on Religious Liberty definitely repudiated the notion that the Church should look for its support to a Concordat with the State. It would do no more than grudgingly admit that there might conceivably be circumstances where a relationship of Concordat was not inadmissible. 'In particular circumstances,' it said, 'one religious community may receive civil recognition in the constitutional organisation of a State, but,' it added, 'where this is the case, the right of all citizens and religious communities to freedom in religious matters must be recognised and respected at the same time. In religious matters no one should be forced to act against his conscience privately or in public, whether alone or in company with others, within due limits.'

One of the major influences of course which has brought about this very great change in the Church's attitude towards its relations with the State has been the vast increase in this century of the general importance of, and of the importance of their Catholic bodies in, the new English-

[1] *The Wit and Wisdom of Pope John.*

speaking overseas countries—in Australia and New Zealand but above all in the United States. Now these countries were built on a formula of absolute separation of Church and State. It was only on such a formula that the rival Protestant bodies of the new United States could have hoped to live together or to form a nation. The Catholics were at the foundation of the country an inconsiderable and not very much regarded minority. There were all through the nineteenth century and indeed right up till modern times considerable bodies in the country— Know-Nothings, Ku Klux Klan and the rest—who were opposed to the granting of full rights to Catholics. They justified themselves—in so far as they condescended to put forward a reasoned case at all—by quoting the saying attributed to Veuillot that Catholics demand freedom for themselves when they are in the minority but refuse it to others when they are in the majority. Therefore it was essential in order that this objection should be refuted that the Catholics should proclaim their full acceptance of absolute religious liberty for all.

The matter came up before the Second Vatican Council. The declaration on religious liberty was strongly supported by bishops from Belgium, France and other continental countries on the ground that respect for personality involves a full recognition of religious liberty. It was as strongly supported by the American bishops on more pragmatic grounds—on the ground that the American Catholics would be in an impossible position if there was any hesitation in the Council's acceptance of a right to complete religious liberty. Most certainly one of the influences which led the American Catholics so readily to accept the principle of religious liberty was that they were so largely Irish in origin and the inheritors of an Irish tradition. By a curious chance Newman could be quoted as the supporter of both of these two streams, moving towards the full proclamation of religious liberty. He had learnt, first from experience when he supported it as an Anglican and later from experience when he suffered from it as a Catholic, of the folly and wickedness of the attempt to impose an alien religion on the Irish Catholics. His own philosophical theories and his belief that decisions were decisions of the whole man had taught him the absurdity on the theoretical plane of attempts to impose beliefs on men. 'It is as absurd,' he was to argue in the *Grammar of Assent*, 'to argue men as to torture them into believing.'

During the closing years of the eighteenth century the formula of *cuius regio eius religio* was almost unchallenged. The notion that a State had the duty to support some form or other of established religion was taken for granted. History had up till then only shown two exceptions to this rule—in America where there was the experiment of an impartial toleration of all religions and a separation of Church and State, and among the French Revolutionaries who for a time opposed all religion. But in Ireland there was an exception of quite a different and a unique sort—a State religion which was the bitter enemy of the religion of the people. Newman in these early days of the 1830's obediently accepted Keble's rhetoric against national apostasy, but it is probable enough that, had he remained an Anglican, he would, like Gladstone and Church, have come to see the absurdity, and to favour the disestablishment of the Church of Ireland. But, as it was, he came to support much more radical policies than either his Catholic or his Anglican friends. Though the Popes even after Pius IX still asserted that the ideal relationship between Church and State was one of concordat and that the Catholic who lived in a non-Catholic State and was offered no more than toleration should accept it but accept it only as a *pis-aller*, Newman came increasingly to feel, as was to be shown later by his comments on the state of religion in Papal Rome, that Catholicism was in greater danger of corruption from an especial relationship with the State than it was in independence. Indeed an English Catholic who remembered that the King who accepted from the Pope the title of Defender of the Faith was to become the King who also repudiated the authority of the Papacy could hardly be expected to feel that the formula of the Alliance of Throne and Altar would inevitably prove a comfortable solution of all problems.

Newman learnt from the Irish and the Irish learnt from him. When the Irish Free State was established, the Irish were careful and wise not to take the opportunity to establish the Catholic Church as a state religion. The Catholics had of course no option but to accept the separation of Church and State in America, but it was left to John XXIII to make it clear that it was no longer a Catholic belief that such a relationship was one merely to be accepted under protest. The Council's Declaration on Religious Liberty reversed the traditional pattern in the direction in which Newman had argued that it should be reversed in his *Lectures on Anglican Difficulties*. 'Where the peculiar circumstances of national history demand it,' the Declaration admits somewhat grudgingly 'the principle of religious liberty does not prevent one religious body being accorded special recognition in the constitution' but only 'provided that the right of all citizens and religious bodies to enjoy religious liberty is acknowledged and secured.' 'Anything that smacks of compulsion or unjust or unfair pressure must always be avoided.' The right to claim freedom was not, as the centuries before Newman would have thought, the right of the Church—whether Catholic or Anglican—but the right of the individual. The statement was one which would have seemed very strange to the generations before Newman and would have been quite impossible without him.

Keble lived in an unreal world. He knew nothing whatsoever about Ireland which he had never visited. For all his courtesy and piety he would not even speak to Nonconformists in his own village, thinking it a sin to do so. Had he been told of the economic grievances of the poor Irish, he would have replied that these grievances were irrelevant. The business of a Christian was not to remedy economic grievances but to give glory to God by serving His Church. But the trouble with Keble's theory of the Church of England was not so much that his enemies attacked it as that it was totally incomprehensible to the very great majority of those who called themselves Anglicans. The average Anglican, then as now, was disposed to agree that God existed. He accepted the Divinity of Christ, though doubtless he was not capable of furnishing any very coherent apologetic account why he did so. As for the Church of England, he called himself an Anglican because that was the religion of most Englishmen. If one must worship God, it was natural for an Englishman to worship Him in an Anglican fashion, but as for theories of what exactly the Church of England was, he had none. If reforms were needed, he thought, let them be introduced. Whether they were introduced by Church or State was immaterial, but on the whole experience had shown that reforms were more likely to come from the State than from the Church.

Keble was singularly ill-qualified to meet this unintellectual approach because his own approach was equally unintellectual. Brought up in pious ecclesiastical circles, breathing their air, it never occurred to him that there was any need to give a demonstration that the Church of England was the Church of Christ—or at the least one branch of the Church of Christ. Was it not obvious that Anglicans were Christians? What need then of further argument? And if inconsiderate people asked, 'Is it not equally obvious that many Nonconformists are

Christians?' he preferred simply not to attend to the question. It was Newman who saw that if the argument was to carry any weight, it was necessary to set it on its legs by giving it a rational content. He issued a *Tract for the Times* in support of Keble, which he entitled *Choose Your Side*.[1] 'Should the Government and the country,' he wrote, 'so far forget their God as to cast off the Church, to deprive it of its temporal honours and substances, on what will you rest the claim of respect or attention which you make upon your flocks? Hitherto you have been upheld by your birth and education, your wealth, your connexions; should these secular advantages cease, on what must Christ's ministers depend? . . . Christ has not left His Church without claim of its own upon the attention of men. Surely not. Hard Master He cannot be, to bid us oppose the world, yet give us no credentials for so doing.' Christianity was not, as Arnold[2] and the liberals taught, merely, or even primarily, about ethics. Christianity of course did incidentally teach its ethical lessons—bade us love one another. But beyond teaching men to love one another it also gave them a reason for loving one another. In the mysterious variety of human nature there were plenty of good men who were not Christians. Christianity had probably on the whole raised the standard of social conduct, but man's conduct was the product of so wide an amalgam of causes that it was difficult to say, with such certainty as to carry conviction to others, what was the cause of what effect.

It was certainly surprising, considering the clear motive for virtue which the Christian faith provided, that Christians were not so obviously better than other people. If you rest your Christian faith simply on ethical consequences, if you say, 'We would be Christians in order that we may behave better,' then there is clearly a danger, every time that we see a Christian who behaves badly or a non-Christian who behaves well, that we should say, 'What then does it matter if we believe or not?' Christianity, though the belief in it ought to cause a man to behave well, is not primarily a religion of behaving well. It is primarily a religion of believing in Christ, and if Christ was God and founded a Church and bade men belong to that Church, then it is our first duty to discover where that Church now is and to join it. We must, if we would convert the world, find definitions much

[1] *Tracts for the Times*, No. 1.
[2] Headmaster of Rugby and a leading Broad Churchman with whom Newman was in controversy.

45

firmer than any that Keble offered of the marks that constitute a body a member of the true Church; and the essential mark, Newman wrote in his pamphlet, was the possession of the apostolic succession. 'We have neglected the real ground on which our authority is built,' he wrote, 'our apostolic succession.'[1]

'Magnify your office,'[2] he wrote in one of the Tracts to his fellow clergy. Newman was, of course, only concerned that they should insist more strongly on the dignity of their priesthood in matters spiritual, but to his secular-minded contemporaries, mainly conscious that clergymen were no longer better educated than laymen and therefore resentful that clergymen should be appointed to many well-remunerated jobs which could be as well filled by a layman, the advice was not attractive. Their desire, for their quite different reasons, was to narrow the gap which divided clergy from laity.

Yet it was thus that Newman laid down what became the central doctrine of the Oxford Movement and what is still the central doctrine of the High Church movement within the Church of England. What was essential was to belong to the Catholic Church—the Church which Christ had founded. Christ had chosen His apostles and given them their power to bind and loose. They had transmitted their power to their successors who had in their turn handed on their authority to other successors and so on down through the ages in an unbroken chain which extended from Christ's time to that of Newman and which was certainly destined to endure until Christ's Second Coming at the end of the world. By that test this apostolic succession was found today in three bodies—the Roman Catholic Church, the Greek Church and the Church of England—which were therefore the three branches which together made up the Catholic Church.

This theory, though a great deal more sophisticated than any that Keble propounded, nevertheless had of course its own difficulties, as some years later Newman was the first to recognise. The Roman Catholic Church did not admit that it was only a branch of the Catholic Church. The great majority of Anglicans had never heard of the 'branch' theory and the Greeks did not recognise the validity of Anglican orders. Was it not strange that the Catholic Church, by definition infallible, should consist of three bodies, each of which gave an account of itself quite different from that which the theory ascribed to it and

[1] *Tracts for the Times.*
[2] *Ibid.*

each of which was therefore presumably in error? If Anglican bishops possessed the apostolic succession they could only possess it because they had inherited it through their Roman mediaeval predecessors. If the Anglican bishops of Newman's day possessed the apostolic succession it was strange that they themselves were entirely unaware of the fact. Newman foretold for the bishops 'the spoiling of their goods and martyrdom'[1] and congratulated them on 'the blessed fate which awaited them for the love of Christ.' But the bishops betrayed singularly little enthusiasm at the reception of such an invitation.

It was this last oddity which was the main obstacle to the spread of the theory, the main stumbling block and cause of ridicule to it, and in the last analysis the reason why Newman in the end came to decide that it was untenable. 'Recollect we are supporting the bishops,' he wrote[1], 'enlarge on the unfairness of leaving them to bear the brunt of the battle.' But did the bishops believe that they possessed the apostolic succession? And, if they did not believe, was it quite certain that they were wrong not to believe? Was there any solid reason for believing that the theory was true? Who can say with certainty that there were no irregularities of ordination through all the dark years of, say, the eighth or the ninth century? Roman Catholic apologists have never pretended that there is sufficient historical evidence to prove the validity of the apostolic succession. They have argued that the Church by the continuity of her life and teaching bears upon herself the marks of the true Church and therefore, accepting her claims in general, they can accept one detail of the claim—the claim to an apostolic succession. The contention of the Oxford Movement that there was sufficient independent intrinsic evidence to prove the apostolic succession, to prove its possessor a Catholic, was quite a different contention and much harder to support. It is not easy to answer the doubts which Macaulay threw on it in his essay on Gladstone's *Church and State*. Roman Catholics believe in the apostolic succession because they believe in the Church. Newman asked his readers to believe in the Church because they believed in the apostolic succession—and the evidence for it, taking it alone, and unsupported, the certainty that there was no single irregularity at any place throughout the Dark Ages of the ninth century was not very convincing. The bishops showed no signs of being convinced. Very much the reverse. '*Non tali auxilio*,'[1] was their shrinking battle cry.

[1] *Tracts for the Times.*

47

Yet of course it was not merely a question whether the theory was true or false. From the point of view of our present study what is almost more important is the recognition of the fact that sincere people believed it. If Christ died for all men and good men are to be found in all denominations, then can it matter so very much to what denomination a man belongs? Or, to the contrary, if in any literal sense *extra ecclesia nulla salus* is true, then can anything else matter other than to get the denomination right? To pick a middle course between the Scylla of intolerance and the Charybdis of indifferentism is very difficult—but above all things necessary. If a man has learnt of other men's theories only out of books which attack them, it is hardly possible for him to understand the strength with which such theories can capture a sincere soul. It is of course very far from true that all converts are good ecumenists. Many a convert, as Newman was to find, is the most bitter and narrow enemy of the denomination which he has deserted. But it was hardly possible that the bridge between the denominations should be spanned save by a convert—by one who had in his time felt the strength and the loyalty and the affections of both systems—who had retained his affection for those whom he 'had loved long since and lost awhile'. A society in which the members of the different denominations were from cradle to grave rigidly restricted in their physical contacts with one another, as Catholics and Anglicans were in the early nineteenth century, could never have produced the frank confession of the Second Vatican Council that a salvific power was to be found in the sacraments of the separated brethren and that the Holy Spirit was to be seen visibly at work among them.

---

[1] 'Not with such help'.

3

Securus Iudicat Orbis Terrarum

NEWMAN'S THEORY of the Church at this time was more coherent than that of Keble but it was not therefore necessarily more palatable. The average Anglican of the day, then as now, was not concerned to pick holes in the details of a theory of belief in the apostolic succession —to ask what happened under Archbishop Parker in Queen Elizabeth's time, what Antonio de Dominis[1] did, whether the Duke of Newcastle's bishops in the eighteenth century had any intention of ordaining consecrating priests. These words and names were unknown to him. His reaction was not to deny that the claim was true so much as to ask how it could possibly matter. To him all this talk about whether sacraments were valid or invalid was without meaning. To be baptised, to be married in a Church, to receive, very occasionally, communion —these were reasonable social customs, much of a kind with taking off one's hat to a lady. It was good form to observe the one sort of custom as it was good form to observe the other. Perhaps if one took vows in a formal and ritualistic fashion they made a greater impression on the mind and thus had a psychological effect that was valuable. The suggestion that there was any especial external grace that came with them from God was without meaning.

It may well be asked why, if they believed no more than this about the sacraments and had no clear conception of grace, did they think it worth while to pray. What did they imagine did happen or could possibly happen when they prayed.? The age of miracles had gone. Did they imagine that God could or would alter His laws and change the weather or bring back to health a man incurably sick simply because a petitioner asked Him? Would they have thought more

[1] Catholic Bishop of Spalato, who in Charles I's reign came over to England and ordained Anglican bishops.

highly of a God who did behave in such an anthropomorphic fashion? It is a curiosity that so many people then or now, who think it superstitious to ask for or expect God's assistance in accordance with some ritual with which they are unfamiliar, do not attend to the retort of the sceptic who will argue that what is really superstitious is not to expect God's assistance in this way or that way but to expect it at all. Why should it be odder to expect God to alter His purpose because you fumble with a rosary than it is to expect Him to alter it because you mumble a prayer? When he came to publish his *Essay on Development* Newman was much criticised for his alleged credulity about miracles—because he refused to dismiss out of hand the claims of St. Januarius or of the Holy House of Loreto. But Newman's attitude towards miracles was perfectly coherent. Any particular claim to a miracle must be approached with all possible objective scepticism. Newman entirely agreed with Hume that it was in itself more probable that a witness was deceived or lying or stupid than that a miracle happened. But he who denied that God could intervene in the affairs of man with a miracle was denying the existence of a God in any sense in which any sort of Christian teaching had ever used the word. It is true that many Victorian Christians sought to have the best of both worlds by arguing that God had performed miracles in biblical times but had since ceased to do so. But this was a position so wholly unsupported by reason, evidence or probability that, as Newman well saw, it was unlikely that men would remain for long in so absurd a half-way house. 'If miracles never happen now,' they would soon be saying, 'is it not most likely that they never happened at all?' As Newman later put it in his *Lectures on the Present Condition of Catholics*,[1] 'To my mind certainly it is incomparably more difficult to believe that the Divine Being should do one miracle and no more than that He should do a thousand.' What is more, if God cannot intervene in the affairs of men, then not only can He not perform miracles, but equally He cannot answer prayers; and with the abandonment of the belief in prayer would go the abandonment of every religious practice ever known to man, Catholic or Protestant, Christian or pagan.

As we look back on the England of those times—particularly if we read about it through the eyes of the Tractarians—it seems to us a time filled with religious controversy. But we have only to turn from the theologians to the novelists of nineteenth-century England—to

[1] Chapter 20, p. 306.

Dickens, or Thackeray or Anthony Trollope—to remind ourselves that the age was not so overwhelmingly theological as one might guess from reading Newman. The problems of the apostolic succession did not loom large in the life of Barchester. To Newman even in the 1830's the age did not appear a deeply religious age. If men still imagined themselves to have preserved a belief in a certain efficacy of prayer, they held their faith with little reason and after having abandoned the beliefs that were concomitant with it. They had no clear belief in grace and it was only too likely that in such an atmosphere the belief in prayer would steadily weaken. The Englishman's religion was mainly derived from the Bible, and the growth of industrialism was making the Bible steadily less relevant and less intelligible. The language of the Gospels, written in an agricultural society with its parables and metaphors all drawn from rural pursuits, had less and less meaning to an urbanised, industrial population whose life was quite divorced from the basic processes of nature. How was it possible to arrest that decline? The Church of England was, as he still thought, founded by Christ as a witness to His truth. Its duty was to maintain all its divine prerogatives—to admit no tampering with the sacramental life.

Thus, shortly after his publication of his *Tract*, Newman, who was by then the Vicar of St. Mary's, was asked by a pastry cook called Jubber, who was resident in the parish, to marry his daughter. Jubber was himself a Nonconformist, but that, though regrettable, did not in itself matter. What did matter was Newman's discovery that Jubber had never had his daughter baptised. Newman could not, he thought, possibly administer a Christian ceremony to someone who was not a Christian. It was argued that Miss Jubber was a Christian—that she believed. But Newman explained that believing had nothing to do with it—or at any rate what did she believe if she did not believe in baptism? Christ's command to all His followers was to be baptised. Those who were not baptised were not Christians. Newman had no personal prejudices in the matter. As James Anthony Froude, by that time in his life by no means generally sympathetic to Newman's point of view, wrote in his *Oxford Counter Reformation*, Newman never at any time treated doubts and difficulties as a form of moral wickedness. He was perfectly willing to baptise Miss Jubber and then to marry her. But neither her father nor she was willing for this, and, if she would not be baptised as a Christian, then, asserted Newman, she could not be married as a Christian. What part her fiancé played, whether he had been baptised and whether that made any difference, does not appear.

Newman, rather to his own surprise, received a good deal of public abuse for his refusal. The abuse took the form of scandalous and wholly false stories according to which Newman was alleged to have called Miss Jubber 'an outcast', bidding her begone. Of course he did nothing of the sort but the stories were sufficient to show how completely the public failed to understand Newman's point of view. They could understand—even those of them who disapproved—personal bigotry and hatred by a man of one denomination for a person of another. They could not understand an objective, dispassionate insistence on a particular ceremony as requisite. The careful thinker might ask why, if Jubber did not value baptism, did he bother so much about marriage in a church, but the answer of the man in the street was that a girl liked to be married in a church—that it made no social odds whether or not one was baptised but that it was to one's social advantage to have a proper marriage—and the man in the street was totally unable to understand one to whom such reasoning was insufficient.

Newman's position in this matter as an Anglican clergyman was not really tenable. While he could perhaps argue on Tractarian lines that he was permitted as an Anglican to believe in the sacrament of matrimony, he could not possibly argue that it was an obligatory tenet of the Anglican Church that marriage was a sacrament. A marriage ceremony on asserted Anglican principles was no more than an exchange of promises between two persons in the sight of God. The only valid reason for forbidding it would be the knowledge that one of these persons either was not in a position to give these promises or quite certainly had no intention of keeping them. Of neither of these was there any suggestion with Miss Jubber. But of course Newman, when he objected to the marriage, thought of himself not as a minister of the national Church to whose services all Englishmen as such had a right but as the priest of a branch of the Catholic Church, to which his branch belonged in virtue of the fact that it satisfied, as he alleged, the very strict conditions of the apostolic succession; and it was Newman's weakness throughout all this period of his life that he held a conception of the Church of England entirely different from that which was held by the vast majority of its members.

Today the problems of marriage present some of the largest problems to ecumenical advancement and satisfactory formulae for the mixed marriage difficulties have by no means been as yet discovered. But the general desire is to make the rules as generous as possible—only to bar out from the religious ceremony those who must be excluded by a real and deliberate rather than a merely technical defiance of the will of God and to think, whatever the theology behind it, that a marriage that is blessed is preferable to a marriage that is unblessed. A marriage is not the better for being forced into a registry office. The mentality of a hundred years ago according to which he who belonged to the wrong denomination held a faith so utterly unpleasing to God that it was hardly preferable to a total lack of faith has passed away. The Second Vatican Council has explicitly stated in the decree on ecumenism that 'there is no doubt that they (our separated brethren) are capable of giving real birth to the life of grace . . . and it must be granted that they are capable of giving admission to the community of salvation.' Even if we suppose that it was true that only social reasons led Miss Jubber to wish for a church marriage, yet most people would agree that a bad reason was better than no reason. In this, as in all relations with those who were not of his communion, Newman was to become a great deal more liberal and generous in his Catholic than in his Anglican days. For the moment the main effect on him was to make clear to him the paradoxical task that he had set himself in attempting to defend his conception of Anglicanism against the overwhelming body of Anglican opinion.

The public philistine abuse was of little importance except as evidence of the wide gap between Newman's mind and that of the general public. Newman did not greatly care about it. What he did care about was the ruling of his bishop, Bishop Bagot, who insisted both that he should marry Miss Jubber and—what is more—that he had no legal right to refuse to do so. The Church of England was a State Church. Every resident in a parish had a legal right to demand the services of the vicar of the parish. If Miss Jubber, a resident in St. Mary's parish, demanded of the vicar that he marry her and if there was no cause or just impediment such as a previous marriage to obstruct it, then the vicar was guilty of a criminal offence if he refused to perform the ceremony.

This ruling of Bishop Bagot, himself a mild and reasonable man and well disposed to Newman, dealt to his theories two shattering blows. On the one hand it was no longer possible to pretend that the

Tractarians, in fighting for the apostolic succession and for the Church's independence of the State, were fighting the battle of the bishops. They might conceivably be fighting the battle of some ideal bishops whose patterns in Platonic fashion were laid up in heaven. The flesh-and-blood bishops of the actual world were against them. Nor could it be pretended that the Church—the Church of England—however it ought to be, was in fact independent of the State. Bishop Bagot was unquestionably right in his interpretation of the law of the land. But, if that was the law of the land, it greatly increased the difficulty of believing that the Church of England was a branch of the Catholic Church. For independence of Caesar was a cardinal principle of the Church of Christ. As the Second Vatican Council was to say, 'In carrying out their apostolic duty ... bishops enjoy essentially complete and perfect freedom and independence from any and every civil power whatsoever.' Did Bagot enjoy such a freedom?

The case with which Newman had been presented over Miss Jubber's marriage was much better as a test case than that of Keble's Irish tithes. For it could well be argued that, however independent the Church might be in doctrine and practice, the State had clearly a right to have a say as to its income. But in the case of Miss Jubber the State directly interfered with a religious practice and—what was worse—the bishop supported its action in doing so.

It was, beyond question, the whole weakness of the Tractarian case that however things ought to be, in fact the law was directly opposed to its contentions. The Church of England did in fact owe its existence and status to a political action. The Jubber marriage showed, as was going to be shown again in case after case—the Jerusalem bishopric, the Gorham case, down to the rejection of the Deposited Prayer Book in recent times—that in law the State had supreme authority over the Church and the Church only possessed such rights of self-government as the State saw fit to concede to it. To a man who found such a situation intolerable there was really no remedy except that he should leave the Church of England. There was no place for him within its communion. His position owing to Parliament's hesitation to use its powers is in practice less intolerable today.

From the time of the Jubber case this was in truth the logic of Newman's position, though in the entirely intelligible human fashion he still struggled a bit before he surrendered. If we consider friends, relations, the climate of opinion of the day, the intimate connection of all the life that he had lived within the Church of England, a certain hesitation was neither surprising nor reprehensible. But of course he had a further reason than that for his hesitation. The fact that he was coming to feel that the Anglican position was untenable did not necessarily prove that the Roman position was tenable, nor indeed would any Roman priest have consented to receive him simply because he no longer believed in the Church of England. Newman felt himself in great danger of finding himself entirely bereft of any spiritual home.

The next controversy in which he found himself involved was that with Hampden, then Professor in Moral Philosophy, afterwards to be successively Regius Professor of Divinity and the controversial Bishop of Hereford. It was concerned with Hampden's proposal that Nonconformists should be admitted as undergraduates to the University. Up till then every candidate for matriculation had to subscribe to the Anglican Thirty-nine Articles and the University was preserved as an exclusive perquisite of the Church of England. Nonconformists or Catholics or the like had to get their higher education as best they could in other and inferior institutions or outside the country. In the temper of the times, when the repeal of Test Acts and Acts of Emancipation had already admitted Nonconformists to take part in the nation's political life, and when a large number of those who called themselves Anglicans were notoriously very careless about their religious beliefs, the continuance of the requirement was an absurdity. It was proper to require a profession of faith from those who were seeking Holy Orders. It was absurd to require it of young men who were only asking to be educated and who had no intention of adopting a clerical profession. One might have thought that Newman would have remembered how deeply he had been shocked by the irreverent spirit in which the Trinity undergraduates had taken the sacrament which the Statutes required, preparatory to getting riotously intoxicated in the evening; and would have been glad that such offensive practices should have been abolished. As an old man he was, in a somewhat similar position, to fight bravely and wisely against Manning and the other bishops when they tried to rally Catholic opinion against a measure for freeing the atheist Bradlaugh from the obligation to take an oath before he could be seated in the House of Commons.[1] But Newman as a Catholic was a much more liberal man than Newman

[1] Walter L. Arnstein, *The Bradlaugh Case*, p. 230, Chapter 20.

as an Anglican—or, if you will, Newman as an old man was much more liberal than Newman in his youth.

Almost all the examples that are given of Newman's intransigence come not from his Catholic but from his Anglican days. Thus Dean Inge in his *Outspoken Essays* quotes[1] Newman as saying that 'A heresiarch should meet with no mercy. He must be dealt with by the competent authority as if he were embodied evil. To spare him is a false and dangerous pity. It is to endanger the souls of thousands and it is uncharitable towards himself,' and comments that Newman spoke thus 'even in his Anglican days'. He should have written not 'even' but 'only'. When Kingsley wished to find words to justify his accusation against Newman that he had taught that a Catholic priest may be indifferent to truth, the only passage to which he could point which had even an appearance of justifying his charge was a passage which Newman had used when he was an Anglican. It was in his Anglican days that Newman indulged in extravagances of hagiography to which he would certainly never have given himself in old age. He showed in his *Inspiration of Scripture* of his closing years a readiness to welcome sane biblical criticism which he would never have accepted in his Oxford days. Newman as an Anglican discussed the theoretical need for suppression in order to save its victims from error. It was only his experience of suppression in practice as a Catholic which showed him the far greater danger of the corruption of those who did the suppressing.

Hampden who had a certain genius for confusing issues confused it now by adding to his proposal that there should be no religious tests for admission to the University the wholly inconsequential rider that differences of religious opinion were in any event unimportant. Newman reasonably enough resented this folly. He found it offensive. That it is not possible to know with any certainty the truth about the ultimate mysteries is an opinion which an honest man may well hold, but such a man would refrain from drawing money from the profession of a faith in whose certainty he had no confidence. A layman might well think it undesirable to disturb the established religion even if he was not certain of its total truth, but Anglican clergymen had subscribed to the Thirty-nine Articles. Those of them who were at Universities or who held positions of high preferment were incomparably more lavishly remunerated than any other clergymen anywhere

[1] *Outspoken Essays*, p. 178, 'Cardinal Newman'.

in the world. It was intolerable that in a casual throw-away they should say that really there is no difference between one opinion and another and yet at the same time continue to hold their positions and to draw their stipends.

In the nineteenth century, and even in the early years of this century, Anglicans would sometimes speak and write as if the truths of Christianity were matters in which only Englishmen had a right to express an opinion and as if issues could be settled by debates in which only Englishmen need be invited to participate. The complacency was, of course, ridiculous but it was intelligible. It was a consequence of Britain's secular imperial position. The Church of England derived its prestige and world-wide consideration from the greatness of the British Empire. The collapse of the Empire has radically changed the nature of the Church of England. It now consists not of one body with its headquarters at Canterbury, but of a number of autonomous provinces in the different countries where it operates, and the voices within it are by no means exclusively the voices of Englishmen. That is doubtless a great advantage, but a considerable amount of the debt for the change is owed to Newman. Though himself the most home-loving and insular of men, he yet tried to teach his fellow countrymen, at a time when they were by no means generally ready to learn the lesson, that the last word on all ultimate questions was not necessarily said by an Englishman—that the appeal was to the world's court—that *securus iudicat orbis terrarum.*[1]

So Newman joined the ranks that were fighting against Hampden, but once again, as at the time of Catholic Emancipation, he found himself fighting in company with allies who were very antipathetic to him. The High-and-Dries—the 'Z's'—were for keeping the Nonconformists out of the University because once they came in as undergraduates, the next thing that would happen would be that they would be clamouring to be elected Fellows, and the existing Fellows would find themselves threatened in their comfortable monopoly. Newman was not at all sympathetic with such men, nor indeed were they sympathetic to him. From their point of view they were by no means sure that Newman himself was not a Nonconformist nor that he himself should not for his equivocal attitude to the Articles be deprived of his Fellowship. Yet for the moment Hampden was defeated by this strange alliance, although when the alliance was renewed a few

[1] The judgement of the world is beyond challenge.

years later to keep Hampden out of the Regius Professorship, it was unsuccessful since this was a Crown appointment over which Convocation had no vote.

It was the argument of the liberals that bigotry and narrow-mindedness were great evils, that virtue was not to be found only in the ranks of one denomination. The 'Z's' were disposed to deny this in effect, if not in these terms. Hiding themselves from the world, they muttered together that Nonconformists were not gentlemen, that many of them were radicals, that they had neither the manners nor the code of honour that one expects of the decently bred. They would not in so many words say that it was a mortal sin to speak to a Nonconformist, but to do so would seem to them an unusual and surprising action of which no gentleman would be voluntarily guilty. Newman's attitude was exactly the opposite. Mindful of the Gospel command that we should not judge, he had no wish to say that Nonconformists were worse than other people, but he along with the other Tractarians thought that, since they were not Catholics, therefore it was wrong to associate with them.

In this he took up an attitude different from that which he had taken when he had first gone as a curate to St. Clement's and when, as he records, he was always very careful to speak well of the Nonconformist minister. It was also an attitude very different from that which as a Catholic he took up in the sunset glory of his days when, at a time when such friendships were not as easy or as common as they are now, he was able to remake and to preserve deep bonds of intimacy with such Anglican friends as Rogers or Dean Church. One cannot but regret that for these passing years, so anxious not to compromise the delicate balance of his *Via Media*, he should have thought it necessary to put on the features of intransigence. The very isolation of his position had persuaded him that Christian faith was a much rarer possession than was commonly thought. As he said in his Sermon on *The Ventures of Faith*, which he preached in St. Mary's in 1836,[1] 'I really fear that most men called Christians, whatever they may profess, whatever they may think they feel, whatever warmth and illumination and love they may claim as their own, yet would go on as they do, neither much better nor much worse, if they believed Christianity to be a fable. When young, they indulge their lusts, or at least pursue the

[1] Oxford University Sermons, February 21, 1836. Heard at the time and recorded in *The Oxford Movement* by Dean Church.

world's vanities; as time goes on they get into a fair way of business, or other mode of making money; then they marry and settle; and, their interest coinciding with their duty, they seem to be, and think themselves, respectable and religious men; they grow attached to things as they are; they begin to have a zeal against vice and error; and they follow after peace with all men. Such conduct indeed, as far as it goes, is right and praiseworthy. Only I say it has not necessarily anything to do with religion at all.'

The argument was coherent enough in itself but it was negative. It was becoming increasingly easy to see what Newman was protesting against. The Church must be autonomous. The State must not order it and its ministers about. The Christian must not be predominantly concerned with the affairs of this world—even with good conduct in this world. He must be concerned with the love of God. Well enough. That shows what he should not do. But what should he do? He should join the Church which Christ had founded. How was he to recognise which was that Church? By its possession of the apostolic succession. The answer did not seem to most Englishmen of the day particularly convincing, but at least it was objective and coherent. But then they went on to ask—those of them, the minority, who followed the argument with any detail or care—if the Catholic Church is, as it seems to be, divided into three branches, why is it so divided? Is there any especial point in belonging to one branch rather than another or ought one simply to adhere to the branch to which one chances to find oneself belonging—much as one is a member of one College rather than another, and no doubt pays to it a decent loyalty, not seriously pretending, however, that it is of a different kind to any of the other Colleges? In particular—for that was of course the question in which Newman's readers were interested—is there any especial purpose in belonging to the Church of England?

To answer this question, Newman next wrote his *Via Media*. In it he argued that the Church of England was valuable as upholding a middle course between the Roman Catholics who had too readily added unscriptural superstitions to the fundamental teaching of Christ and the Nonconformists who, anxious to purge religion of Roman superstitions, had in fact destroyed too much and destroyed some things that were an essential part of Christ's teaching. The Church of England stood in the middle, retaining what should be retained and abolishing what should be abolished. It was her Prophetical Office to bear witness to the Middle Way. Without becoming involved in arguments about details, it was clear from the first that there were two major difficulties in this thesis. First, it in no way proved that the Church of England was a *Via Media*. The most that it proved was that Newman—and a few of his friends—were perhaps Viae Mediae. They may, if you will, have struck the balance exactly right, but, if so, the rest of the Church of England had struck it wrong, for they could not pretend that they were carrying the Church of England with them. Secondly, 'media' could not on any theory of Newman be the correct word with which to describe the Anglican position. It certainly did not stand in the middle. For, on Newman's own terms of reference, what was of supreme importance was to belong to the Catholic Church. The Romans along with the Anglicans belonged to the Catholic Church. The Nonconformists did not belong to it. Therefore the Anglican, it might be, stood between Rome and the Nonconformists, but he did not stand in the middle between them. He stood much nearer to Rome.

Naturally enough such a demonstration did not increase his popularity with the average Anglican who took the exactly opposite point of view—who thought that he stood much nearer to the Nonconformists than to the Catholics and indeed thought of the Church of England as a body especially formed in the sixteenth century to protest against the corruptions of Rome. The apostolic succession was to this average Anglican's eyes simply an irrelevance. What could it matter if the Anglican bishops possessed it or not? Newman, now a little despairing of public approval, was more concerned with discovering the truth for himself than with converting others. Differences had appeared even in the ranks of the Tractarians themselves, and what was necessary, therefore, was to establish not merely who had the apostolic succession but what was positive Catholic doctrine. The only court of appeal in a divided Christendom was that of the appeal back to the days before the division. What did the Church teach in its undivided days? He had already from his study of the Arians derived the conclusion that it was wholly false to think that there was a simple, primitive Christianity which had been subsequently corrupted. On the contrary the record from the first told of a voice which spoke with authority and defined doctrine. It was because authority had spoken that the Arians were defeated, and similarly it was the voice of authority which had rescued the Church from the other early heresies which attacked it. It condemned impartially the heresies on the one side and the heresies on the other. Arius claimed that Christ was begotten in time and less than fully God and the Church condemned him. The Monophysites claimed that Christ had only one nature and was less than fully Man and the Church condemned them. It was not in those days the Church of England that was the *Via Media*. It was Rome which was the *Via Media*, condemning the extravagances first of the one side and then of the other.

Yet there still remained the obstinate question of the man in the street. What can all these things matter? Who cares about Arians and Monophysites today? What bearing can their theories or the refutation of them have on our modern problems? It occurred to Newman—in the insular, constricted life that he led it seems hardly to have occurred to him before—that it was absurd that either he or his antagonists should argue out these problems as if they were purely English problems. The problems were of their nature universal problems. There were Christians in every country of the world. Anglicans, for all practical purposes were at that time still only found in England.

> To foreign lands no sound of her is come,
> Humbly content to be despised at home[1]

Dryden had written a hundred and fifty years before with a bitter pertinence. Was it not common sense in settling Christian doctrine to look to what the general body of Christians said? He was studying the history of the Donatist heretics in North Africa and reading on them an article in the *Dublin Review*,[2] written by Dr. (afterwards Cardinal) Wiseman, and in that article he came across the quotation of St. Augustine's refutation of the Donatists by the appeal to universal consent. '*Securus iudicat orbis terrarum*,' wrote St. Augustine. The sentence rang like a bell in Newman's ear. Was not this universal consent the test of truth? And, if it was the test that could be invoked against the Donatists in the fifth century, could it not equally be invoked against the Anglicans in the nineteenth century? He had appealed to the teaching of the undivided Church, and what had he found? 'My stronghold was Antiquity,' he wrote. 'Now here in the middle of the fifth century I found, as it seemed to me, the Christendom of the sixteenth and the nineteenth centuries reflected. I saw my face in that mirror and I was a Monophysite.'

[1] *The Hind and the Panther.* Part I. 22, 404, 405.   [2] Summer, 1839.

The strength of the argument is self-evident. As self-evident is its peculiar danger. The appeal of general consent might indicate that it was more reasonable to be a Catholic than an Anglican. But Christians of any sort inhabited only a small part of the world and had inhabited even that for only a minute proportion of the world's history. If general consent showed that it was more reasonable to be a Catholic than an Anglican, did it not even more clearly show that it was more reasonable to be neither—that most men and women had got along without any faith in Christ at all? It was arguable that there was some sort of general consent through the ages to the existence of God: that by and large almost all men had always had some sort of a sense of God; that even polytheists believed that there was a God behind the gods, much as Virgil in more casual moods talked about the gods but always dropped into monotheistic language in moments of deep intensity; that even those who were most anxious to deny the existence of obligation could not express themselves without constantly employing, willingly or unwillingly, the language of good and bad and 'ought' and 'ought not'. Such beliefs, it could be argued, were a necessity of thought, an inescapable part of man's manhood. But it could not possibly be pretended that either in Newman's own day or throughout history there was any general consent to the Divinity of Christ.

The Jesuits of the sixteenth and seventeenth centuries, when they came across in India and China civilisations that had been built with no knowledge of Christ, had understood that here was an intellectual challenge which they had to meet: that, for reasons that were far more than mere reasons of necessary convenience they had both to show the Indians and the Chinese and to show themselves that the beliefs of these non-Christians were in some ways beliefs of men groping towards the Christian truth, of which they had not yet heard, little though they knew it themselves. Their efforts did not meet with favour at Rome and were condemned. Official policy for a century and a half preferred to meet the non-Christian with a *non possumus* of total rejection. But Newman challenged the purely negative and obstructive and what he called Novatian opposition. To him the Christian's duty was to go out into the world conquering and to conquer, expressing Christian truth in so far as it was possible to express it in the language of those to whom he was speaking. Such tactics did not meet with much favour in Rome in the time of Pius X and the campaign against Modernism. But they were adopted and embraced by John XXIII.

It would of course be insolent to say that such a man as Newman had not even in these earlier years meditated on this point. Later in life he was to express most fruitfully the results of such meditation. Such a man as he must in the nature of things have considered the problem even in earlier years. Passage after passage in his early sermons bear witness to the depth and reality of his faith in Christ and it is not to be believed that such a man would have used such words idly or without considering deeply with himself what they meant and why they were true. But all that we can say is that we know a good deal from his own confessions about his private thoughts, and he has left us plenty of record at this stage that he believed in Christ but no account why he believed in Him. But it was natural that others asked the question. Common opinion at that time believed in God, regardless of whether it derived the belief from St. Thomas or from Paley or whether (as was more likely) it did not clearly know whence it derived it—because it was convinced of the evidence for design, convinced of the great Watchmaker, who arranged and sustained and must therefore in the first instance have created the universe. The Kantian argument which found the fundamental reality in conscience rather than in matter was a moral argument. In Kant the relationship between God and Man which it established had no concern with Christ. No one could pretend that only Christians had consciences.

Was there any reason to think that it had necessarily any such concern for Newman? No man of sense or decency challenged the sincerity of Newman's profession of faith in the historical claims of Christ. His sermons were proof of his sincerity but, it was argued, they were not proof of the validity of his reasoning. Scepticism was in the logic of his argument, whether he wished it to be so or not, whether he understood it to be so or not. Here was a man proposing a belief in an infallible Church, consisting of branches all of which were gravely in error, and unable to find a secure resting place for himself either in Anglicanism or in Catholicism—believing in fact in an infallible Church which did not exist. What more likely than that such a man would end finally in scepticism and despair?

The clearest and most certain of the dogmas of the Church, argued Newman, was that of original sin. If there was any good at all, then it was certain that Man had a divided nature—that he had indeed within him some impulses which urged him to identify himself with the general good and others which put him selfishly at enmity against the good of others. Of those two sorts of impulses there could be no question. The absurd optimism of some of the eighteenth-century thinkers who imagined that some purpose was served by saying that Man was purely good, when it manifestly was not true, seemed as silly to Newman as it did to Voltaire. The alternative to a belief in original sin was not a belief that Man was absolutely good but that he was absolutely evil, or at least amoral—or at least that the world was absolutely evil in the sense that there was no purpose in it; that some of a man's impulses were such that it would be convenient to other men if he satisfied them and others were such that it would be inconvenient if he satisfied them; but that was all that could properly be said of them. It was without meaning to say that in themselves they were good or bad.

Whatever others might say about this risk of incipient scepticism, Newman never wavered in his belief in Man's double nature, in the reality of obligation and the reality of original sin. Corruption was in his view in the will. If men fell from virtue they did not as a rule fall because their temptations were of overwhelming strength. They fell because they did not wish to conquer. As he said in a Sermon on *The Power of the Will*, which he preached in 1840,[1] 'Wherever men complain, as they often do, of the arduousness of a high virtue, at least it were well that they should first ask themselves the question whether they desire to have it. We hear much in this day of the impossibility of heavenly purity. . . . Are you sure that the impossibility which you insist on does not lie not in nature but in the will? . . . Say not . . . that you cannot be other than Adam made you; you have never brought yourself to will it—you cannot bear to will it. You cannot bear to be other than you are. Life would seem a blank to you, were you other; yet what you are from not desiring a gift, this you make an excuse for not possessing it.'

That might be the condition of many men. It doubtless was their condition, but it was not Newman's condition. From a very early age —from a time long before he had come to a religious position which would entitle him to advocate it as a general precept—Newman had felt himself called to a life of celibacy. He was not without sympathy and understanding of those whose more common difficulties were of

[1] Oxford University Sermons, March, 1840.

the opposite nature, but his difficulty was not that he lacked the will to be pure. He possessed such a will in abundance. What he wanted was an assurance that such a will had some validity behind it, some virtue in it, that it was not merely some fad of physical repulsion with which he happened to be afflicted. He wanted an authority which would assure him that his aspirations were of value. Others wanted by nature to be incontinent but thought that religion forebade it. Newman wanted by nature to be continent but wished to discover from religion a reason which would make his wish valuable.

Obviously if we are able to accept the claims and authority of Christ, then we receive such a reassurance, but the difficulty about an appeal to what might be called the naked Bible is that, if we turn to the Bible alone, the Gospels are so short, the sayings attributed to Christ are often so difficult to understand—taken in isolation one text is so often contradictory of another—that it is not possible without an interpreter to know on many points what Christ taught. The internecine battles among those who profess to base their faith solely on the Bible are sufficient evidence of this difficulty. But fortunately, thought Newman, we have such an interpreter. One of the clearest lessons which the New Testament teaches is that Christ founded a Church and left with us the Holy Spirit who shall guide us into all truth. Therefore the most urgent task was to discover where that truth was to be found. Yet where was the Church? These years of the first half of the 1840's, the years of his retirement at Littlemore—years during which he had so largely lost his faith in the Church of England and was not yet able to give his faith without hesitation to the Church of Rome—were for him very sad years.

His first attempt was to bridge the awkward gulf between the Church of England and the Roman Catholic Church by arguing that it was not as wide as was generally thought. In his famous *Tract 90* he argued that it was possible to hold the full cycle of Catholic beliefs and yet to sign the Thirty-nine Articles. The Thirty-nine Articles, he argued truly enough, were not intended to be a creed telling a man what he ought to believe. They were a statement of the limiting conditions of a Church, which it was intended to make so comprehensive that all Englishmen could be included within it, and, argued Newman, its articles were so widely drawn that, while outspoken Protestants could indeed sign them, those who wished to remain Catholics could also sign. The Articles did not condemn Catholic doctrines. The Articles condemned not Roman, but 'Romish' practices, by which was meant, he asserted, not the essential Roman doctrines of, say, Mass or purgatory or indulgences or the invocation of saints but the corruptions of practice that had been allowed to creep in in the days before the Reformation.

Newman's argument was sound up to a point. It was true enough that most Elizabethan Englishmen did not think of themselves as Protestants in the sense in which Victorian Englishmen had come to think of themselves as Protestants. The Church of England up till the death of Laud was a very different place from the Church of England after 1688 and Newman was within his rights in reminding his contemporaries of the fact—in rebuking them for their bad history when they appealed so confidently to the Elizabethan example. Whether he pressed his argument too far, whether the distinction between Roman and Romish was far fetched and sophistical was a matter for argument, but learned men, like Dean Church, who remained with the Anglican body and indeed rose to the highest honours in it, continued to maintain until their dying days that the argument of *Tract 90* was a just argument. But what was certain was that whether or not the argument was sophistical, it would inevitably be greeted as sophistical by the greater number of Anglicans of the day. It was this incapacity to judge public reactions that was so strange a defect in Newman and the other Tractarians. They were surprised that people were surprised at what they had to say. Yet it was surely not surprising. These men in the street thought of themselves as Protestants linked together to fight against the tyranny of Rome. To them frank enemies—confessed Catholics —were very bad, but far worse were the secret traitors within their own ranks who took the very title deeds of Protestantism and by sophistical argument twisted the words of them to make them appear not to say what in plain language they most obviously did say. Doubtless this was not a just interpretation of *Tract 90*, but it was an interpretation which was to be expected in the England and the Oxford of that day.

It was Newman's discovery that a main obstacle to ecumenism then, as indeed to a large extent it is today, was an obstacle of the will. It was not merely a problem of comparing documents, of showing that this and that position of the one side or the other had been misunderstood. Such attempts were doubtless valuable but in the last resort people were much more divided by their will to be divided than by any genuine intellectual incompatibilities. It is not a matter of explaining to Mr. Paisley in Belfast the meaning of certain theological formulae and then he will speak more kindly of the Pope. And so in the 1840's it was not a matter of explaining to the average Anglican clergyman that he could sign the Thirty-nine Articles and yet be a Catholic if he wished. It was the last thing that he wished, and if it was shown to him that the Thirty-nine Articles were patent of a Catholic interpretation, his only reply was 'So much the worse then for the Thirty-nine Articles. Let us rewrite and strengthen them so as to make certain that they say what they should mean.' Equally it must be admitted that there was at this date little ecumenical will on the Catholic side. Whatever modifications were admitted of the most uncompromising interpretation of the maxim *Extra ecclesiam nulla salus*,[1] they were admitted only most grudgingly. It was not imagined that Catholics could have anything to learn from those outside the Church. Their only business was to protect themselves against the dangers of these persons' attacks.

Nor can it be pretended that in these days Newman's own position was so widely more liberal. If conscience is the supreme evidence of God's existence then it must be admitted that, while it may be contended that every man who is fully a man has a conscience, yet their consciences tell different things to different people. The difficulty of the traditional or Thomist proofs of the existence of God was that not everyone found them cogent. It could not be pretended that they were universally accepted. The difficulty about the derivation of God from conscience was that it was not easy on its terms to see how any honest opinion could be condemned as invalid. By what test is one voice to be called the voice of God and another denied that title? Newman's conscience may have told him that Miss Jubber should be baptised, but Miss Jubber's conscience apparently told her that she should not be baptised. What should decide which was right? By what test could Hampden's contention that differences of religion were unimportant be refuted? It might be—probably was—that Miss Jubber was an ill-educated person who could not clearly marshal the arguments for her position but that, even if true, got the case no further. There were plenty of ignorant people, but there were also plenty of learned people, who did not agree with Newman.

The Vatican Council of today in its decrees on ecumenism, on non-

[1] No salvation outside the Church.

Catholic and non-Christian religions, has approached these problems in a very different spirit from that of the Church of a hundred and forty years ago and has paid tribute to the influence of Newman in leading it to do so. It has shown no ambition merely to denounce those who differ from it as wrong or to exclude them unnecessarily from avenues of grace. Its anxiety has been rather to find how far they are right. This ambition has sprung partly from charity but partly also from a proper curiosity which seeks to discover what must be the purpose in the scheme of things of those from whom God has withheld His full gift of faith.

Certainly there has been—through many influences no doubt but largely through the influence of Newman's spirit—a very marked change in official Catholic policy towards those outside its ranks. Whereas in previous years ecclesiastical authorities had been mainly concerned to defend the Church's position by definitions of exclusion, the modern age has seen a change. Pius IX had issued his *Syllabus Errorum*. Leo XIII had condemned Anglican orders. The English Catholic bishops of the day had thrown cold water on Cardinal Mercier's talks on reunion with Anglican ecclesiastics. But today the Church, concerned indeed to assert the certainty of grace in its sacraments, is careful not to deny that grace is found wherever there is good faith. The constitution *De Ecclesia* admits the reality of sacraments outside the Church. Plenty who are not Catholics, it says, 'recognise and receive even other Sacraments (than baptism) in their own churches or religious companies.'

In accordance with the Council's Declaration on Religious Liberty, if Miss Jubber's conscience told her that baptism was wrong, then, informed or uninformed, she had not only a right but a duty to refuse it. The State, far from rendering the Church a service by insisting that even such a marriage as this should be in church, would have a duty to provide a registry office or to license a Nonconformist chapel in which Miss Jubber could go through the forms to which her conscience led her. It was neither Anglicanism as such nor Catholicism as such which brought Newman in his maturer years to an understanding of these truths but the experience within himself that truth could on occasions only be attained as a result of dialogue and that its cause could not be furthered by rigid authoritarian rules. It was of course by no means true that all converts came to such comprehending conclusions. Plenty turned with bitter recrimination against the faith in which they had been reared and even Newman himself was for a time guilty of words of violence which many would have wished unsaid.

Tract 90 was not on its own merits a very satisfactory document. For, prescinding from any detailed verbal arguments about its distinctions of Roman and Romish, what did it say, on the interpretation most favourable to itself? It said that it was possible for one who held the whole cycle of Roman doctrines to sign the Thirty-nine Articles. If so, so what? No one pretended, Newman never pretended, that only Catholics could sign the Thirty-nine Articles. What then was the Church of England, this amorphous body, some of whose members were Catholics and some of whom were not? Whatever Christ founded, no one had ever pretended that He had founded a Church, 25% of whose members were to be His disciples. If one would be a Catholic what was necessary was to join the body which Christ had founded—the body which bore witness to Christ's teaching—not to tabulate one's own beliefs and then to discover a body within which the profession of those beliefs would be perhaps tolerated. The proper question to ask was not 'What body will Christ allow you to belong to?' but 'What body would Christ wish you to belong to?'

So Newman's critics were perhaps wiser than his friends in seeing *Tract 90* as in reality an act of resignation from the Church of England. The Church of England, perhaps, ought to be the sort of body which Newman described, but manifestly it was not such a body. Twenty-four bishops with Bagot at their head joined in condemning the Tract and by doing so underlined the contradiction of Newman's position, and it is hard to say that the bishops were not on their terms of reference right.

Of course there still remained the ultimate difficulty, which so few people understood, that to become a Catholic it was necessary not only to believe the Church of England to be wrong. It was—which was far more difficult—necessary to believe the Church of Rome to be right. Rome, as he put it, had about it, as far as he could see at that time, 'none of the marks of sanctity'.

Newman had a strange faculty for asking the right questions even when he did not give the right answers. He was of course quite right to warn himself and his disciples of the danger of losing themselves in Pascalian *esprit de géométrie* or in merely historical arguments about apostolic succession and the like. Wherever the truth might be in these arguments, the fundamental business of the Catholic Church was to be the home of holiness. It was of course true of that day, as of today or of any other time, that the vast majority of Catholics were far from being saints. But, if it had indeed been true that sanctity was wholly wanting in the Catholic ranks, that would have been a refutation of the Church's claims far more important and far more final than the discovery of any gap in the chain of apostolic succession. Fortunately it was not true and a few years later there was to come to his house at Littlemore a simple-minded Italian Passionist whom he was to accept as the refutation of his fear that the day of saints had passed.

Tract 90 had an important bye-effect that it brought Newman his first Catholic friend. Up till then he had for some years taken the line —as many would think and as has already been argued in this book, unfortunately—that it was wrong to hold communication with those who were not of his communion. This had caused him to avoid Nonconformists—even his own brother. Roman Catholics were from his point of view of course members of the Catholic Church. One might therefore have expected him to show a wider tolerance to them, and from his point of view Roman Catholics outside England were indeed to be accepted. He was willing enough to call on Wiseman in Rome, for in Rome the Roman was on his own territory. But a Roman Catholic in England was an intruder—an emissary of the Italian mission. He had refused to meet at dinner the convert Father Spencer when he called on him in Oxford, though willing to talk to him in private. But a consequence of *Tract 90* was that Newman received a courteous letter from a Maynooth professor, Father Russell, explaining to him that Newman had mistaken Catholic teaching about the nature of the sacrament. Newman thanked him and accepted correction but added, 'That your communion was unassailable would not prove that mine was indefensible.'[1] It was as much as Newman as an Anglican clergyman could decently be expected to admit to a Catholic controversialist. But the truth of the matter was of course that he was by then coming more and more to feel that his position was in fact 'indefensible', not on sacramental grounds but for quite other reasons. Therefore Father Russell in removing an objection to the Roman position was striking a very important blow—a blow more important than he at the time probably guessed.

Newman's most fundamental difficulty to the Anglican position was not of course to its sacramental teaching but to the increasing absurdity

[1] *Apologia*, p. 240, Part VI.

of a situation which ascribed to the bishops an authority which the bishops themselves were so anxious to repudiate. This absurdity, which had already been so adequately exposed by Bagot's behaviour over the Jubber case, and over *Tract 90*, was brought to a final head by the Jerusalem bishop controversy.

It was thought desirable to have in Jerusalem a bishop who could look after the Christians there who were neither Greek nor Roman, and therefore it was decided as a common sense measure of compromise that the Prussian Lutherans and the Anglicans should share a bishop, taking it turn and turn about to make the appointment. To Newman and the Tractarians, who taught that Anglican bishops had the apostolic succession and Lutherans did not have it, the arrangement was of course one of blasphemous impropriety. Anglicans were to be asked to receive invalid sacraments from false priests who had been ordained by a man who had not valid orders—and this arrangement was countenanced and abetted by the English bishops who were specifically and divinely commissioned to protect their flocks from heresy. In the ecumenical mood of today conversations are at the moment going on both between Methodists and Catholics and between Methodists and Anglicans to see if ways can be found to heal the divisions between them. The obstacles to full success are formidable but at least these conversations are held in the spirit that the full reunion of Christendom is to be desired. The Jerusalem arrangement was made in quite a different spirit—in the spirit that theological differences were merely unimportant and could cavalierly be expected to give second place to administrative convenience. To the ordinary Englishman, clergyman or layman, talk about validity of orders was without meaning. A bishop to them was simply a man who had a job of administration to do. If there was only sufficient congregation and enough work for one bishop, it was an absurd waste of money to keep two—just as it would have been an absurd waste of money to pay the salaries of two sanitary inspectors if one could do the work.

It was to Newman the parting of the ways. He thought of writing in protest, but abandoned the project. What good could protest do? The bishops were quite determined on their ways. A protest would not cause them to turn from it. There was no alternative but to throw up all his posts and to retire to his refuge at Littlemore where he could live in quietness and solitude until the way ahead was made clear to him. The retirement of course meant to him a considerable financial sacrifice which he could ill afford. He had henceforward no regular source of income, but that was not a consideration which caused him at all to hesitate.

Just as Keble's proclamation of national apostasy has had an adventitious consequence quite different from any that he had intended, so has Newman's appeal to the apostolic succession of bishops as a proof of catholicity. Whatever may be said about Newman's history, whether or not we decide that Anglican bishops have the apostolic succession, he was certainly correct in the proposition that he stated—that the possession of the apostolic succession was one of the traditional tests of catholicity—and. Newman, writing as an Anglican, had necessarily to appeal to the authority of the bishops because in the nature of things there was no Pope to whom he could appeal. Now the Catholic Church in the years after 1815 was, for very intelligible reasons, dominated by the fears of Gallicanism and of an excessive interference in ecclesiastical affairs by secular national politicians. It may be argued that, if they were obsessed by this fear, they were a little foolish to rely so much on the support of the State, and that was indeed a point that Newman was often to make in later years when the controversy about the Pope's temporal power was so vigorously alive. Yet, logical or illogical, they had this fear of secular interference, and local bishops, it was thought, had often in the past proved themselves and might well prove themselves in the future, too subservient to their political masters. Therefore as a remedy against Gallicanism it was necessary to concentrate as much power as possible at Rome, where, it was thought, the secular arm could not reach.

At the First Vatican Council some of the minority bishops argued that it was wrong to assert that the Pope had a universal primacy of jurisdiction because any bishop derived his authority not from the Pope but from Christ and had full authority in his own diocese. Pius IX challenged this view, encouraged appeals to Rome, on occasion reversed rulings that bishops had given in their own dioceses, lifting cases out of the local ecclesiastical courts and bringing them directly under papal jurisdiction. He insisted on the Council adopting a statement that the Pope has 'the full plenitude of this supreme power.' In the years of his captivity the sentiment of pity for the old Pope throughout the Catholic world was such that there was no way of stopping him from annexing to himself any further powers that he wished. As a result by this century there was, as is now generally accepted, a gross overcentralisation at Rome and intolerable delay as the inadequate bureaucracy there struggled with the multitude of petty decisions that it was called upon to take on cases that reached it from every quarter of the world and, when the present Council met, it was generally agreed that one of its main tasks must be to devise for the Church policies of sensible decentralisation. For that purpose it was necessary to carry through the task which the First Council had never completed when it was dissolved by the Franco-Prussian War, and to redefine the rights of the individual bishop.

To do so it was pertinent to go back to Newman, for, though his theories of the apostolic succession had been propounded when he was still an Anglican, his work on it was primarily historical and well *à propos*. The Second Vatican Council issued its decree on the Pastoral Office of the Bishops. The practical suggestions of the Council for a reform of the Curia, for the establishment of a Synod of Bishops or for the establishment of national episcopal conferences could not in the nature of things have been derived from Newman, but his influence is evident in the strong assertion of principle. In his own day the strong assertion of episcopal independence, which was for one reason novel teaching in the Church of England, was equally, though for quite a different reason, novel teaching in the Church of Rome. But it has in our time become accepted in the Catholic Church. 'The bishops,' decreed the Council, as we have quoted, 'exercise full and supreme authority.' No secular authority must hamper their freedom. Gallican domination is fully repudiated. 'In carrying out their apostolic duty, which has the salvation of souls as its end,' runs the decree, 'bishops enjoy essentially complete and perfect freedom and independence from any civil power whatsoever.' There was some dispute whether the word 'full' should be allowed to remain in the definition but in the end it was retained.

This assertion of the bishops' rights has been criticised on two grounds. On the one hand, while no one can sensibly deny the necessity for decentralisation, yet it would be indeed dangerous to create a situation in which the Pope could no longer speak effectively *Urbi et Orbi*. Few would deny that at the time of the First World War the bishops of every nation with hardly any exceptions merely echoed the fashionable opinions of their country. Those on the Allied side supported the Allied cause, those on the German side the Germans, and neutrals championed neutrality. Few today would deny that the one truly Christian voice was that of the Pope Benedict XV. It would be indeed a tragedy should that voice be silenced and it was a moving moment in the Second Vatican Council when the Ukrainian, Archbishop Slipyi, but recently released from prison in Siberia, bore witness to the passionate desire of Catholics in captivity and behind the Iron Curtain for a strong Papal voice which could speak to them at a time when perhaps their own bishops were silenced.

The other criticism came from those who said, 'If we are to decentralise, why stop at bishops? It is the whole Church which is the people of God. Has not every Christian a right to his opinion?' This criticism came most strongly from Protestants and it corresponded of course very much to the sort of criticism which was levelled at Newman and the Tractarians by the man-in-the-street in the 1830's.

Thus Dr. Lindbek, for instance, Associate Professor of Historical Theology at Yale, has written in *Dialogue in the Way*, a composite volume of Lutheran theologians, 'the *De Ecclesia* asserts that episcopal consecration confers the fullness of the sacrament of orders. This excludes the traditional view, found in the germ as early as St. Jerome, in the fifth century, that there is no fundamental sacramental difference between priest and bishop and that consecration is more a juridical than a sacramental act which, so to speak, releases powers conferred in ordination . . . However if this is all that distinguishes a bishop from a priest, why should bishops be considered the successors of the apostles in a unique way? How can one argue that because Peter together with the other apostles constituted a "college", so the Pope and bishops, but not the priests, constitute a similar supreme college? In view of these difficulties it is necessary to affirm the sacramentality of the episcopacy in order to assert collegiality . . . It is strange that practically none of the Catholic bishops and theologians at the Council showed awareness that this affirmation of episcopal sacramentality can be considered unfortunate from the ecumenical point of view. It is perhaps the only point at which the Council has increased the gap between Catholics and Protestants. For the Protestant the highest office in the Church *de iure divino* is that of pastor, that of preaching the word and administering the Sacraments. We cannot but regret this exaltation of the episcopal office at the expense of the pastoral one.'

The criticism might have had some force had it been levelled at the Council's decree on the Pastoral Office of the Bishops alone. I do not think that it has much force when we set side by side with that decree the decrees on the Ministry and Life of the Priests and on the Apostolate of the Laity. I think rather that, considering that they were bishops, the Fathers almost fell over themselves in their readiness to recognise the rights of people other than themselves. In the same way if we look to the Tracts alone—incidentally of course the works of his Anglican days—we might think that Newman exalted the position of bishops somewhat excessively. But, if that was at that time his fault, he certainly changed his tune when he had had a little more experience of actual bishops, whether Anglican or Catholic and when, in an age when clergymen for the most part associated almost solely with clergymen, he had on the contrary over the Achilli case and the Irish University found more sympathy among laymen than among his fellow clerics. As we shall later see in his *Considerations on Consulting the Faithful in Matters of Doctrine*, he argued that truth could not be mechanically discovered by merely taking the majority opinion of the bishops at a given moment, that there had been times in history when the laity and the common people had been for the moment more faithful guardians of Catholic truth than the episcopacy; indeed he had himself delated by a bishop to Rome and nearly condemned for saying so.

4

Development and Conversion

AS AN ANGLICAN Newman was now on his deathbed. But the Roman position still had its difficulties. Yet to live suspended, the full adherent of no communion, was to him an agony. There was no getting over the fact, as it seemed to him, that the Roman Church did on some points teach doctrines that were unknown to the primitive Church. But then, as he came to argue, was that necessarily an error? Christ, departing, had left the Holy Spirit with His Church and left to His followers the promise that the Holy Spirit would lead them into all truth. Of course the notion that the Church should invent new doctrines on which Christ had in no way spoken was intolerable. But did the Church do that? Was not the story rather than in the natural human way Christians both debated about the nature of their faith and indeed made new discoveries and raised new problems in the secular order. The faithful had the right to ask of the Church, 'What ought we to think about these problems, these new speculations, whether they be theological or secular?' The faithful had the right to ask of the Church, when it thought fit and when the time was ripe, to issue new definitions of doctrine which were not definitions of total novelty but which were developments that arose logically out of the original deposit of faith, even though no recorded word of Christ gave a direct ruling on them. In face of new speculation the Church was not compelled woodenly to remain silent because no text of the Gospels could be found to give a direct ruling on the matter, nor compelled to declare itself the enemy of all progress simply because progress involved change, nor to allow the world to go on its new ways without its guidance. On the contrary it had the right to recognise the facts of new discoveries and speculations and to say on them 'This is Christ's teaching', because it possessed the Holy Ghost through whose authority it spoke.

It was in these Littlemore days that Newman was working out his *Essay on Development*. He was not working it out in order to persuade others. He was working it out in order to clear his own mind. At the time when he was writing, Darwin's theories of evolution had not yet been popularised and there is no reason to think that Newman had evolution in any way especially in his mind. But of course the doctrine of development proved a doctrine singularly well suited to enable religion to meet with such ideas. The Church through the ages, taught Newman, had developed through assimilation. It had considered the great secular discoveries of the different ages and restated its own doctrine in their language. Thus the early Church had taken into itself the truths of Greek philosophy. After a struggle it had annexed to itself the achievements of the Renaissance. It would indeed be a tragedy if in face of the great discoveries of his own age the Church should allow itself to be purely reactionary, should merely reject and abdicate from its function of sifting out truth from falsehood.

Newman embarked on these speculations in order to find where the truth lay as between Catholics and Anglicans on comparatively narrow points, such as the nature of the authority of bishops. The Vatican Council a quarter of a century later was to define the Papal headship of the Church and then owing to the Franco-Prussian War to adjourn before it had gone on to define the position of the bishops. The assertion of the rights of the bishops—of what it is the fashion to call their 'collegiality'—was to be one of the main tasks of the Second Vatican Council. Newman wrote his *Essay on Development* at a time before he himself had been received into the Church and before Papal infallibility had been defined. The prime test of Catholicism to his mind at that time was, as we have said, not acceptance of the Pope but the possession by its bishops of the apostolic succession. It was more important that a Church's bishops should be bishops than it was that the Pope should be at its head. Newman eventually abandoned the Church of England much more because he could no longer accept the authority of its bishops than because those bishops did not accept the authority of the Pope. As a consequence and to some extent as a matter of accident Newman's Essay became the all-important guiding test, as Cardinal Gracias put it,[1] when the Second Vatican Council came to consider the position of bishops and their collegiality.

But it had an importance beyond that—considerable as that import-

[1] Michael Novak, *The Open Church*, chapter 8, p. 111.

ance was. He began his inquiries when he seemed to the ordinary man to be obsessed with trivial and irrelevant problems that had no bearing on the real issues of the day. His speculations led him to conclusions so enormously pertinent that it is hardly an exaggeration to say that had his influence not come to shape all Christian apologetics they could hardly have survived in the obscurantist form which their protagonists alike in the Catholic and in the Anglican world were allowing them to assume. He who had seemed in youth the least relevant of Christian apologists was destined in the end to become the most relevant of all.

Both the Protestants and the Tractarians had thought that Christianity had been wholly revealed once and for all. All that was needed was to appeal back to the past and to the early Church and to discover what had been there revealed. They differed from one another in their interpretation of the past but they agreed in their method of treating it. Modernists and secularists on the other hand despised the past and proclaimed as truth the fashion of the moment. Newman held that truth had been revealed in the past but that we had been left with a Voice which could, as needed, develop the teaching of the past and draw out of it the necessary lessons to meet the problems of the present. He propounded a religion that was both traditional and topically relevant.

The Church, he argued, developed new teaching out of old teaching. The tests of the validity of development were: preservation of type, continuity of principles, power of assimilation, logical sequence, anticipation of results, tendency to preserve the old, chronic vigour. There are two theories Newman had argued in his *Essays Critical and Historical*.[1] 'The advocates of the one imply that Revelation was a single, entire, solitary act or nearly so, introducing a certain message; whereas we who maintain the other consider that Divine teaching has been in fact what the analogy of nature would lead us to expect "at sundry times and in divers manners", various, complex, progressive and supplemental of itself. We consider the Christian doctrine, when analysed, to appear like the human frame "fearfully and wonderfully made", but they think it some one tenet or certain principles given out at one time in their fullness without gradual enlargement before Christ's coming or elucidation afterwards. They cast off all that they also find in Pharisee or heathen; we conceive that the Church, like Aaron's rod, devours the serpents of the magicians. They are ever

[1] p. 234, 'Milman's View of Christianity'.

78

hunting for a fabulous primitive simplicity; we accept and use what even they acknowledge to be a substance. They are driven to maintain on their part that the Church's doctrine was never pure; we say that it never can be corrupt. We consider that a divine promise keeps the Church Catholic from doctrinal corruption; but on what promise, on what encouragement they are seeking for their visionary purity does not appear.'

In the *Essay on Development*[1] he returns to the same point. 'I observe then that if the idea of Christianity, as originally given to us from heaven, cannot but contain much which will be only partially recognised by us as included in it and only held by us unconsciously; and if again Christianity, being from heaven, all that is necessarily involved in it and is evolved from it is from heaven, and if on the other hand large accretions actually do exist, professing to be its true and legitimate result, our first impression naturally is that these must be the very developments which they profess to be: moreover, the very scale on which they have been made, their high antiquity, yet present promise, their gradual formation, yet precision, their harmonious order, dispose the imagination most forcibly towards the belief that a teaching so consistent with itself, so well balanced, so young and so old, not obsolete after so many centuries but vigorous and progressive still, is the very development contemplated in the Divine Scheme. These doctrines are members of one family and suggestive, or correlative or confirmatory or illustrative of each other. One furnishes evidence to another and all to each of them; if this is proved, that becomes probable; if this and that are probable but for different reasons, each adds to the other its own probability. The Incarnation is the antecedent of the doctrine of Mediation, and the archetype both of the Sacramental principle and of the merits of Saints. From the doctrine of Mediation follows the Atonement, the Mass, the merits of Martyrs and Saints, their invocation and cultus. From the Sacramental principle come the Sacraments properly so called; the Unity of the Church, and the Holy See as its type and centre; the authority of Councils; the sanctity of rites; the veneration of holy places, shrines, images, vessels, furniture and vestments. Of the Sacraments Baptism is developed into Confirmation on the one hand; into Penance, Purgatory and Indulgences on the other; and the Eucharist into the Real Presence, adoration of the Host, Resurrection of the Body and the virtue of relics. Again the

[1] pp. 93, 94, Section III.

doctrine of the Sacraments leads to the doctrine of Justification; Justification to that of Original Sin; Original Sin to the merit of Celibacy. Nor do these separate developments stand independent of each other, but by cross relations they are connected and grow together while they grow from one. The Mass and Real Presence are parts of one; the veneration of Saints and their relics are parts of one; their intercessory power and the Purgatorial State are correlative; Celibacy is the characteristic mark of Monachism and of the Priesthood. You must accept the whole or reject the whole; attenuation does but enfeeble and amputation mutilate. It is trifling to receive all but something which is as integral as any other portion; and on the other hand it is a solemn thing to accept any part for, before you know where you are, you may be carried on by a stern logical necessity to accept the whole.'

Newman's belief that revelation was not static—at one time and once and for all—was not a novelty. His own quotation shows that from St. Paul's time it had been recognised that God spoke 'at sundry times and in divers manners', and a multitude of quotations from such Fathers as St. Augustine bear witness to the survival of that belief through the early Christian centuries. There have in all ages been two tendencies in Christian teaching—a tendency to stand still and a tendency to develop. We saw them in the Early Church in the debates at Jerusalem whether the full Jewish law should be imposed on all converts. We saw them in the thirteenth century in the debates whether the Church should use or should denounce the metaphysics of Aristotle. We saw it at the Renaissance when extreme conservatives rejected all the novelty of the new learning and the new discoveries, and the Jesuits insisted that they must on the contrary be incorporated to broaden the Christian apologetic. Yet the advances of one generation have easily become the obstinately held conservative positions of its successors. Wise men even in Newman's day remembered the necessity for development, but wise men were few and it is doubtful if they would ever have had the courage to sustain their position had it not been for Newman, just as it is doubtful whether men of such a sort would ever have had the courage to sustain their position today had it not been for Pope John. The Council of Trent which in its day had been a text-book of change had come to be looked on as a guarantor of immutability. Newman saw the necessity of moving the Church from the position on the absolute Right, into which its leaders were attempting to put it, to its true and traditional position of a *Via Media*, holding the balance between obstinate conservatism and a fatuous surrender to every novelty simply because it called itself progress.

This was but little remembered in the post-Napoleonic Christian world where it was so desperately needed if the forces that called themselves the forces of progress were to be successfully and intelligently confronted. It was a belief that in our time has been reasserted alike by such thinkers as Teilhard de Chardin and by the Vatican Fathers in their Declaration on Non-Christian Religions. Their debt to Newman, who reintroduced a line of thought which was at first widely suspect in orthodox circles but has today been almost without question accepted as orthodoxy, is beyond measure.

Although it was not completed or published until he became a Catholic, yet the greater part of the *Essay on Development* was composed when Newman was still at any rate nominally an Anglican. It would not, it is true, be just therefore in any way to call it an Anglican work written for Anglicans. It was, as has been said, of course a work composed by Newman to clear his own mind and the conclusion of his study was to lead him to the Catholic Church. Yet it is sufficiently remarkable that a work composed by one who was not at the time a Catholic should be accepted, to use Cardinal Gracias's phrase, as the test by which a General Council of the Catholic Church should proceed. It is the more remarkable since Newman's mind had been so largely influenced—and indeed continued even in his Catholic days to be so largely influenced—by Anglican writers like Bishop Butler, and his method of thought, even if not his conclusions, by sceptics like Hume. Hurrell Froude among the Tractarians went to the mediaeval scholastics, but Newman was never deeply influenced by them. He found his spiritual home among the early Fathers.

It is not difficult to trace the marks both of the *Essay on Development* and of Newman's other works in the all-important document on the Dogmatic Constitution of the Church. Neither Newman's works nor the Constitution in any way argue the case for Christ's divinity. That, as far as these documents go, is taken for granted. 'Christ is the light of the nations,' begins the Constitution as a flat statement without qualification. Its concern is to describe the nature of the Church that Christ founded. There, while of course careful not in any way to challenge the authority and infallibility claimed for the Pope at the time of the First Vatican Council, it is careful also to assert the collegiality of the bishops. The Apostles, it argues, went about as a company. When the place of Judas had to be filled it was the whole body of the Apostles who took part in the election of Mathias. Of course it was fully recognised that Peter was the head of the Apostles and there could be no conflict between the acceptance of the primacy of the Pope and of the collegiality of all bishops, since the bishops could not act as a college save in agreement with the Pope. 'Together with its head the Roman pontiff—and never without its head—' ran the Constitution, 'it also exists as the subject of supreme, plenary power over the universal Church. But this power cannot be exercised except with the agreement of the Roman pontiff.'

In the debate there were integralists who argued that, though indeed the New Testament spoke of the Apostles as going about as a body, there was no phrase which exactly defined their juridical nature as a college. But Cardinal Gracias, maintaining that 'arguing for collegiality is like flaying a dead horse', suggested that Newman's essay ought to be the test whereby the Council proceeded. And a week later Cardinal Frings pointed out the danger of the integralist argument against evidence for the bishops' collegiate power. When we came to that, he asked, was there in the New Testament any phrase which exactly defined the authority of the Pope? If it could not be absolutely demonstrated that the Apostles' powers were transmitted to later bishops, could it be absolutely demonstrated that St. Peter's powers were transmitted to later Popes? Not all the truths of faith, argued Cardinal Frings, were clear from the beginning. The nature of the authority, the relationship in Christ of Manhood and Godhead, the nature of Our Lady—all these doctrines were gradually developed and defined as need called for them over the ages.

This was of course pure Newmanism. But while Cardinal Frings was able to trace the use of the phrase *collegium episcopale* as far back as Optatus Milevitanus, who wrote in about A.D. 366, he did not explicitly note that such a view of the episcopacy was in the early half of the nineteenth century far more likely to be found in a Tractarian Anglican, who based the validity of his orders on the genuineness of his apostolic succession, than in most Catholics; these latter were at that time only concerned to exalt the central authority of the Pope at the expense of local bishops who might, it was thought, be too easily subject to the pressure of national governments. The Constitution, while proclaiming the collegiality of bishops, is careful not to substitute an oligarchy of bishops for the autocracy of the Pope. It proclaims fully and with eloquence the doctrine of the apostolate of the laity and explains the nature of the universal priesthood. 'The work to be achieved,' it says in an exuberant phrase, 'is the drenching of the world in the spirit of Christ.' The Pope, if he defined doctrine, spoke only as the mouthpiece of the Holy Spirit. He did not invent new doctrine and impose it on the people. He merely expressed and defined the general mind of the Church. It was language very closely based on Newman's *On Consulting the Faithful in Matters of Doctrine*, and language which would have seemed very strange and temerarious to Monsignor Talbot's belief that the sole functions of the laity were 'to shoot, to hunt and to entertain'.

The three issues, since the time Newman wrote, on which the question of new definitions has been raised have been those of the Immaculate Conception, the Assumption of Our Lady and Papal Infallibility. Though Newman was one of those who doubted whether the definition on Infallibility was opportune, yet it was certainly a very exact example of his principle of development. It was universally admitted throughout the Catholic Church both that the teaching of the Church was infallible and that the Pope was the Head of the Church. What did this mean? Did it mean that under certain circumstances the Pope could speak infallibly? The definition defined the exact circumstances under which he could do so. The definitions about Our Lady were manifestly definitions of beliefs that had been widely held since the earliest times, which had not up till then been of faith but which were then declared to be so. The Council in its turn called on the theologians 'to develop the study of sacred scripture, the Fathers and Doctors and the Liturgies of the Church under the guidance of her magisterium, and throw a correct light on the functions and privileges of the Blessed Virgin'. It is the exact Newmanesque word.

The *Essay on Development* is within its own limits a work of extraordinary competence and cogency. In it Newman shows most clearly that if there is a revelation it is not to be expected on general grounds and not supported by the historical evidence that God should reveal Himself unaided and then depart, leaving the world to its own devices to make the best that it could of His Gospel. He refuted the belief both of Protestants and High Churchmen that all that was required was to discover and adhere to the original deposit of faith. But what the *Development* did not prove and did not attempt to prove was that the original revelation was valid—that Christ was God. Newman asserted that of course but he did not prove it.

The importance of the influence of Father Russell in all this can hardly be exaggerated. It was Father Russell who more than any other had removed the great obstacles of misunderstanding which, long after he had lost faith in Anglicanism, yet prevented Newman from accepting Catholicism. By 1843 he had moved so far that he thought it necessary to issue a Retraction of the charges that he had made against Rome. It was not the sort of task at which Newman was very adept. He had a strange incapacity to understand the immediate reactions and prejudices of the public mind. He ought by then to have plumbed the deep anti-Catholic prejudice of the English of the 1840's and to have understood how strong was the suspicion that they must inevitably have felt alike towards an Englishman who joined the Church of Rome and towards an Englishman who, remaining nominally within the Church of England, appeared to be undermining its Protestantism—with what ineradicable assurance they would feel such a man must inevitably be lacking in candour. In his difficult position it would have been wisest for Newman, if he must say anything at all, merely to have baldly stated that he had found through further study that some of his opinions which he had previously held against Rome were erroneous. Instead he must go on to explain that as an Anglican he had 'thrown himself into their system'. He had used language which he now saw to be indefensibly violent from 'a hope of approving myself to persons I respect and a wish to repel the charge of Romanism'. Language less fortunate could hardly be imagined. To the plain blunt Englishman, unacquainted with the agonies of a subtle conscience and accustomed to call a spade a spade, this appeared simply to mean that all the time that Newman was pretending to be an Anglican and (as they did not scruple to add) was accepting Anglican emoluments, he was in reality a secret Romanist.

Unpopularity against him ran high. Only a curious and typically English accident in some measure turned a certain amount of sympathy back in his favour. Through all this state of obloquy he had of course his small band of faithful friends. Newman, though he attracted so much hostility at different periods of his life, had the capacity of arousing the devotion of friends to an extent that few could equal, and the Tractarians, though they were generally unpopular, had their devoted and indeed fanatical defenders. Of these defenders none was more devoted and more fanatical than the young Fellow of Balliol, William Ward.

Ward, who dearly loved *épater le bourgeois*, took advantage of the outcry against *Tract 90* to issue a far more startling and outspoken work, the *Ideal of a Christian Church*, in which he claimed without any sort of qualification that an Anglican clergyman could sign the Thirty-nine Articles and at the same time hold 'every Catholic doctrine'. Newman was living in retirement at Littlemore, holding no preferment and making no attempt to influence anybody. Ward was still an active Fellow of Balliol. The authorities thought that action must be taken against him. In order to hold a Fellowship it was of course necessary to accept the Articles and, though a reasonable latitude in their interpretation was permitted, was not this going too far? The conservatives, only anxious to humiliate Ward, were for circumventing his argument by concocting new tests—demands which he would certainly be unable to meet. The liberals who disliked tests and who only a few years before had been supporting Hampden's demand for their abolition acutely insisted on the folly of such a demand. To impose new tests would, they justly argued, be to concede the contention of Newman and Ward that the Thirty-nine Articles admitted of different interpretations. If Ward was to be condemned he must be condemned on the present tests. It must be decided that the Thirty-nine Articles which he had signed did not admit of the interpretation which he had put on them, and an excited Convocation, meeting on a snowy day, did after a heated debate reach this conclusion.

It is true that a majority is not a proof, but few today would wish to deny that Ward's argument was somewhat exaggerated and in places sophistical and that the Convocation was justified in deciding by a substantial majority that his interpretation was unacceptable and by a sufficient, if much smaller, majority that, as a consequence which the Statutes of the University required, he should be deprived of his degree. Ward, revelling in the knockabout of controversy, was fair game. Whether it was decent to subject Newman, wrestling in seclusion and in agony with the subtleties of a divided conscience, to the judgement of philistine, or what Aristotle would have called banausic, men who were in every way his inferiors in learning or in spiritual perception was wholly another question.

Newman did in fact not greatly care for Ward's approach. Newman believed that 'a man thinks with the whole mind'. Like Pascal before him and Jung after him, he thought that the heart had reasons that the reason knew not of and that one brings to a decision the whole animus of the personality, not a merely logical process. He distrusted such abstract demonstrations whether they were employed in defence of or against the faith and did not much care for Ward's smart-alec logic-chopping, his 'solitary, naked, external, logical process' as he called it with some derision.[1]

'The condemnation of N.,' wrote Pusey,[2] who had no sympathy with the step which he knew it to be all too probable that Newman would soon take, 'when he has retired successively from every means of influence and has won more souls to Christ than any beside in England is beyond measure dreadful. I should expect some dreadful chastisement to follow.' Gladstone,[3] whose sympathy with Newman's intellectual position was limited, was appalled at 'this prospect to treat Mr. Newman worse than a dog'. Yet academic men rarely show much pity or sensitivity in their political controversies, and there is little doubt that, had it been put to the vote, the condemnation of Newman, though the majority for it would have been less than that for the condemnation of Ward, would nevertheless have been carried. However it chanced that one of the Proctors of the year, Church of Oriel, was one of Newman's closest friends and disciples—and destined to remain so till their deaths. The Proctors have according to the constitution a right to stop any proceedings in Convocation by their veto, and this Church decided to do. Before the debate on Newman began he and his fellow Proctor announced, '*Nobis procuratoribus non placet*',[4] and the proceedings were inevitably at an end. The company stamped out of the Senate House and outside all soon dissolved into almost a comic opera.

The great majority of the undergraduates probably had little understanding of the finer points at issue and, had they understood them, would in all likelihood have been opposed to Ward. But Ward was a genial, enormous, good-natured man, uproarious, fat, fond of jokes and, what is more, he was making fun of the Establishment and above all of the very stuffy and unpopular Vice-Chancellor. By a strange

[1] *Letter to Mrs. Froude.*
[2] Letter to a Friend. See *Pillar of the Cloud*, Meriol Trevor, p. 345. '1845—Scattering of the Ashes of the Dead.'
[3] *Pillar of the Cloud*, p. 345.
[4] We Proctors object.

paradox Ward, pleading for the extremes of Ultramontanism, gained the popular cheers as the derider of authority. The undergraduates were on Ward's side and when he came out they cheered him. He slipped on the snow and dropped all the sheets of his notes which were scattered to the winds. The undergraduates cheered him again and then those that had snow to spare made balls of it and pelted the Vice-Chancellor. Thus ended that peculiar day.

Newman, when he learnt of it, expressed with characteristic courtesy his gratitude to Church for his support and indeed continued to repeat that gratitude throughout his life—as for instance twenty-six years later when he dedicated to Church his *University Sermons*. But in truth it must remain doubtful whether Church really behaved correctly in imposing his veto. The Proctors have a veto in order that they may prevent the Convocation from discussing and voting on matters that are beyond its jurisdiction. Whatever the rights and wrongs of the matter, it clearly was not beyond its jurisdiction to consider whether Newman was complying with the conditions of a degree, and it must be very doubtful whether Church's use of the veto simply to protect a private friend was a proper use, even though a Proctor who was Hampden's friend had employed the same tactics in his favour a few years before. Newman, from his point of view, though he thanked Church for his support, had in fact by then ceased to care about the issue very much. He no longer believed in the Church of England. It was therefore no longer of much interest to him what the Articles said or what interpretation they might bear. He did not mind whether the Church of England condemned him or whether it did not. The Convocation won its victory in so far as it succeeded in degrading Ward, but it was a very pyrrhic victory, for the result of the debate was to show that the Thirty-nine Articles were so dubious and unclear that it was not possible to base any demand for faith on them and, though the signature is still legally required from an Anglican ordinand, they have never, as a distinguished Anglican clergyman said to me a little time ago, since that day been taken seriously.

The stories of the last years at Littlemore, of Newman and his companions, of the last sermon, of Father Dominic's visit, the last night in Oxford at the Observatory, these are some of the great and moving stories of those times. Their place in any biography of Newman is of course essential and all his biographers have done justice to them. But they are not within the terms of this book. We are concerned with

Newman's mind. It was fairly clear by these closing years that the final victory must be with Rome. To return to the Church of England was no longer possible. The only alternative—to hold a vivid belief in Christ and a vivid belief that Christ had founded a Church to which it was the first duty of a Christian to join himself and yet to remain for any length of time without an attachment, havering uncertainly between the two communions—was hardly thinkable. 'I think that the English Church is in schism,' he wrote at this time to his brother Frank;[1] 'I think the faith of the Roman Church the only true religion. I do not think there is salvation out of the Church of Rome. This of course does not interfere with my thinking an exception is made for those who are in involuntary ignorance.' But then he added the dreadful sentence, 'I am no longer in such ignorance.'

Two cardinal points must be understood in judging Newman's mind at that time. The first is that which is hinted at in the above quotation. We today in these more tolerant, ecumenical times do not attach a very desperately literal interpretation to the phrase *Extra Ecclesiam Nulla Salus*. We easily explain that there is a baptism of desire, that those who are in good faith belong to the body of the Church, whatever the tenets that they may think themselves to profess, that they are good men and at least as likely to be saved as those in the Church. Let us hope that it is all true. Certainly, as we have seen, even the Vatican Council assures us that it is. It would certainly seem to our modern moods almost an affront to the loving kindness of God to believe that something of the sort was not true. But it is important to understand that the Victorians had no such easy-going complacency. that those who are in good faith belong to the body of the Church which Christ had founded. The fate of an immortal soul was at stake in the taking of the decision. If it was Christ's will that a man should become a Catholic and he refused the gift of faith through laziness or cowardice or wordly advantage he was in peril. If on the other hand, it was God's will that he should protest against the corruption of Rome and he failed and faltered in his task he was also in peril. The decision was a terrible one which could only be taken in the deepest agony of soul.

Secondly, we must note one very peculiar feature about Newman's conversion. As we have shown, with the exception of Father Russell, he had for all intents and purposes never had any communication with

[1] August, 1845. *Pillar of the Cloud*, p. 348.

a Catholic. Today Catholics mix in English society and most Englishmen, whatever their interests or opinions, are acquainted with a number of Catholics. A hundred and twenty years ago Catholics in England were few and far between and they lived a life of their own, separated from the rest of society. The average Englishman never met a Catholic, and Newman had of course felt under a special compulsion during his Anglican days to have no communication with one. As a result, his conversion was to a peculiar degree a literary conversion and, as one might put it, conversion by history. His concern was with what happened in the fourth century and what happened in the fifth century and what happened in the sixteenth century. He paid before his conversion strangely little attention to what was happening within the Church in the nineteenth century. It never seemed that in those days he had much curiosity to look to contemporary Rome and see how it was shouldering its tasks, and perhaps, to be quite frank, it was in many ways fortunate that he did not have this curiosity. For he did not join the Catholic Church at any very glorious moment in that Church's history.

Gregory XVI was on the Roman throne. After the defeat of Napoleon the Papacy, under the influence of Cardinal Consalvi, had reclaimed its temporal states. Its rule there during those years was not very enlightened or very glorious. Under Pius VIII and Leo XII the Papal provinces had been in chaos and order of a sort had only been preserved by letting loose on the populace what were virtually brigands who under the title of Sanfedisti imposed their reign of terror and rapine. The Austrian troops had come in shortly before, and the French troops were to come in shortly afterwards, to protect the Pope against his own subjects. In 1866, while Manning was pronouncing that the belief in the Pope's temporal power would beyond question before long be made an article of faith, Newman was being threatened with the Index for the moderate views that he had expressed in his sermon on *the Pope and the Revolution*. There might be something to be said for the temporal power of a Pope, living at peace and beloved by his subjects and holding himself aloof from the rivalries of the Powers. It was hard to see what there was to be said for the temporal power of a Pope who had to be protected against his own subjects by foreign bayonets.

The state of the Papal dominions was indeed a considerable embarrassment for those Catholics who maintained that the temporal power was a necessary part of the Papal prerogative. Newman, as we have said, never was of that school. To him the temporal power was at the best a convenience and, as he thought, by that time an inconvenience. The possession was not part of the promise of Christ to Peter, and Newman, who was not very politically minded, frankly neither knew nor very much cared whether the Papal dominions were well governed or ill governed. It could not matter to the truth of the Christian claims. Gregory XVI was succeeded by Pius IX in 1846 and Pius ascended the throne with great promises of constitutional reform. 'A pretty state we are in altogether,' wrote Robert Wilberforce to Mozley,[1] 'with a Radical Pope teaching all Europe rebellion! Every post brings a fresh argument for the duty of securing the middle classes if possible.' Newman was not much moved either by Pius's early promises of liberalism or by his later actions of repression.

It was also beyond question true that a consequence of the obsession of the early nineteenth-century Popes with the preservation of the temporal power was that they gave no attention at all to the grave social problems which were being created by the rising industrialism in North Europe and the United States. It was not until Leo XIII and the end of the century that the Papacy gave its mind at all to these problems. But there is no evidence that Newman either at this earlier date had especially given his mind to them and the Pope's silence then did not at all bother him. What would have bothered him, had he at all understood it, was the discovery that the Papacy's obsession with the temporal power, coming on top of the Gallican subordination of the Church and the conflict with the French Revolution, and going hand in hand with the absolute monarchs' alliance of throne and altar had caused the Papacy completely to mistrust and to abandon reliance on evidence or reason for the support of the Catholic cause. The Church was so certain, it felt, to get the worst of any battle of reason that it was best not to allow the faithful to reason at all. It was not so much false thinking as thinking that was to be condemned. Newman, it is clear from the letters that he sent back from Rome in the next year, had had no idea of the depth to which Catholic apologetics had sunk under Gregory XVI.

Monsignor Ronald Knox would sometimes speak in jest of 'that most dangerous of all Protestant libels which speaks of the Catholic Church as an efficiently managed organisation', and it is certainly true

[1] B. A. Smith, *Dean Church*, chapter III, p. 92.

that English Protestant writers in their combination of fascination and distaste have often tended to write with an almost comical exaggeration of the subtlety and cunning astuteness of Catholic policies. It has in some ways been by no means an evil that the story of the late Vatican Council, so full as it has been of noble and worthy achievement, has also given us so many examples of organisational incompetence, sufficient to free the Church for ever from any danger of an accusation of mere efficiency. So readers will remember the coloured and generous, if highly critical, account of the *History of the Papacy* in Macaulay's famous Essay. 'It is impossible to deny,' wrote Macaulay, 'that the polity of the Church of Rome is the very master-piece of human wisdom.' It is amusing to note that these words were written during the pontificate of Gregory XVI when by Newman's experience, and indeed by general consent, the affairs of the Church were managed with an unintellectual incompetence that was without parallel in its history.

What, then, did Newman find about Catholics when he joined their communion, and what did he expect to find? As we have shown, he had hardly met any Catholics and knew nothing from experience of Catholic countries or Catholic practices. The Catholics in England were few in numbers, played little part in the political or social life of the nation and kept very much to their sequestered selves. They were of course still excluded from the universities. Only a few years before they had still been excluded from Parliament and from all positions of responsibility. They still lived under the shadow of the penal system, grateful to have been recently relieved of its incubus, fearful that any act of ostentation would bring the reimposition of disabilities. They used language which as far as possible concealed from the world the practices in which they were indulging, speaking of 'Mass' as 'prayers' and the like. It was 'Oxford itself that made us Catholics,'[1] Newman used to say. The Old Catholics did not very well understand what he meant, but they suspected that he meant that he had become a Catholic as a result of an intellectual process, and indeed an intellectual process undertaken under non-Catholic auspices, and they were deeply suspicious. Although their faith forbade them to say so in so many words, they did not really believe that anyone could become a Catholic. Catholics were born, not made. They should be seen and heard as little as possible. The popular outburst a few years

[1] Wilfrid Ward, *The Life of John Henry Cardinal Newman*, 1912. Vol. 2, chapter XXI, p. 57.

after Newman's reception at the time of the restoration of the hierarchy showed that their fears were not ridiculous.

Therefore Newman was prepared to find his co-religionists, through their exclusion over the generations from the corridors of power, ignorant and innocent of the ways of the world. Those whose ambitions were at all worldly had already preferred the world and over the years dropped off from the practice of religion. The remnant were simple, rigid and pious. Their exclusion from schools and universities meant that they were not well instructed. Their religion was not an intellectual religion. They had no ambition to engage in debate with non-Catholic fellow citizens, being, like the Pope, convinced that they would in all probability get the worst of such a debate on its intrinsic merits and that, even if they conquered, the issue would be so reported as to do their cause no good. They could not of course in the least talk the language of Oxford. Newman, having breathed that air for some thirty years, probably, as dons so often do, a little exaggerated the necessity of an academic training, and above all a formal academic training, for intelligence and wide reading. Universities, as he had every reason to know, sometimes broaden and sometimes disastrously narrow the mind in accordance with how the discipline is used. The majority of men, if they are not allowed a formal education nor given an opportunity to use their talents in positions of responsibility, allow themselves intellectually to decay.

> These vegetables of the Catholic creed
> Are apt exceedingly to run to seed

he had read in his Byron,[1] and Newman was certainly right in thinking that the majority of the Old Catholics were men of no great intellectual capacity. Power corrupts but the absence of power corrupts all but as absolutely. But Newman did not sufficiently recognise that unfavourable conditions, while they discourage the great majority, act as a stimulus to the exceptional man who can see life the more steadily from the fact that he does not see it through the blinkers of the Establishment. The Old Catholics, dim as they generally were, had produced in those years in Lingard one of the outstanding men of the age. It is very curious that Newman never seems to have met and indeed hardly to have heard of Lingard.[2]

[1] *Don Juan*, xiv. 81.

[2] Secular priest and Professor of Ushaw. Author of the first modern documented History of England.

Newman was therefore hardly surprised to find that the Old Catholics among whom he now found himself thrown were not familiar with the problems which occupied his mind. How could such men be expected to concern themselves with the details of the Arian heresy? Newman did not complain that the Old English Catholics talked a different language from him and that he found it at first difficult to get on terms with them. He understood why this should be so—why it was perhaps inevitable that it should be so. But what did surprise him and a little sadden him was the discovery that to some of the Old English Catholics his conversion was by no means entirely a thing to be welcomed. Newman was by far the most distinguished convert to come to the Catholic Church from Anglicanism since Dryden a hundred-and-fifty years before. Newman cannot for all his lack of self-importance have failed to know this. It would have been asking too much of human nature that he should not at the least have expected to be welcomed by his fellow Catholics. Nor indeed would it be fair to say that they refused him a welcome. They were both too decent and too Catholic for outright repulsion. Yet he could not but fail to notice that, mixed with Christian welcome, was a feeling that nothing but harm could come to Catholicism and to them from the adherence to their ranks of so very controversial a figure. The one thing that they hated was a fuss, and there would be a fuss.

Yet he did not join the Catholic Church with any desire or expectation that he should rebuild it. It is most important in estimating his character to understand how completely at the time of his reception all that was before him was unforeseen. He was forty-five at that time. He was of course to live for another forty-five years and his long life to be almost exactly divided into its pre-Catholic and its Catholic periods. But he had no suspicion of that at the time. 'I think I have now passed into my autumn,' he said in 1853, not guessing that there were even then another forty years before him. Even at forty-five he thought of himself to an exaggerated extent as an old man. He thought that his life was behind him—that his work had been to find for himself, and perhaps to point out to others, the road to the Church. But, arrived there, he had arrived at his destination. He had come home. He would live a few years and then die in the Church of his conversion. It never occurred to him that he had a mission to remould that Church.

5

The Roman Hope

NEWMAN REMAINED for six months after his conversion at Maryvale near Oscott. Almost alone among the Catholics in England, Wiseman, who had come recently from Rome, filled with exaggeratedly optimistic visions of the imminent conversion of England, was excited about Newman, and he understood nothing at all about Newman's mind. To Wiseman, Newman was simply a trophy to be exhibited, a preliminary triumph which carried with it the promise of further triumphs to come. This did not make things any easier for Newman with the Old Catholics, who were by no means enamoured of Wiseman and his exuberance. 'How dreary my first years at Maryvale,' wrote Newman, in his private journal,[1] 'when I was the gaze of so many eyes at Oscott as if some wild incomprehensible beast, caught by the hunter and a spectacle to Dr. Wiseman to exhibit to strangers, as himself being the hunter who captured it.'

His co-religionists thought it a considered part of charity to break his spirit. He recalls in the *Apologia* how he had to stand in a queue along with the Oscott schoolboys at Wiseman's door to wait his turn for confession. Ullathorne, his bishop, afterwards to be a friend, was at first magisterial. He wrote to Newman[2] in connection with the Oratorian *Lives of the Saints*, 'I am pained to observe the acute sensitiveness with which several little matters have been viewed of late. Believe me, dear Mr. Newman, this cannot be without a hidden ingredient of self-love, a most subtle spirit and the object of the fears and combats of the humble saints of God.' As Newman wrote to his friend Allies in 1851,[3] 'We have been (necessarily) treated as children,

[1] Written seventeen years later.

[2] In 1848. *Pillar of the Cloud*, p. 449; '1848—Old Catholics, New Converts and Saints.'

[3] *Ibid*, p. 546: '1846—Snow and Surprises at Rome.'

being grown men. This is not a trial to one's pride in the common sense of the word, but it is to one's desire of sympathy and to those habits of refinement and good breeding and mutual consideration which University life more or less creates.'

After six months at Maryvale Newman was bidden to go to Rome to the College of Propaganda. He went to Rome, confident that there at any rate things would be seen in proportion. It was understandable that the English Catholics, living under those very peculiar circumstances, should have developed their peculiar qualities. But at Rome surely it would be possible to find the full richness of the Catholic faith. Politically, Newman quite understood, the Pope was having his difficulties, but the problems of the temporal power were in Newman's eyes always problems of quite secondary importance in which he was not deeply interested. It was the full Catholic gospel that he was anxious to learn. What had the Pope to tell the world about these new developments in social arrangements, in industry, in political theories with which the world was full? It was a surprise and a dismay to him to discover that by and large the Pope had nothing to tell the world on these matters. There were indeed some intelligent men in Rome. He met some of the Jesuits of whom he thought highly and whom he compared to Oxford dons. The Jesuits, though they were the strongest supporters of repression and Ultramontanism and their views were, in Newman's opinion, mistaken, at least used arguments to support their conclusions. He heard that Perrone, the most learned of them, was picking out passages from his *Essay on Development* to condemn in his lectures, but Perrone was at least capable of reason and Newman, calling on him and offering a personal explanation, was able to some extent to set his mind at rest. Cardinal Barnabo, who was the Cardinal in charge of English affairs, was from the first hostile, mimicked Newman and complained, when the Birmingham Oratorians were formed, that they were 'unwilling to throw themselves into the age and work to purpose'.

By working to purpose Barnabo meant exactly the opposite of anything that Newman could possibly mean. He meant abandoning any attempt at reasoned apologetics as in itself dangerously liberal— intransigently denouncing any criticism of any clerical activity. By and large Newman found Rome simply was not interested in a Catholic apologetic. Since Innocent XI's death in 1689 the Papacy had in effect retired from the task of teaching the world. The world was to it a very wicked place, growing rapidly more wicked. All political developments, all new speculations in thought were almost automatically condemned. The weapons that were to be used were exclusively the weapons of proscription, censorship and excommunication. Even the great Catholic champions of the past were under suspicion because in order to refute error they had described it, and so deep was man's folly and wickedness, they thought, that it was not to be believed that if he heard of an evil thing, he would not embrace it. The works of St. Augustine were unknown to them. So was St. Thomas Aquinas. It was a very different spirit from that which Leo XIII was to infuse at the end of the century. Apologetics at this earlier date consisted of little but quotations of text-book maxims which in fact begged questions rather than answered them but which it was considered temerarious to question. Newman when he joined the Catholic Church joined it in a spirit of total humility. He joined it in order to learn and to be taught. He had no notion of imposing a new method of apologetics on the Church. The notion would have seemed to him appalling arrogance. But experience at Rome forced upon him, whether he wished it or not, a conclusion to which up till then strangely few had come. The liberal case against repression and censorship and the conservative case in favour of them were both familiar enough. But few who had visited Rome before Newman seem to have adverted to the more important truth that a policy of repression, whether it corrupted those who suffered it or whether it preserved them from the contamination of infection, most certainly corrupted the intellect of those who imposed it. Heretics were sent, as St. Augustine truly said, so that we—so that the Catholic authorities—should not remain in infancy. Nowhere does original sin reign more potently than over the intellect. Few people will think clearly and honestly unless they are compelled to do so by the challenge of antagonists. The temptation to leave apparent contradictions unresolved—to prefer anathema to reasoned answer—is overwhelming. A hierarchy that does not allow itself to be challenged is not likely to be a hierarchy that has frequent truths to enunciate.

It was Newman's fortune that he joined the Church at one of the lowest moments in its history. The Papacy of Gregory XVI and Pius IX lived in a condition of peculiarly absurd ambivalence. It was its habit to speak always in a language of extreme triumphalism, claiming total authority over the world and calling for the obedience of princes and peoples, much as the Emperors of China used to use language that pretended that all kingdoms of the world were subject to them when in fact their writ hardly ran effectively outside their own palace. At the same time the Papacy also spoke as if the world were entirely given over to evil and irreligion, as if death and persecution were all that the faithful could expect in this godless age and as if the most that the Pope and the few remaining Catholics could do was to take refuge in their catacombs and pray that the saving hand of God might avert total destruction from them.

To Newman both these forms of language seemed absurdly false and exaggerated. He agreed indeed that a rising tide of atheism was threatening the world and that it was almost certain that the strength of religion would decline yet further in the future. But, when Newman spoke of the decline of religion, he meant by the phrase something entirely different from what the Roman ecclesiastics meant. He did not mean that the Pope would lose his temporal power. He thought that the Pope would probably lose his temporal power—as indeed he did—but he thought that on the whole that would be a good thing rather than a bad thing. At any rate it certainly was not a matter of first importance. Rome, by which, when he saw it as an Anglican, he had on the whole been agreeably surprised, now seemed to him an appalling place. 'I never saw any city with a tenth part of dung in the streets as Rome,' he wrote to Frederick Bowles.[1] 'When the rain comes this is formed into a thickish fluid. Last Sunday it rained hard and, when we came in, our mantellas had a deep fringe of the nastiest stuff I ever saw and all wet.' Rome, the centre of the world, he told a shocked and very aristocratic congregation of Catholics and Protestants when he preached the panegyric on Lord Shrewsbury's niece, was 'the very place where Michael and the Dragon might be seen almost visibly in battle'.

If the Church was threatened by the modern national States and if the Catholic Powers were likely to repudiate their concordats, what did it matter? It was much more probable that the Church would be corrupted by placing excessive reliance on the support of a State that was not truly Christian, as was happening even then in France and was to happen yet more flagrantly in a few years' time when Napoleon III was to be on the French throne. What Newman meant by the growth of atheism was the growth of a spirit in which men, whether

[1] *Pillar of the Cloud*, p. 399: '1849-50—Bugs, Smells, Cholera, Heavenly Favours.'

they gave verbal assent to the existence of God or not, yet really ceased to believe that there was any possibility that God could or would intervene in the affairs of men. Perhaps only a small minority was anxious to proclaim itself dogmatically atheist, and it might well be that not many more would wish to do so in the future. What purpose was there in troubling to proclaim unequivocally that one did not believe in something in which nobody did in fact believe?

If the world was going atheist, it was not, thought Newman, primarily because the Church was attacked by wicked men from outside but because its own champions, relying on repression rather than reason, had ceased to state the case for it and indeed, though they did not understand as much themselves, had to a large extent ceased to believe it themselves—ceased to believe that the Church should rely on the promises of Christ rather than on the support of Governments. The Church had much more to fear from unbelievers within its own ranks than from the unbelievers outside precisely because the former did not guess that they themselves were unbelievers. There is perhaps an inevitable difficulty in all established, firmly organised, firmly supported Christianity. It is that the historical claims of Christianity are extraordinary and should always be seen as extraordinary. He who forgets to be surprised at the story of Easter Sunday can hardly be said really to believe it. Yet, man's imagination being so weak as it is, it is almost inevitable that most people, if brought up in a Christian atmosphere where regular church-going is the fashion, will come to take the Christian story for granted and think it a natural story which all men of common sense believe.

The difficulty of the position is clear. The New Testament story is a story of divine and miraculous interventions in the course of history; it does not contain any hint that God after a short season was going to cease to intervene in the affairs of the world. He who rejects the possibility of the miraculous rejects the Christian story. Yet, cogent as that reasoning may be, the fact remains that the vast majority of us as we go about the affairs of life are perhaps willing enough to accept the metaphysical possibility that there is a God Who is the First Cause and Creator of the universe, but we think that if He acts in this world He only acts through His laws. The belief is indeed the very condition of our thinking. It is the very condition of our thinking that whatever happens happens in obedience to some physical law or to some decision of a will. How many do really believe in the possibility of even occasional divine miraculous interferences with the normal course of nature? More perhaps in these days with the evidence before us in a very few instances of the utterly inexplicable cure at Lourdes, or with the physicists and Sir Arthur Eddington telling us that the ultimate atom does not split in obedience to an unalterable law but for no reason at all. Yet it is still beyond the capacity of the average man of today to believe in the possibility of miracles—that is to say, to believe in what Newman would have called real God. Yet, if that be so, what becomes of Newman's appeal to general consent as the test of truth? It appears that, so far from belief in God being the general opinion of mankind, what Newman would have considered a real belief in God is a very rare achievement.

Writing as always in a popular rather than a technical language, Newman over the stretch of his work sometimes gave different meanings to the same word. Thus there are at least two senses in which he used the word 'reason' as we shall see. So when he speaks of belief in God, he sometimes means a very vague belief such as can with plausibility be said to be possessed by all men. He sometimes means a very rare belief in a God who acts, such as is only found with a very small number of persons.

The secular world had in his time frankly abandoned the belief in the possibility of miracles. The Roman world babbled of the possibilities—indeed was too credulous in its professions of belief—but in its practice showed very clearly that it did not really believe that miracles would happen and that it relied for success on policy. Consalvi by his alliance of Throne and Altar had dealt not only a grave political blow to the Church. He had dealt also a grave intellectual blow. Authors like Montalembert who tried to work out a genuinely religious policy for the Church—who put forward policies much nearer to those of Pope John XXIII than were the policies of Gregory XVI or Pius IX—were out of favour at Rome. The authors who were in favour were such men as de Maistre and Châteaubriand who advocated for the Church romantic and conservative policies that were not really Christian at all—who saw the Church not as the spouse of Christ but as the defender of order or the preserver of culture.

Newman had left the Church of England because he had found as he thought that it was at bottom a political and a social rather than a religious society. Was the Church of Rome anything different? The truth was that, so long as the Papacy held and was possessed by the

Temporal Power, political considerations—and rather petty political considerations—did inevitably bulk inordinately in its mind, and it clung even in the intellectual sphere to old and outmoded schemes of philosophy simply because it was afraid that, if it once began to allow change anywhere, there was no knowing where that change would end. It was only the loss of the Temporal Power which made inevitable a reassessment not merely of the political situation but of every sort of situation—which created an atmosphere where a purely religious answer to purely religious questions was both needed and accepted and thus gave an opportunity for Newman's restatements. Even then things moved slowly as is the Roman way. It was not until Leo XIII ascended the throne that things even began to move and it was not till John XXIII ascended the throne that they had in any way achieved a completion.

There was of course about John a naturally buoyant optimism which enabled him, in his inaugural address to the First Session of his Vatican Council, confidently to rebuke the 'prophets of doom' who foretold the imminent catastrophe of the world. It was in a similar spirit that Teilhard de Chardin was able to look forward so confidently to Omega Point or in an earlier day Juliana of Norwich to assert that 'all manner of things shall be well.' Was there any justification for this optimism? Would Newman with his frequent prophecies of the growth of atheism have accepted it? Above all, if the world can judge *securus*, is there not all too much reason today to think that the world is complacently judging against religion? that, as Nietzsche put it, 'God is dead'?

Newman's answer was that, when we appeal to a general consent, we should look not merely to a general consent over the world at one given moment but to a general consent in time and through the generations. It was the major folly of the Modernists, for whose spiritual paternity Newman was sometimes most unjustly held responsible, that they thought that a particular generation could sit in judgment on the traditions of mankind. There is of course much sense in using as far as possible the fashionable phraseology of the day simply in order to make yourself more easily intelligible. But it is a folly to think that mere fashion is likely to be right. It was not for the Modernist to sit in judgement on the traditions of mankind but for them to look to those traditions and see how far their teaching bade the Modernists correct their own extravagances. They did not do so and as a result no one could be more completely out of date, behind the times and irrelevant today than the Modernists of the early years of the century. So Newman was in no doubt that he was living in a uniquely irreligious age and that that phase of irreligion would continue for some time. But he was in as little doubt that such irreligion was opposed to the permanent and enduring habit of mankind and that in the end the tide which had gone right out would come right back again. It will be for our grandchildren to see whether his confidence is justified.

6

Achilli

IN THE MIDDLE of the last century the Church was losing ground in all Catholic countries and the Christian religion was losing ground all over the world. To meet that attack there lay a choice between two policies. One policy was to magnify every difference in belief and practice between the Church and the world; to resign oneself to the fact that there were many, and there would be far more, who were disillusioned with the world; and to fancy that these would turn most readily to an alternative that was as starkly different from it as possible. The other was to assert that God had created and loved and died for all mankind—such of it as was Catholic and such of it as was not Catholic; that it was both foolish and false to condemn without distinction and qualification all the achievement of the modern world; rather, that it was desirable to study carefully what modern man was saying, to understand why he was saying it and, without compromising truth, to accept its discoveries where neither intrinsic reason nor the Christian faith forebade; to rephrase Christian truth where it was necessary and where it was possible in language more easily intelligible to the modern mind than was, at times, the language of the ancient formularies. The second method of approach is the method to which the Church is now committed by the Vatican Council's documents on Ecumenism and on the Non-Catholic and Non-Christian religions, in which it is careful to pay tribute to the degree of truth that is to be found among those outside the Church. To quote again the words of John XXIII in his inaugural address before the Second Vatican Council: 'The deposit of faith itself, that is to say, the truths contained in our ancient doctrine, is one thing, but the form in which these truths are announced is another.'

Newman also in his day took it for granted that the second was the correct method of approach. *The Essay on Development* advocated it, but it was his surprise and dismay to discover that his co-religionists at that time did not by any means generally agree with him. He found the Old Catholics suspicious at Oscott. He found the Roman ecclesiastics suspicious at Propaganda. At least, he thought, educated converts must see things as he saw them, but then from across the Atlantic came a furious attack from the most eminent American convert of the moment, Orestes Brownson, a convert from Unitarianism. He accused Newman of whittling away the faith by his theory of development. Newman, exasperated and losing patience, replied by condemning Brownson as 'a half-converted Yankee'. It sounds, it must be confessed, suspiciously like a schoolboy '*tu quoque*'. It was in fact more than that. Newman meant that the Protestant faith, in the form of a belief in the literal verbal inspiration of the Bible in which it was then commonly held, was a faith that could not adjust itself to modern developments. Such a faith was a declaration of war on reason in the crude abrupt sense, since there were statements here and there both in the Old and the New Testament that were in verbal contradiction to one another and thus could only be held by a repudiation of the rights of reason. Catholicism, according to Newman's conception of it, was capable of such an adjustment to modern developments.

But the trouble was that Newman discovered that the very great majority of Catholics at Rome and elsewhere seemed to take a view of Catholicism that was much more similar to that of Brownson than to his view. It was not until Leo XIII's *Providentissimus Deus* that the Church was in any way definitely committed to a scholarly approach to the Biblical documents. It was not until Pius XII's *Divino Afflante Spiritu*, and perhaps not finally till the Vatican Council's Constitution on Divine Revelation that the hermeneutic approach and the abandonment of literalism were final. But at Newman's first writings as a Catholic the tide was running in the opposite direction. Only a few years after Newman was writing Pius IX, in his *Syllabus Errorum* was to invoke anathema on those who asserted that the Holy See could 'accommodate itself' to 'modern civilisation'! What should be done?

Some men of course, in disgust at finding that the Church of Rome in its human personalities was so full of folly, would have turned from it as easily as they turned to it. There were people in England outside the Church who did not hesitate to prophesy that Newman would do this, or sometimes even that he had done it. Newman of course, as his great Anglican friend, Dean Church, unswervingly bore witness, never dreamed of doing such a thing. 'Never for a moment,' wrote Church,[1] 'did his loyalty and obedience to his Church, even when most tried, waver and falter. The thing is inconceivable to anyone who ever knew him, and the mere suggestion would be enough to make him blaze forth in all his old fierceness and power.'

Indeed, in order to give the lie to any such rumours he twice during these years—first in his novel, *Loss and Gain*, and the second time in his *Lectures on Anglican Difficulties*—exposed with an almost painfully withering sarcasm the contradictions of the Anglican position which he had so recently abandoned. A few years before, in order to prove the sincerity of Anglicanism he had employed language, which he afterwards retracted as too bitter, in criticism of the Church of Rome. Now to prove the sincerity of his Catholicism he employed language which was too bitter against the Church of England. His attitude towards Anglicans he had explained in unexceptionable language to his sister at the time of his reception. 'Of course,' he wrote, 'I must think any other body [than the Catholic Church] to be a usurper,' but he added, 'all this is quite consistent with believing, as I firmly do, that individuals in the English Church are invisibly knit into that True Body of which they are not outwardly members!' 'There are two reasons,' wrote Newman to his old doctor's wife, Mrs. Wootten,[2] 'why I should not dream of avoiding a member of the Church of England; first because he may not be formally and really a heretic, secondly because, though he were, he is to be loved and reclaimed by love, not by repulsion.' It was a more charitable attitude than that which he had taken towards Catholics when he was still an Anglican. Yet in *Loss and Gain*, a novel of Oxford life which he wrote in retrospect in Rome, the Tractarians to whom he had so recently belonged were held up to some ridicule. Newman had a power of satire and invective which had not been seen in English literature since Swift, and he was engaged in a continual battle not to use that power unnecessarily, unworthily and without charity. He did not always win his battles.

If he was glad enough to shock the worldly by bidding them to consider what was the depth of the reality of their religious faith he was equally glad to shock them by reminding them of the rigour of

[1] Obituary notice in *The Guardian*.

[2] Dr. Wootten had been his doctor at Oxford.

the demands of the moral law. It was in one of his *Lectures on Anglican Difficulties*[1] that, to refute the notion that Catholics were unduly accommodating, he said that it would be 'better for sun and moon to drop from heaven, for the earth to fail and for all the many millions on it to die of starvation in extremest agony, as far as temporal affliction goes, than that one soul, I will not say should be lost, but should commit one single venial sin, should tell one wilful untruth or should steal one poor farthing without excuse.' In a similar spirit he had said that 'a lazy, ragged, filthy, story-telling beggar woman, if chaste, sober, cheerful and religious, had a prospect of heaven that was absolutely closed to an accomplished statesman or lawyer, or noble, be he ever so just, upright, generous, honourable and conscientious, unless he had also some portion of the divine Christian grace.'[2] The sentences startle and are intended to startle but on examination they say less than they appear to say at first sight.

We are inclined to use the phrase 'venial sin' to describe actions which are against the formal rules but which are not really sins at all. That is not its true meaning nor was that the meaning in which Newman used it. He did not mean to say that it was better that the world should expire in agony than that a guest should tell his hostess that it had been a lovely party when in fact he had been bored stiff. The verbal untruth, when courtesy required it, he would not have considered a sin at all, whether venial or otherwise. He spoke of 'wilful' untruth, of the stealing of a farthing 'without excuse'. All that he said was that no physical evil as such could be a valid excuse for the acceptance of any moral evil as such—which is surely unexceptionable. Or again it would be false to draw from the second judgement the conclusion that Newman was indifferent to education. It would indeed be surprising to have found such a conclusion from the pen of the author of the *Idea of a University* and he was very clearly in agreement with, if he was not indeed to some extent the inspirer of, the judgement of the Vatican Council's Constitution on the Church that 'layfolk ought to apply their skill in deepening their understanding of revealed truth.' Nor could it in itself be a virtue in the filthy beggar woman that she was illiterate and superstitious. All that Newman was arguing was that education ought to be used in order that the student might deepen his religious understanding. As such it was good, but, if he did not use it

[1] Quoted in *Apologia*, pp. 50, 51, Appendix.
[2] *Apologia*, p. 340, 'What Then Does Dr. Newman Mean?'

for that purpose, he was better without it. Worldly advantages were in themselves advantages, but no worldly advantage could of its nature weigh against a spiritual blessing. The two sorts of benefits were simply not comparable with one another.

Newman had joined the Catholic Church because he believed it to be the Church of Christ. If some of its instruments were irritating people, then they were irritating people, but that could have no bearing on the duty of a man who had received the gift of faith to remain loyal to his gift. Others thought that he should stretch the duty of obedience so far as to do nothing to criticise and better that which he found amiss. He had no wish to put himself forward as the corrector of others. Yet he could not think it right to retire into complete impassivity. Without advertising himself to the world he nevertheless thought it his duty to bear a full witness in whatever humble sphere he might find himself. Therefore, casting about what society he should join, he toyed indeed for a time with the Jesuits but—obviously rightly —thought that it would be a folly to put himself under obedience to a Society which was devoted to policies in so many ways the opposite of his own. He decided for the Oratorians of St. Philip Neri on the ground that theirs was not, strictly speaking, an order: that he would be tied by no vows of obedience, that he would live there in a small company, quite independent of all other houses, and that he would in fact have a greater freedom than he could expect elsewhere. A short experience had shown him that he could not expect instant and general acceptance for his ideas and that therefore it was essential for him to live a life of freedom not subject to an excessive immediate discipline.

The decision proved to be a wise one. Returning to England, he soon discovered, somewhat to his surprise, that, as with Brownson in America, so with a large number of the English converts, they were by no means anxious to take advantage of their past Protestant experiences in order to smooth the path for others who might be thinking of following them on the journey. It was among the converts that he often found those who were most anxious to exaggerate in what seemed to him unnecessary ways the differences between Catholics and other Englishmen, and in contrast to their extravagances he came more and more to appreciate the common sense of the Old Catholics' undemonstrativeness, and they, comparing him with other converts, came to appreciate him. He had no special reverence for the mere fashions of the age. They would doubtless pass as those of the previous generations had passed. But it was common sense, in so far as it was possible, to adopt the language and the artistic habits of the society in which one found oneself. There was no purpose in being wantonly unintelligible. Thus he had no sympathy with Pugin's faith that all architecture must be Gothic or with Faber's ambition to introduce into English Catholicism unnecessary Italianate customs.

'Charissime,' he wrote to Faber, 'I cannot see that we have any call whether as Oratorians or as converts to begin our course by preaching to the Old Catholics—and a good part of your argument is that.' No one in Newman's view had a right to demand of the Catholic more than the Church demanded of him. Where the Church had left freedom, it was essential that that freedom should be scrupulously respected. To demand in the name of Catholicism conformity with fads of one's own was a very grave fault, and—particularly in nineteenth-century England, in a population whose members were passionately convinced that the teaching of the Church was erroneous—the only hope of conversion lay in a rational demonstration that that teaching was true. If the Catholic teaching was mixed up with private fads which the average Englishman had every right to reject, the chances of converting him were negligible.

Thus he was critical of the plan for the restoration of the English hierarchy in 1850 and particularly of the flamboyant way in which Wiseman advertised it. The Pope, he was careful to argue, had of course the right to establish organised dioceses in England or anywhere else. But, as in the question of papal infallibility twenty years later, it was a matter not of what was right but of what was expedient. Was there any advantage in upsetting public opinion in order to establish a new organisation that might well not work any more efficiently than the old? Yet, once the step was taken, it was necessary to defend it unflinchingly. No victory could be won by an army in retreat. 'The people of this great country,' he wrote to Talbot,[1] 'are such [moral] cowards that nothing is so likely to prevail with them as firmness. They will rush forward if you retreat, but they will be cowed and fall back if you calmly keep your ground. We must not budge an inch, nor will anyone I am sure.' His rule was, as he explained in his sermon on Ullathorne's enthronement, 'to be a lightning conductor to attract the odium that would otherwise have fallen on the ecclesiastical authorities.' It was not a very grateful role but he accepted it.

[1] *Pillar of the Cloud*, p. 535: '1850—No Popery Down with the Oratorians.'

Newman's first years as a Catholic were, then, years of unforeseen and dreary loneliness. He was criticised abroad and he was criticised at home even among his own Birmingham Oratorians, where Dalgairns, the most turbulent of his fathers, complained that he had no sense of community. Into the responsibility for his catalogue of quarrels such a book as this is not required to enter. His loyal champions, such as Miss Trevor, examining the details, are able to find that it was always the other party that was to blame. Others, arguing perhaps more from a general experience of human nature than from the particular facts, tend to think that, if a man is consistently quarrelling, a large part of the responsibility must in the nature of things be his. Historians make the point—as indeed a number of foreigners did at the time—that from the sixteenth and seventeenth centuries onwards Catholics in England have always been abnormally quarrelsome and have dissipated their energies and ruined their cause by internal squabbles.

In 1851 Newman stumbled into a controversy which looked for a time as if it might bring him to utter ruin of the most humiliating kind but which in the end probably improved his public reputation. Achilli was a very unsavoury Italian priest. He had in fact been unfrocked because he had been found guilty of numerous acts of seduction of young girls. But he saw fit to pretend that he had been condemned by the Roman Inquisition because he had come to hold unorthodox opinions and had had the courage to proclaim them. He took advantage of the excitement in England over 'papal aggression' and went about the country giving lectures on the iniquity of Rome to low-grade societies of the Protestant underworld. Out of these he hoped to make a considerable sum of money. It was an age in which it was still possible to find a certain market for any conceivable absurdity about the Church of Rome. The pretended revelations of Maria Monk about the scandals of convent life were enjoying an enormous circulation. A Member of Parliament, a Mr. Spencer, had accused Newman of keeping 'underground cells' at Edgbaston for the incarceration of monks. Cardinal Wiseman wrote an article in the *Dublin Review* in which he exposed the real truth about Achilli's life. But the *Dublin Review* had of course only a very small circulation—and that entirely among Catholics. Achilli, thinking that there was little risk that any of the audiences which he was preparing to address would ever hear of it, thought it the wiser plan to ignore it. Newman for that very reason thought it desirable to give further publicity to Wiseman's charges. He took trouble to repeat them in a public lecture which he gave in the Birmingham Corn Exchange on *The Present Position of Catholics*, and saw to it that the secular press published what he said. Newman of course understood very well that in acting thus he was taking a certain risk. But he argued that, if Achilli had not dared to sue when Wiseman first published the charges, he would not dare to sue if Newman repeated them. He took legal opinion before he spoke and the lawyers advised him that the risk would be small. This expectation was quite a reasonable expectation. But it could obviously not be certain that things would turn out thus. The wider publicity which Newman received might compel Achilli to act. His supporters might demand that he should do so. Therefore it was perhaps but a precaution of common sense that Newman, if he decided to go forward, should, before he spoke, make certain that his case was absolutely fool-proof—that he had a total substantiation of every charge that he was proposing to make.

In fact he relied entirely on Wiseman's article—which was clearly unwise and which the event proved to be extremely unwise. Nevertheless, it was reasonable to assume that Wiseman had chapter and verse for what he said and that the Roman records could substantiate the charges. Therefore, when he heard that Achilli was proposing to sue him, Newman was not greatly concerned. All that was needed, he thought, was to write off to Wiseman and obtain the evidence.

The event proved the unwisdom of such reliance. Wiseman's conduct is to this day almost incomprehensible. The future of the most distinguished member of his flock was at stake. Apart from that the reputation of the Church, then so desperately assailed, was at stake. His own reputation was at stake since it was on his word that Newman had relied, and all that Wiseman was required to do to save Newman was to put himself to the trouble of answering a letter, telling Newman where the evidence was to be found. If by any strange chance he could not remember or could not lay his hands on the evidence, all that he had to do was to write to Rome to ask them to furnish Newman with it. The event was to prove that the evidence was all there at Rome. Had it not been there, had Wiseman misstated or exaggerated the evidence it would have been another story, but the whole oddity of the tale was that Wiseman in his original charges was entirely correct. Yet neither Wiseman nor Monsignor Talbot in Rome, to whom Newman appealed in despair, could put themselves to the trouble of answering a letter furnishing him with this simple information. As Newman wrote again and again, requesting the information and receiving no reply and as the date for the case came nearer and nearer, it began to dawn on Newman that, far from having the overwhelming evidence which he had imagined, it was all too likely that he would have to appear in court unsupported by any witness who could justify his accusations, and such accusations, if unsupported, would constitute a very serious criminal libel which would involve him in a long term of imprisonment.

It did not in the event turn out quite as badly as that, as his devoted friend, Miss Giberne,[1] at great inconvenience to herself had ransacked Italy and was able to produce a number of witnesses who could testify to Achilli's evil practices. But their testimony was not altogether satisfactory for, though it was quite sufficient to ruin Achilli's reputation and convince sincere and good Protestants, like Lord Shaftesbury, that he was no man whom they should wish for as a champion, yet they were not able to substantiate every one of the charges that Wiseman had made. The outcome was still uncertain right up till the time of the verdict. Newman quite expected that he would have to go to prison and had made every preparation. In the event, Mr. Justice Coleridge contented himself with reading Newman a lecture on the deterioration of his character since he had become a Catholic and fining him £100.

The conduct of Coleridge, one of whose sons was to become a Catholic and eventually a Jesuit, was unquestionably outrageous, and his lecture convinced many men in England who had never thought of it before, or who would before have denied that it was so, that the Establishment in England was still imbued with a fiercely anti-Catholic prejudice. *The Times*, which had rancorously attacked the Catholics over the Ecclesiastical Titles Bill, commented with disgust on Coleridge's treatment of Newman that 'such a trial would give substance to Catholics' complaint that they would not get justice in their own country'. A subscription to pay Newman's costs was heavily oversubscribed and Newman was able to pay for the erection of the University Church of St. Stephen's Green in Dublin out of the surplus.

It is commonly said, and truly said, in these days that the first condition for a fruitful dialogue is an atmosphere of courtesy, respect

[1] A family friend who had made Newman's acquaintance in his Over Worton days at Oxford. Subsequently became a nun in France.

and friendliness. Little of value is likely to come out of controversial arguments between disputants who distrust one another, where each is merely watching to catch the other out in contradiction.

> The man convinced against his will
> Is of the same opinion still,

and it is also very commonly said and with patent truth that Newman did incomparably more than any other man to bring about these relations of courtesy in England. Today it would happily not be surprising to find men of one denomination visiting at the houses of men of another and received there as friendly guests. But it would have been very rare until the last years, and in the nineteenth century such an incident as that of Newman staying at the Deanery of St. Paul's as the guest of Dean Church was an incident entirely unique. The Achilli story shows how very different was the atmosphere in the middle of the nineteenth century. Newman's name today is such that we read almost with incredulity of the insolence of a Judge in venturing to lecture him on the failings of his moral character.

But what is the lesson to be drawn from the Achilli story? It did indeed show the strength of an almost insane hatred and suspicion of Catholicism. About that there was little that Newman or any other Catholic could directly do. But the Catholics could do much indirectly. So long as there was an almost total social cleavage between the denominations the abatement of suspicion was not likely. For antagonists did not meet one another as people. One man only heard of another what he read about him in the literature of men who were attacking him, and the effect of the friendships which Newman was able to recapture and to retain in later years with Anglican associates was clearly of immense ecumenical importance—even though the discourse that tired the sun with talking was often not on theological topics at all—perhaps even because the talk was often not on theological topics at all. But while the faults of misunderstanding were predominantly on the Anglican side, they were by no means entirely on the Anglican side. The Catholics too had their faults. The penal memories made the Catholics understandably reluctant to throw themselves into general society and invite rebuff. But it was Newman's lesson that, though this reluctance was understandable, it must be overcome. The Catholics must meet their fellow citizens and, to avoid misunderstanding, they must meet them not only with courtesy but also with competence.

The great Catholic vice was not answering letters. 'Popish religion creates,' said de Souligné, a seventeenth-century Huguenot 'an unaptness for trade.' A part, if only a small part, of the prejudice against Catholics was due to the fecklessness of Catholics in their business arrangements and the awkwardness of their response to approaches. That must be remedied. The Catholics most sorely needed the qualities which were to enable John XXIII to break a sound barrier and speak to men and women of every nation and creed in accents that convinced them that to him at any rate love was not an abstract theological dogma but a universal passion with which he was aflame.

The Achilli story showed the strength of anti-Catholic prejudice but there was no news in that. The important lesson that it taught was the lesson on the slackness and discourtesy in Catholic ecclesiastical circles. The First Vatican Council, held in the mid-nineteenth century atmosphere, was the Council of a still segregated body. No journalists and no observers from other denominations were invited. At the Second Vatican Council, whatever its defects of arrangements, those defects were at any rate remedied and the Schema on the Church in the Modern World was addressed, as Pope John's encyclical *Pacem in Terris*, had been before it, not only to the Catholic community but to the whole world.

7

Ireland, and the Idea of a University

IF THE PUBLIC VERDICT on the Achilli case in England was not indeed favourable to the Catholic cause, yet on the whole favourable to Newman, the verdict in Ireland on him was much more simply enthusiastic. It is safe to say that fewer people in Ireland even than in England followed the intricate details of the charge. To the Irish public the issue was simple. Here was a Catholic priest who had defended the honour of the Catholic Church before an English (and of course Protestant) jury. Naturally in their eyes he was condemned. They would have been very suspicious of any priest whom an English jury did not condemn. Equally naturally he was of course in the right. Newman found himself hailed by Irish opinion as a hero—a man who had boldly defied the British oppressor. It was of course the last aspect of the case that had presented itself to him. In his Anglican days he had been a strong opponent of Irish nationalism. It had been one of his complaints against the Catholic Church that its leaders did not unequivocally condemn O'Connell, whom he looked upon as a wicked agitator and a wanton disturber of the peace.

His subsequent change of religion must inevitably have brought him to a changed view, though there is no evidence of any especial meditation on this point. The great secular catastrophe of Ireland—the famine —does not seem to have impressed itself on his mind with anything like its full horror. Only a small minority of Englishmen ever travelled in Ireland in those days. The great majority regarded Ireland as their nation's private property and were willing to leave it to those whose business it was to decide what in detail were the policies by which it should be governed. They no more pretended to know about Ireland than they pretended to know about India. Both to them were utterly foreign countries. The real Irish problem, as the average Englishman came across it, was not the problem of the Irishman in Ireland but the problem of the Irishman in England; and this, after the famine in the middle of the 1840's, as the Irish immigrants poured into England and into the new industrial towns, was a very real problem indeed. It was a real problem to all Englishmen but it was a particularly real problem to the English Catholics. For from the middle of the century the proportion of Catholics in the population of Great Britain began very rapidly to increase. This increase was to some extent due to converts, but only to a very small extent. Influential as some of the converts were, their number was not large. The increase in the proportion was predominantly due to Irish immigration. The Catholic body in England became, as it has ever since remained, a predominantly Irish body.

This Irish immigration was greeted by Englishmen in general, and by English Catholics as much as any other, with language that differs little from the language with which today extreme racialists greet the coloured immigrants. There seems little reason to think that there is an absolute bar between black and white of quite a different kind to other racial bars. Rather to the contrary; immigrants almost always come in the first instance to take the most menial jobs. They live in conditions of poverty. They are denounced by the native inhabitants on the ground that they are alleged to be introducing insanitary habits, to be an element that defies assimilation into the national life. Then by the next generation people have got a little more accustomed to them. A few of them have made a success in life and raised themselves up into the middle class. It may be that some new race of immigrants has come in to drain off the animus of prejudice. In any event the original prejudice does somewhat abate. It is thus for instance that the various waves of immigration have got themselves accepted into the national life of the United States.

Certainly in the middle of the nineteenth century Englishmen and English Catholics commonly spoke of Irishmen as if they were almost another and an untouchable race of beings. The papers of the Oratorians bear as vivid an evidence to this antipathy as any other source. 'The Irish are swamping us,' wrote Faber from the London Oratory.[1] 'People are made physically ill by the stench and dirt—old Ward even is made ill in our chapel and as a result collections are falling off.' The

[1] Faber's Letters. August, 1849, *Pillar of the Cloud*, p. 500: '1849-50—Bugs, Smells, Cholera, Heavenly Favours.'

suggestion was made that the congregation should be divided off—into rich and poor—by a system of tickets. Newman, it need hardly be said, did not like the suggestion that a Christian congregation should be treated in such a fashion. Yet he did not deny the problem. They had it in Birmingham too, though there he could plead that it did not take such an offensively nationalist form. For in Birmingham all the Catholics were poor—Irish or English—and to be frank, all smelt. Newman himself had recently had personal experience of the conditions under which so many English Catholics lived when he went to visit the cholera victims at Bilston and, though he honourably did his duty, he did not pretend to like it and was unfeignedly glad that he only arrived when the worst of the epidemic was over. In Birmingham there were no rich Catholics to be offended and yet, even so, he confessed,[1] 'Coming up our passage last night at midnight (as I was accidentally taken out) it smelt like one of the For Gentlemen on the railroad station. Brother Frederick, without my noticing it to him, said that it arose from the Irish who had been there at four—eight hours before.'[1]

It is not to our purpose to examine into this not very savoury problem nor to attempt to decide to what extent the English Catholic prejudice was justified. The only point that it is important to make is that Newman did not in any very marked degree fail to share it. That was important, for the lesson that Newman had drawn from his first few years of experience as a Catholic was that what the Church needed above all was an educational programme. This was in itself an important lesson. The Catholics in England were still excluded from the universities. The question whether the Catholic authorities should allow Catholics to go to Oxford and Cambridge was still for the future. In the 1850's the universities themselves by their requirement of a signature to the Thirty-nine Articles excluded the Catholics. Therefore there was a common sense case for it that some institution should be established where the Catholic could receive a higher education. But of course Newman had larger ideas than that. He was not merely concerned that there should be an institution to which Catholics should be permitted to go. The Catholics, according to his view, were losing the battle for the modern mind because of the deficiencies of Catholic education. Newman was anxious to establish not merely a Catholic institution but a Catholic institution whose policy was shaped to meet the battle of the modern world.

[1] *Ibid*, p. 500.

To Newman the political and social problems of Ireland were of secondary importance—problems to which he had never deeply given his mind. To him Dublin was primarily the one great city in the world that was both Catholic and English-speaking. It was therefore the city that was ideally suited for the great experiment of an English-speaking free Catholic university—a university shaped according to Newman's ideas. In Dublin Trinity College was of course Establishment and Protestant. The attempt to found 'godless' non-denominational colleges had proved a failure. There seemed at first sight an ideal opportunity for Newman's experiment. And, when Archbishop (later Cardinal) Cullen asked him to come over and preside at such a college, he jumped at the opportunity. Here surely at last was the finger of God, the task to which he had been called.

In the event, as we know, Newman's work at the university proved fruitless. It led him to formulate the *Idea of a University* by which Catholic education in coming years was so largely moulded and by which, it is much to be hoped, it will be increasingly moulded in the years to come. The battle is as yet by far from completely won but, if the Catholic mind all over the world is coming increasingly to turn away from the old idea of a regimented university and increasingly to turn towards a university which encourages and requires freedom of thought and freedom of inquiry, the development derives far more from Newman than from any other one man. For the Irish University, failure as it was in practice, was yet the cause of the production of one of the great seminal works of the modern world. Yet it appeared, for the moment, only to add one more to the long list of enterprises which had been entrusted to Newman and had met with unsuccess.

It is important to understand why it did not succeed and why, looking back with the advantage of hindsight, one is tempted to say its failure was from the first inevitable. In the first place Newman went to Ireland with no understanding of and no real interest in Irish problems. What interested him was the infusion into the Catholic world, and the English-speaking Catholic world in particular, of a new and deeper understanding of Catholic truth. It was a tenable proposition that such a task was more important than nationalist obsessions and that nationalistic Catholics should be urged to rise above their lower to their higher interests. Such a demand could hardly be presented with success unless it was presented by an Irishman—by, for instance, Newman's firm ally, Moriarty. Moriarty[1] was the Bishop of Kerry who had lived through and shared the sufferings of the Irish in the past years. It was not likely to find an easy hearing when taught by an Englishman who had never previously been in Ireland. For, when Newman launched his experiment of educational reform, Ireland was only two years removed from the most devastating famine in which men and women and children had died of starvation by the million and in which the population was reduced by a half. How far English callousness, injustice and folly were responsible for that catastrophe was perhaps a matter for argument, though the most impartial of critics could hardly deny that they were very largely responsible. But in any event the pertinent point for the moment was that at any rate Irish opinion thought that the English were entirely responsible. The Irish thought of themselves as a peasant population reduced by England to misery and starvation, and as they saw it, then here comes an Englishman who, when they ask for a potato, offers them a university curriculum.

It was not an exciting invitation, and it must indeed be confessed that Newman showed himself strangely insensitive to Irish memories of the famine. There is hardly any mention of it anywhere in his letters from Ireland. He writes back to Birmingham gossiping in a good-humoured way about the crudities of Irish cooking, the bleeding meat which he was compelled to eat, and accepts the hardships without undue complaint, but there is little hint that he at all understood that most of his hosts, though it may be that they were too courteous to say so, thought that it was English tyranny and English incompetence that was responsible for all this Irish poverty. MacHale, the 'lion of the West', the grand and intransigent Archbishop of Tuam, the most outspoken Fenian of the hierarchy, while he greeted Newman personally with a hearty handshake when he met him at Maynooth, never made any bones about it that he was opposed to the university plan. MacHale surely had a stronger case than the biographers usually credit to him.

If Newman was insensitive to Irish social problems, very much the same might be said of Cullen, the Archbishop of Dublin, at whose invitation Newman had come over. Cullen, like Wiseman, had had his training in Rome. He was more a Roman than an Irishman. He had

---

[1] Moriarty was a great opponent of the Fenians, whom MacHale supported. At the Vatican Council he and MacHale joined to oppose the infallibility decree, which Cullen championed.

little sympathy with Irish nationalism. Nationalism was to him a word which he naturally associated with Mazzini and Garibaldi and hostility to the Church. Such an evil spirit had shown itself in Ireland in 1798. The leader of the rising of 1848, Smith O'Brien, was a Protestant. Cullen had no wish to see the spirit of nationalism abroad in Ireland. The only political questions that seemed to him interesting or important were ecclesiastical questions. Political pressure must be brought to bear that the Catholic Church be freed of disabilities. Thus Catholic Emancipation was important. The abolition of tithe was important. The disestablishment of the Church of Ireland must be demanded. A full system of Catholic education under rigid clerical control must be established. But, those reforms achieved, legislation had done almost all that it could usefully do. It was not desirable that the legislature should reform the landed system, for would not such reforms involve the confiscation of private property, which was forbidden by the laws of the Church? Still less was it desirable that the Act of Union should be repealed. Cullen's policy was to get the Liberal party to pass the desirable ecclesiastical reforms and in return to get the Irish members to enrol themselves as obedient Liberals and to pass no further reforms. He wanted to marshal the bishops in support of the Union.

Therefore to Cullen, as opposed to other bishops, it was no defect in Newman that he was an Englishman and that he was not interested in Irish politics. But soon it became apparent that Newman had a failing which was in Cullen's eyes even more serious than that of the Irish politicians: it was indeed a bad thing to believe in nationalistic education, but it was even worse to believe in liberal education. Cullen had brought from Rome the belief that education should be rigid and under absolute clerical control. Young men should not be encouraged to ask questions, which were tantamount to entertaining doubts. They should be taught as certain facts the teachings of the Church. It was not for them to distinguish between what was of faith and what was not of faith. It was for their professors to draw such distinctions as might in that sphere be necessary. It was for the young men to learn and to accept and, if any should be so temerarious as to ask the reason why, it was sufficient to explain to him as answer that hell was the penalty for disobedience. 'The prelates,' scornfully concluded Newman,[1]

[1] Dean Inge, *Outspoken Essays*, p. 176: 'Cardinal Newman. Roman Catholic Modernists.' See 'Memorandum About my Connection with the Catholic University.' *Autobiographical Writings*.

'regard an intellectual man as on the road to perdition.' Rigid censorship must keep from the student's ears and eyes any impious speculations that in any way threw doubts on the teachings of the Church and in the same way his conduct must be controlled by strict rules and religiously spied upon by superiors who saw to it that he was never allowed to encounter any dangerous occasion of sin.

Newman's ideas of education were of course almost directly the opposite of these. To him a university should be as nearly as possible autonomous. Hierarchical control over it should be minimal. A university, he wrote in an amusing private paper in 1872,[2] 'is not a place to get up petitions for the Pope's temporal power and be deposed if a man won't sign it, or to print in its Gazette the Pope's dogmatic Bulls, or *docete gentes* in Mathematics, or oblige a dissector ever to be bringing in Providence.' So far from it being sufficient to teach the young their religion and a matter of indifference if they learnt anything else, to Newman's mind a man could not properly understand the Christian religion unless he understood what man was capable of without the aid of it. 'It seems,' thought Newman,[2] 'that the human mind is ever seeking to systematise knowledge, to base it upon a principle and to find a science comprehensive of all sciences.' If it is not offered a true system then it will prefer bigotry to 'a fluctuating and homeless scepticism'—or resign itself to some insufficient formula of economic determinism or of art for art's sake. Merely to teach the young to recite a catechism, unsupported by any general base in culture and apologetics, will not save him from this bigotry. A man cannot live by a variety of unconnected beliefs in 'a sort of bazaar, or pantechnicon, in which wares of all kinds are heaped together for sale in stalls independent of each other.'[3] 'Excellence must have a centre,'[4] and to provide that centre is what mere education can do. It can produce the 'gentleman' but to be a gentleman was not sufficient. 'Human knowledge and human reason' were not sufficient to conquer 'these giants, passion and the pride of man'. 'Philosophy, however enlightened, however profound, gives no command over the passions,

[1] J. Coulson, *Theology and the University*, p. 58: 'Newman's Idea of an Educated Laity.'

[2] *Ibid*, p. 30.

[3] *Ibid*, p. 50.

[4] *Ibid*.

no influential motives, no vivifying principle. Liberal education makes not the Christian nor the Catholic but the gentleman.'[1]

What exactly was the point of being a gentleman?

'A gentleman,' he wrote in the *Idea of a University*,[2] 'is one who never inflicts pain. This description is both refined and, as far as it goes, accurate. He is mainly occupied in merely removing the obstacles which hinder the free and unembarrassed action of those about him; and he concurs with their movements rather than takes the initiative himself. His benefits may be considered as parallel to what are called comforts or conveniences in arrangements of a personal nature; like an easy chair or a good fire, which do their part in dispelling cold and fatigue, though nature provides means of heat and rest without them. The true gentleman in like manner carefully avoids whatever may cause a jar or a jolt in the minds of those with whom he is cast—all clashing of opinion or collision of feeling, all restraint or suspicion of gloom or resentment; his great concern being to make everyone at their ease and at home.

'He has his eyes on all his company; he is tender towards the bashful, gentle towards the distant and merciful towards the absurd; he can recollect to whom he is speaking; he guards against unreasonable allusions, or topics which may irritate; he is seldom prominent in conversation and never wearisome. He makes light of favours while he does them and seems to be receiving when he is conferring. He never speaks of himself except when compelled, never defends himself by a mere retort, he has no ears for slander or gossip, is scrupulous in imputing motives to those who interfere with him and interprets everything for the best. He is never mean or little in his disputes, never takes unfair advantage, never mistakes personalities or sharp sayings for arguments or insinuates evil which he dare not say out.

'From a long-sighted prudence he observes the maxim of the ancient sage that we should ever conduct ourselves towards our enemy as if he were one day to be our friend. He has too much good sense to be affronted at insults, he is too well employed to remember injuries, and too indolent to bear malice. He is patient, forbearing and resigned on philosophical principles; he submits to pain because it is inevitable, to bereavement because it is irreparable and to death because it is his destiny. If he engages in controversy of any kind his disciplined

[1] Coulson, *Theology and the University*, p. 51.
[2] pp. 208–210.

intellect preserves him from the blundering discourtesy of better, perhaps, but less educated minds; who, like blunt weapons, tear and hack instead of cutting clean, who mistake the point in argument, waste their strength on trifles, misconceive their adversary and leave the question more involved than they find it. He may be right or wrong in his opinion but he is too clear-headed to be unjust; he is as simple as he is forcible and as brief as he is decisive. Nowhere shall we find greater candour, consideration, indulgence; he throws himself into the minds of his opponents, he accounts for their mistakes. He knows the weakness of human reason as well as its strength, its province and its limits. If he be an unbeliever he will be too profound and large-minded to ridicule religion or to act against it; he is too wise to be a dogmatist or fanatic in his infidelity. He respects piety and devotion; he even supports institutions as venerable, beautiful or useful to which he does not assent; he honours the ministers of religion and it contents him to decline its mysteries without assailing or denouncing them. He is a friend of religious toleration; and that not only because his philosophy has taught him to look on all forms of faith with an impartial eye but also from the gentleness and effeminacy of feeling which is the attendant on civilisation.'

As we can see, there was a good deal of quizzical ambivalence in Newman's estimate of the value of the gentleman's character. But it appeared evident a hundred years ago, even if it is not quite so evident today, that there must be gentlemen in a society in order that it may go on. Therefore it was important to train them. But gentility is not of course a substitute for religion. Still less, as some modern humanists would have it, is education a substitute for religion. Yet accomplishments such as these, while they did not in any way make a man a Catholic, made a Catholic who possessed them a more useful Catholic.

It is only possible to produce either a gentleman or an educated man in an atmosphere of freedom. It was essential that he who was going to lay claim to be an educated Catholic must be given a good general education—must learn what man had achieved in literature and the arts and science—and he must be taught these things on their intrinsic merits, not with a twist to wrest out of them an apologetic argument. 'The great point,' he wrote to Richard Simpson, the editor of the *Rambler*,[1] 'is to open men's minds, to educate them and make them

[1] A liberal Catholic paper with which Newman was for a time associated. Richard Simpson was a convert, clergyman, author of *Campion*.

logical. It does not matter what the subject is ... If you make them think on politics you will make them think on religion.' As he put it in his first sermon preached before the Irish University,[1] 'I wish the intellect to range with the utmost freedom and religion to enjoy an equal freedom; but what I am stipulating for is that they should be found in one and the same place and exemplified in the same persons. I want to destroy that diversity of centres which puts everything into confusion by creating a contrariety of influence ... I want the same roof to contain both the intellectual and the moral discipline. Devotion is not a sort of finish given to the sciences; nor is science a sort of feather in the cap ... an ornament and set-off to devotion. I want the intellectual layman to be religious and the devout ecclesiastic to be intellectual.' Sanctity was of course important, but so was intellect. 'The influence of sanctity,' he said, 'is greater in the long run; the influence of intellect is greater at the moment.'

On a more pragmatic plane it was, he thought, idle to attempt to stop the young from reading any literature that described sin. Literature was concerned with the doings of human beings and man was born in sin and a large part of his life was spent in sin. Suppress all literature that speaks of sin and you suppress all literature. 'If literature is to be made a study of human nature,' he writes in the *Idea*,[2] 'you cannot have a Christian literature ... Give up the study of man, as such, if so it must be; but say you do so ... Man is a being of genius, passion, intellect, conscience, power. He exercises these various gifts in various ways, in great deeds, in great thoughts, in heroic acts, in hateful crimes. ... Such is man; put him aside, keep him before you; but whatever you do, do not take him for what he is not.'

So scientific truth was the product of free inquiry. Scientific truths were not revealed in the Bible. The youth must be taught to investigate and he could only investigate if he was left free to speculate. Truth, he believed, could be achieved only 'by many minds working together'. Newman was first concerned to show what he meant by a university. A university, as he used the word—it is a mere matter of nomenclature —was a place where pupils should be taught. He did not consider it as a centre for research. That was another function, with which in these studies he was not concerned. A university again was a quite different place from a technical college. A technical college was a place that

[1] 'Intellect. The Instrument of Religious Training.'
[2] pp. 229, 230.

taught its pupils how to do certain things—make certain machines or use certain processes. It was of no concern to it whether these processes were good or bad, useful or useless. Thus he quotes[1] from the Inaugural lecture of Oxford's Professor of Political Economy, who said of his subject that 'it will rank in public estimation among the first of moral sciences in interest and in utility' as 'the science which teaches in what wealth consists, by what agents it is produced and according to what laws it is distributed and what are the institutions and customs by which production may be facilitated and distribution regulated, so as to give the largest possible amount of wealth to each individual.' Newman pertinently argued that political economy may tell us how to accumulate the greatest possible wealth, but it is not the economist but the moralist who tells us how far it is desirable to accumulate wealth. Therefore a university, while it teaches other things, must also teach ethics, and therefore philosophy and therefore religion. For religion, if true, is by its nature the master of all other disciplines.

But then he was careful to draw a distinction. To teach religion by no means meant to submit the student to a cleric-dominated, restrictive, bowdlerised discipline. Christianity was the religion of God acting in the world and it could therefore only be properly taught by a teacher who gave a full account of the world in all its aspects, good and bad. 'Why,' he asked,[2] 'do we educate except to prepare for the world? Why do we cultivate the intellect of the many beyond the first elements of knowledge except for this world? Will it be much matter in the world to come whether our bodily health or whether our intellectual strength was more or less, except of course as this world is in all its circumstances a trial for the next? If then a university is a direct preparation for this world, let it be what it professes. It is not a convent, it is not a seminary; it is a place to fit men of the world for the world. We cannot possibly keep them from plunging into the world with all its ways and principles and maxims, when their time comes; but we can prepare them against what is inevitable; and it is not the way to learn to swim in troubled waters never to have gone into them. Proscribe (I do not merely say particular authors, particular works, particular passages) but secular literature as such; cut out from your class books all broad manifestations of the natural man; and those manifestations are waiting for your pupil's benefit at the very doors of

[1] *Idea of a University*, p. 89.
[2] *Ibid*, p. 232.

your lecture room in living and breathing substance. They will meet him there in all the charm of novelty and all the fascination of genius or of amiableness.'

Thus, as we see, to Newman a university was not only a different place from a study for research or from a technical college. It was also a different place from a seminary. In a seminary the prime purpose was not to educate the seminarist. Its concern was not so much to form his mind as to make certain that he did not make mistakes. The seminarist when he became a priest would have to sit in the confessional and to pronounce on the morality of his penitents' actions. It was of vital importance that he should not make mistakes—that he should not say that certain actions were sinful which the Church did not authorise him to call sinful. Therefore for him it was of overriding importance that he be right. But with the undergraduate the considerations were different. He was being trained not for the confessional but for life, and he could only be so trained in conditions of freedom—in a condition of freedom that was, as Newman soon discovered, quite unknown to the traditions of Irish life. 'The office of a university,' he said, 'is to teach faith and of colleges to protect morals.'

Thus Newman mixed with the students. He encouraged them to keep horses and even rode out with them. He started musical societies, debating societies. He put billiard tables in their common rooms—defending himself by saying that if they had billiard tables at home they were less likely to go to taverns to discover them. Cullen was horrified. He found that Newman was even employing laymen to teach—and some of them Young Ireland men and liberals of very dubious reputation. He even wanted a layman to be appointed Vice-Rector. He either thought that the young were responsible people or that the clergy were not—Cullen was not quite certain which nor which was the more subversive. Newman suggested the formation of a lay committee to manage the university's finances, rather than have them mismanaged by clerics after the orthodox Roman fashion. It was best to bring up the young in Catholic principles but then not to worry too much if they made incidental errors in adolescence. If they had the roots of the matter in them they would discover for themselves the insufficiency of error and recovered faith would be all the stronger because the recovery was made by the young man for himself and out of an independent spirit. All that he demanded was that the young be willing to accept rebuke when their error was shown to them. The young men, Cullen complained in horror to Propaganda,[1] 'are allowed to go out at all hours, to smoke, etc., and there has not been any time for study. All this makes it clear that Father Newman does not give attention to detail.'

Cullen of course had a certain point. If religion is dogmatic and to be taught dogmatically and if all other subjects are to be taught freely and the greatest possible free investigation connected with them encouraged, how are we to draw the line? What are we to say where opinions honestly differ? The moral law has no bearing on the rules of mathematics. Twice two is four alike for the just and for the unjust. But there are intermediate disciplines between the dogmatic and the wholly secular—history for instance. People's views on history have varied in accordance with their religious opinions, but how far are such differences really necessary? Scholars of competence and honesty should be able to tell us the story of what happened irrespective of their own opinions, and indeed it can be said that scholars of today are giving us 'fair' history to an extent that would have been unthinkable in Newman's time. But on religion, in spite of the welcome growth of ecumenism and the dialogue of courtesy, men still differ from one another. Should we then be content to concentrate on a highest common factor of the general good, say that that is all that we require our general educators to invoke and leave any special denominational instruction for special periods and for those who desire it? Newman was later in life to come to think that this was the least bad plan—at any rate in universities. There was, sad experience had taught him, at least as great a chance that the Catholic apologists would twist the truth as there was that their antagonists would do so and the danger to faith of the inaccurate Catholic apologist was in the long run greater than the danger from his opponent.

By 1867 he had come to think, if we may judge from his correspondence with Sir Justin Shiel,[2] that the Catholic young man would do better at a non-denominational university, and in 1872 he wrote to Lord Howard,[3] 'On the whole I do not know how to avoid the conclusion that mixed education in the higher sense is as much a necessity

[1] Letter from Cullen to Father Kirby, Rector of the Irish College at Rome. October, 1855.

[2] Coulson, *Theology and the University*, p. 57: 'Newman's Idea of an Educated Laity.'

[3] *Ibid*, p. 60.

now in England as it was in the East in the days of St. Basil and St. Chrysostom. . . . In a large university there are good sets and bad sets; and a youth has a chance of choosing between them. In a small exclusive body there is no choice; and one bad member ruins for a time the whole community. Thus the open university, when complemented by a strong mission, may be even safer than a close Catholic college.'

Yet at this earlier date Newman still argued for a special Catholic university for Catholics. The university authorities should tell their students what the Catholic teaching was. They should endeavour to see to it that they obeyed that teaching in their conduct, but they must on no account make the fatal mistake of attempting to conceal from those students the fact that Catholic principles were not universally held and the knowledge of what the world was like.

'It was,' Newman wrote later in a private paper, 'not Ireland that was unkind to me. The same thing would have happened in England or France. It was the clergy moved as they are in automaton fashion from the camarilla at Rome.' The experience taught him that the project of a Catholic university was hopeless. Yet, whatever the truth about nationalism or about ideal systems of education, Newman's plans were mainly frustrated by a third handicap of a more pedestrian quality. Mid-Victorian society was a society which required the great majority of its citizens to earn their living by manual labour. Neither Newman nor anybody else at that time had any notion that a university education was desirable except for the small minority of what are today called 'white-collar workers'. His educational theories were entirely directed to the development of the mind. He had no notion of vocational training in any direct sense. Did not his theorisings about the nature of a gentleman prove as much? Now in Ireland at that time a quite overwhelming majority of posts of responsibility and of 'white-collar' jobs were of course in Protestant hands. The Protestants owned by far the greater part of the land in a country that was almost entirely agricultural. Therefore it was an inevitable difficulty for an institution that was specifically designed to educate middle-class Irish Catholics that these middle-class Irish Catholics simply did not exist in any sufficient numbers.

The Jesuit Provincial, Father Curtis, told him that the 'mechanics' whom he was seeking to educate were a figment of his imagination and that he had better abandon his enterprise.[1] Almost all the Catholics

[1] Memorandum About My Connection with the Catholic University.

in Ireland were peasants. They were in no position—indeed they had no wish—that their sons should go to a university at all. It was a tradition in which they took great pride that one member of the family should go to the priesthood, and they understood that a training was required for that vocation. They did not understand nor aspire to criticise the details of its curriculum—and they did not see at all the purpose of any higher education for a boy who was going to be a layman. It was simply a waste of money and of time that should be employed working on the land at home. Nor without disrupting family life would it have been possible to introduce the young, even had young of such a sort existed, so rapidly to those free ideas which were entirely unfamiliar to their parents. General English literature was so overwhelmingly anti-Catholic that there was grave reason to fear that a general education, without the balance of a cultured home, would turn out to be an anti-Catholic education. Science, which New-man was anxious to teach, might not be in itself at warfare with the Church, but the scientific revolution was in fact entirely the work of non-Catholics. A student who was indoctrinated with it was likely to think that brains and free thinking were more commonly found among the critics of the Church than among its champions and the prestige of Catholicism in their minds was likely to be weakened.

It is true of course that over the years and with the economic and social and political developments of Irish life a Catholic middle class has by today grown up. There is today and of recent years a different situation. In that different situation—in an Ireland politically free, with a land-owning peasantry, with a considerable urban and industrial population, much more frequently in contact with the rest of the world —there is a much greater scope for Newman's notions of a free education. Newman, though he himself did not guess it, was writing his *Idea of a University*, as in different ways he has written many of his other works, much more for a world that was to come a hundred years after his time than for the world of his own day.

Newman immediately, though not, as I think, finally, failed in Ireland. When, as will surely happen, Irish education is finally freed it will be to Newman more than to any other that the debt is owed. Yet for the moment rebuff after rebuff left him in a sad state. In 1856 he had written to Ambrose St. John,[1] 'I go to Rome to be snubbed. I

---

[1] His closest friend among the young Oratorians. Had St. John not predeceased him Newman had intended that he should be his biographer.

come to Dublin to be repelled by Dr. MacHale and worn away by Dr. Cullen. The Cardinal taunts me with his dedications and Father Faber insults me with his letters. I would be let alone but I have no means of defending myself more than if my hands and tongue were tied . . . What is to be the end of it?'[1] 'I am nobody,' he wrote,[2] 'I have no friend at home. I have laboured in England to be mis-represented. I have laboured in Ireland with a door ever shut in my face . . . Oh, my God, I seem to have wasted these years that I have been a Catholic. What I wrote as a Protestant has had far greater force, meaning, success, than my Catholic works—and this troubles me a great deal.'

Snub followed snub. The invitation to him of the English hierarchy to make a new translation of the Bible was withdrawn after a muddle about copyright. Bishop Ullathorne requested him to abandon his editorship of the *Rambler*. He got into what seemed for a time likely to be the most serious trouble of all about his article in that paper *On Consulting the Faithful in Matters of Doctrine*. Dr. Gillow, theologian of Ushaw, wrote, 'it is most painful to see published by one whom we regarded as the best of our converts allegations and arguments . . . which might now seem to be the writing of a Calvinist'[3] and Bishop Brown of Newport delated the article to Rome.

On no point has Newman's prescience been more dramatically justified than here. For this theory which earned him his episcopal censure and so nearly earned him condemnation in the middle of the last century has now been adopted by the Church as a central teaching. His influence has brought the Church right round. 'What is the province of the laity? To hunt, to shoot, to entertain. These matters they understood but to meddle in ecclesiastical matters they have no right at all,' said Monsignor Talbot with the voice of the Vatican of a hundred years ago. 'The universal body made up of the faithful, whom the Holy One has anointed, is incapable of being at fault in belief,' teaches the present Vatican Council's Constitution on the Church.

One of the major achievements of the Second Vatican Council has been its assertion of the Apostolate of the Laity. The Church, the Fathers there proclaimed, does not consist of the clergy and their subjects. The Church is the Church of all Christians. The laity is the

---

[1] *Light in Winter*, p. 153: '1853—The Task is to Soothe and Butter me.'

[2] Autobiographical Writings. The Journal. January 8, 1860, pp. 251–2.

[3] Letter to Bishop Brown. Coulson, *On Consulting the Faithful*, p. 37, Introduction.

people of God. Cynics may suggest that the shortage of priests has made ecclesiastical authorities more ready to allow the laity to perform functions which up till now have been closed to them. Whether for that reason or for a more worthy, it is certain that even as late as the beginning of this century clergymen, alike in Catholic and in Protestant countries, were still able to claim a virtual monopoly of all important educational posts. They kept in their own hands the management of their finances, and this, if the case fifty years ago, was of course still more completely the case fifty years before that.

As we have seen, Newman's suggestion that laymen should be allowed to teach and to manage finances in a university was rejected by Cullen as dangerously revolutionary, and Cullen's opinion was of course only the usual opinion of the day. Laymen took a part in the teaching at the Oratory School quite out of proportion with any that they would have been allowed to take in any other Catholic School of that time. The revolution today has been so complete that we almost forget that there has been a revolution, but the change over a hundred years has been enormous and here as elsewhere the modern fashion was largely formed by and is largely indebted to Newman. It is thought desirable to give a university education to a vastly larger proportion of the population than it was a hundred years ago and a greatly increased number of Catholics have raised themselves into the class that demands this education. A hundred years ago education was entirely in the hands of the clergy and only given grudgingly to laymen in any higher form. 'Ought the principle to be admitted that the laity should be more highly educated than the clergy?' asked the questionnaire circulated by Propaganda in 1864. Whether or not the principle is admitted, the fact has come to happen and steadily over the years there has been a growth in the number of laymen holding teaching posts and in recent years a flight from clericalism has been a main mark of Catholic education.

The Church's policy here as in other fields had in the middle of the last century been largely the product of Italian experience. All the posts in the Papal States were in clerical hands and Pius IX's brief experiment of giving power to laymen had proved wholly disastrous. Even after the fall of Rome there was no change in this respect. On the contrary Catholics were forbidden to play any part in the political life of the new Italian kingdom. They were to be neither *eletti* nor *elettori*, and when under Pius X a very restricted political freedom was allowed to those who called themselves Christian Democrats, the fact that one of their first leaders, Murri, happened also to be a Modernist meant that they were only allowed to operate under very strict episcopal control. Down to most recent times the only sort of action wholly approved of for the lay Catholic was the very strictly organised and controlled Catholic Action and even so excellent and wise a Catholic layman as de Gasperi was thought of as dangerously independent. The Italian experience had its effect even in other countries.

When the first draft of the Council's decree on the Apostolate of the Laity was presented to the Council, the Fathers congratulated themselves that this was the first time that an attempt had been made at a General Council to sketch out a scheme of Catholic lay action, and quotations were given to show 'that the lay apostolate has always existed in the Church' (even in apostolic times). Nevertheless the particular scheme was harshly criticised on the ground that it was too exclusively concerned with official and directed action. There was little said of the free Catholic lay action which Newman thought so important. The first draft was withdrawn and an amended draft, which was finally passed by a very large majority, was substituted for it. This draft stated it to be 'the proper duty of the lay state to live in the midst of the world and worldly affairs, where they are called by God to exercise their apostolate like a leaven in the ardour of the Christian spirit.' 'The laity must use these aids [of religion] in such a way that while they fulfil their worldly duties in the ordinary conditions of life, they do not separate their union with Christ from their ordinary lives, but live in accordance with the will of God in their daily life.' The Fathers neither called on the layman to make himself a mere sacristy man nor did they share Monsignor Talbot's fear[1] that 'if a check be not placed on the laity of England they will be the rulers of the Catholic Church in England instead of the Holy See and the Episcopate.'

What then was it exactly that Newman meant when he claimed that the laity had a right to be consulted? In his support he pointed to Pius IX's inquiries shortly before at the time of the definition of the Immaculate Conception when he wrote round to the bishops of the world inviting them to inform him of their congregations' opinion on this doctrine. Newman thought it desirable that laymen should teach in schools and universities. He thought that they had a right to be consulted on the Church's policy towards secular authority. They were more likely to know how to deal with the non-Catholic layman than were

[1] Letter to Manning. Coulson, On Consulting the Faithful, p. 41, Introduction.

the priests and they were less likely to be suspect. The great political issue of the day was, as so often, that of education. What treatment was the State to give to Church schools? Newman wrote[1] in an unsigned contribution to the *Rambler* on the Catholic attitude towards the proposed Royal Commission on Elementary Education, 'we do unfeignedly believe ... that their lordships desire to know the opinion of the laity on subjects in which the laity are especially concerned. If even in the preparation of a dogmatic definition the faithful are consulted, as lately in the instance of the Immaculate Conception, it is at least as natural to anticipate such an act of kind feeling and sympathy in great practical questions.'

It was the conditional clause that aroused all the fuss. What did it mean? Eight years before in 1851 Newman had referred to the laity as at all times,[2] 'the measure of the Catholic spirit. They saved the Irish Church three centuries ago.' It was the Catholic bishops who had betrayed Catholicism in England under Henry VIII. But Bishop Ullathorne argued that Newman's appeal to Pius's inquiries about the Immaculate Conception was little more than a debating point. Pius IX might have used words of consultation as a matter of courtesy but in reality, argued the Bishop, it was 'absolutely unnecessary that the reasons for our own actions should be explained and that the Catholic community should be informed of the grounds of our proceedings.' Cardinal Wiseman, as alleged truly or falsely by Simpson, Newman's predecessor as editor of the *Rambler*, had said that 'the only function of the laity is to pay.'[3]

Therefore Newman, under fire, had to dig more deeply into history to show what it was that he meant. He did not mean, he explained, that the Church was a congregationalist society which decided its doctrines by a majority vote or that the laity should usurp the function of authority to teach and rule. The laity, he argued, were consulted by Pius IX not in the sense that they were invited to make up their minds or to give advice but 'as a thermometer' is consulted. They were consulted in order to discover what in fact they did and believed. The Pope, when he defines a doctrine, does not invent a doctrine and impose it upon a public that has never previously heard of it. He speaks—or the Holy Ghost speaks through him—giving definition to

[1] Coulson, *On Consulting the Faithful*, p. 8, Introduction.
[2] *Ibid*, p. 21.
[3] *Ibid*, p. 17.

what is already the general mind of the Church. The *ecclesia docens* has 'the power and prerogative of definition', as he wrote in his correspondence with Gillow, but that does not mean that infallibility in the Church is to be found exclusively in the *ecclesia docens*. No one but a fool indeed thought of the Church as a slave society in which laymen had no duty except to ask of the priests what they should believe. But Newman stated their rights much more explicitly than was at the time the general fashion. They had, he asserted, a sort of instinct or *phronema* of Christian doctrine. They had a jealousy of error, and naturally reacted from it as a scandal.

The clergy of course had such a *phronema* as well and in all the happiest periods of the Church clergy and laity acted together, stood together and thought alike. But God has only given to his Church a guarantee against error over the long run. In the long run truth conquers. But there is no guarantee that truth will appear to be predominant over a short run. Sometimes it appears to be losing in a certain part and sometimes it appears to be losing in the whole Church. Athanasius did not have a majority. He had to stand alone against the world of authority. Yet his was in the long run the Catholic voice. There were plenty of occasions in history when the episcopacy had witnessed to truth against an unfaithful laity. But there were also occasions when it was the laity which had proved faithful and the episcopacy faithless. Newman took as his great example the Arian period of the fourth century when the world groaned to find itself Arian and when the man in the street stood for Catholic truth against the bulk of the bishops. With a weight of instances he overwhelmingly proved his case.

There was at that time, he argues, not indeed a 'failure' but 'a temporary suspension' of the *ecclesia docens* and the true witness to the faith was found in the *consensus fidelium* of the *ecclesia discens*. He added with some irony 'as to the present, certainly if there ever was an age which might dispense with the testimony of the faithful and leave the maintenance of the truth to the pastors of the Church, it is the age in which we live.' We know of course well enough what he really thought of the 'Novatianism' into which the Church was in danger of falling, of the habits of bishops and of that belief in a special providence in the Papacy in which he had once so fondly believed but which his experience of the ways of Pius IX had, as he confessed, so completely dissipated. In any event there is, he thought,[1] 'something in the *pastorum et*

[1] Coulson, *On Consulting the Faithful*, p. 104.

fidelium conspiratio, which is not in the pastors alone', and the *ecclesia docens* is happier in a period of full partnership than 'when she cuts off the faithful from the study of her divine doctrines and the sympathy of her divine contemplations and requires from them a *fides implicita* in her word, which in the educated classes will terminate in indifference and in the poorer in superstition.'

There was of course a risk in freedom but it was a risk that was worth taking. 'It is the property of life,' he quoted from his *Anglican Difficulties*[1] 'to be impatient of any foreign substance in the body to which it belongs.' But these risks must of course be taken in a responsible manner. A layman had no right to cast a vote carelessly on matters to which he had never given his attention. The layman must be ready to learn. The priests must be ready to meet him. It was such a meeting that he had hoped would be effected in a Catholic university—'a middle station where clergy and laity can meet and from which as from a common ground they may act in union upon an age which is running headlong into infidelity.'[2]

[1] Coulson, *On Consulting the Faithful*, p. 23.
[2] *Ibid*, p. 35.

8

The Apologia

FOR THE MOMENT Newman found to hand another task of education, in which, though success was not entirely outstanding, it was not at least an immediate and total failure. As long as the penal laws were on, Catholics were not of course allowed to establish a school in England. Those parents who wished a Catholic education for their sons had either to make for them some private and secret arrangement or else to send them overseas to one of the English Catholic schools abroad. Then with the French Revolution these continental schools were suppressed and the Fathers had to find refuge in England. A slightly more tolerant age was willing to take account of the fact that the Fathers were being persecuted by the French for their patriotism rather than for their religion and to allow them therefore to settle down in England for—as was thought to begin with—a temporary refuge. But when at last the long French wars were ended and Napoleon beaten, there seemed no point in returning to France. They were allowed to stay on in England, and the aristocratic English Catholics of the first half of the nineteenth century got their education at English Catholic schools—along with the Church boys at Ushaw or Oscott, from the Benedictines at Downside or from the Jesuits at Stonyhurst.

Newman thought that these schools had not sufficiently broken with their continental habits. His experience at Rome had not given him a very high opinion of the quality of contemporary Catholic thinking, but it was not that defect that so much bothered him in this context. He did not wish or expect that the young teenage Catholics would set themselves up as amateur theologians, but he thought that the Continental system sought to keep boys under a covert espionage which was not healthy or desirable in England. He thought that these schools ruled their pupils with an excessively savage discipline. So he started a school of his own at the Oratory at Birmingham. The truth is, of course, that Newman had not been to a public school and was not very well informed on what went on at them. He had that reverence for the public schools which is so commonly found among Englishmen who have not been to one of them. Mid-nineteenth-century discipline may have been too severe at Stonyhurst. It is hard to believe that it was more brutal than was that at Eton. In fact, as might be expected, the effect of introducing ex-public-school men as masters into his new Catholic school and bidding them to treat the place as if it were an English public school was rapidly to brutalise it and complaints soon began to be raised—not of course against Newman but against Darnell, the Headmaster, a Wykehamist—that the flogging at the Oratory was excessive.

In any event what was important was not so much whether these prejudices against the schools that had come from the Continent were justified as that they were in fact entertained. There were, thought Newman, some of the converts who had come into the Church along with him and the Oxford Movement who had themselves been at public schools and who would not be willing to entrust their sons to those schools with a Continental tradition. The event proved that he was up to a point right. The Oratory school had plenty of its troubles —troubles of the kind with which every school's history is peppered— quarrels between the headmaster and the matron, rows with assistant masters and the like. His critics on the Oratory staff did not scruple to spread about rumours that not only was Newman past his zenith but even that he was going mad. At one time the whole staff resigned and Newman and St. John had to take the school on themselves. Wiseman, now totally under the influence of his Provost, Manning, who was uncompromisingly opposed to any lay influence in education, wrote that he 'had washed his hands of the school plan'. Yet it survived. It is only necessary to record with regret that Newman should have become involved in these squabbles. He had a strange incapacity for keeping out of a row, however petty. We need not here attempt to disentangle the question. It by no means proved in the event that all of the converts were unwilling to send their sons to the older religious schools. The greater number of them was content to do so and the older schools always had larger numbers than the Oratory school. Still, the Oxford Movement had brought into the Church a number of professional families. The Catholic body, which had previously consisted predominantly either of aristocrats or of proletarians, now had a considerable middle-class membership and there was therefore plenty of room for a new school which could cater for them.

In those days the public examinations were little known and less regarded. Catholics were not admitted into Oxford and Cambridge and there was therefore no list of scholarships gained by which a school's merit could be easily, if unsatisfactorily, estimated. There was thus no simple statistical test by which one Catholic school could be set against another. So it is hardly possible to say how the Oratory school compared with other Catholic schools in academic merit. Doubtless none of them was very good. How could they be? The complaint was made that, in reaction from the excessive catechisms of the Jesuits, religion at the Oratory was under Darnell's leadership hardly taught at all. Yet obviously it was desirable that Catholic parents should be offered a variety of schools from which to choose and the Oratory school proved by the event that it satisfied the wishes of a certain number of them. It survives but it has never established itself as a major school.

These years of the early 1860's were, as we learn from Newman's own journal, the years of his supreme desolation. It is true that some of the Old Catholics, contrasting him with other converts whose rabid Ultramontanism they so much disliked, spoke of him with respect. But what comfort was there in that? He did not know them. He did not mix with them. He respected their sense of restraint but his mind was not as their minds. They with their simple gentleman's code had no sense of those deep questions about which his mind was concerned. In face of the Anglican world he had forced himself to be more aggressive than he would otherwise have been because it would have seemed to him a disloyalty had he in any way acquiesced in a use of him as a foil to the other Catholics. 'I certainly,' he wrote,[1] 'am under the temptation of looking out for, if not courting, Protestant praise . . . I am tempted to look back. Not so, O Lord, with Thy grace not so.' Therefore to absurd suggestions that he was thinking of returning to the Church of England he replied with an unnecessary brutality in a letter in which he said that the thought of the Thirty-nine Articles made him 'shudder' and 'shiver'.

Except for a very few dear personal friends Newman felt that he was left utterly alone. The great issue of the day in the eyes of most

[1] *Light in Winter*, p. 216: '1859–60—I am the Scapegoat.'

Catholics—the great battle to which every loyal Catholic was called—was that for the Pope's temporal power. In 1859 the Piedmontese had seized all the Pope's dominions except Rome itself and there was little doubt—as of course happened in 1870—that before long a convenient opportunity would be taken to seize Rome, too. But Newman, unlike the great majority of his co-religionists, was simply unable to see in this threat a supreme catastrophe. The Ultramontanes did not hesitate therefore to claim that he was not really and never had been a Catholic, and they pointed as proof of it to the statistical fact that he was not making converts, as they were making them.

Newman felt the strength of that taunt. Of course any Catholic must wish to make converts. But truth was deep and subtle. It was not permitted to take short-cuts with truth or to attract converts by equivocations. Newman wrote for a century ahead. 'When I am gone,' he wrote,[1] 'it will be seen perhaps that persons stopped me from doing a work which I might have done,' but added, 'it may be God's will it should be done a hundred years hence.' There is no more vulgar test of apostolic worth than that of the statistics of immediate conversion. Those who set their sights on distant targets can hardly expect immediate appreciation. What was needed was to persuade the age that it could matter to real issues what did or did not happen in Palestine two thousand years ago—that the Christian revelation was relevant. Formal conversion was not in itself necessarily a solution of this problem. There were plenty of people within the Church, even as there were plenty of people outside the Church, to whom—except perhaps at the point of death—the whole Gospel was, whether they understood it or not, in fact irrelevant. How could they be made to see it as relevant?

Faced with such problems Newman felt himself utterly alone. Who was it who could understand what was troubling him? He was unsupported by the bishops in Ireland and the bishops in England, unsupported at Rome, unsupported by his fellow Oratorians in London, unsupported even by many of the Oratorians at Birmingham. No one likes to be left alone, compelled to battle without a friend by his side. Lack of support is particularly difficult to bear for a Catholic who believes that he is divinely commissioned to live under authority.

'And now, alas I fear,' he was to write in his journal for October 30, 1867,[2] 'that in one sense the iron has entered into my soul. I mean that

[1] Coulson, *On Consulting the Faithful in Matters of Doctrine*, Introduction, p. 20.
[2] *Autobiographical Writings*, p. 262: 'The Journal—October 30, 1867.'

confidence in any superiors whatever never can blossom again within me. I never shall feel easy with them. I shall (I feel) always think they will be taking some advantage of me—that at length their way will lie across mine and that my efforts will be displeasing to them. I shall ever be suspicious that they or theirs have secret unkind thoughts of me and that they deal with me with some *arrière pensée*. And as it is my happiness so to be placed as not to have much intercourse with them, therefore, while I hope ever loyally to fulfil their orders, it is my highest gain and most earnest request to them that they would let me alone—and, since I do not want to initiate any new plan of any kind, that, if they can, they would keep their hands off me. Whether or not they will consent to this is more than I can say, for they seem to wish to ostracise me. . . . God forbid I should liken them to the Scribes and Pharisees—but still I obey them as Scribes and Pharisees were to be obeyed, as God's representatives, not from devotion to *them*.'[1] He obeys but, if he obeys where he cannot have confidence, obedience is bitter and servile. If he fights a battle under such auspices he fights without spirit.

The Catholic authorities were in his opinion themselves strangling the traditional and necessary freedom of Catholic life and were its most dangerous enemies. 'This age of the Church,' he wrote,[2] 'is peculiar—in former times, primitive or mediaeval, there was not the extreme centralisation which is now in use. If a private theologian said anything free, then it went to a Bishop, a theological faculty or to some foreign University. The Holy See was but the court of ultimate appeal. Now if I, as a private priest, put anything into print, *Propaganda* answers me at once. How can I fight with such a chain upon my arm? It is like the Persians driven to fight under the lash. There was a true private judgement in the primitive and mediaeval schools—there are no schools now, no private judgement (in the religious sense of the phrase) no freedom, that is, of opinion. That is, no exercise of the intellect. No, the system goes on by the tradition of the intellect of former times.'

The policy of Propaganda and the episcopate was to admit that a wicked world was full of atheism and infidelity, to abandon it to its devices but to protect the faithful remnant from contamination by a thorough censorship and proscription. Newman saw that such tactics must inevitably fail. The rot had gone too far. It was not merely that

[1] *Autobiographical Writings*, p. 263.
[2] Coulson, *On Consulting the Faithful*, p. 44.

atheism had captured the non-Christian world. Even those who were not professed atheists had become pragmatic atheists: whatever idle guesses they might make about a First Cause, they took it for granted that God had never interfered and never would interfere with the affairs of Man; and what was frightening, of course, was that this assumption was made not only in the world outside the Church but also all too often by Catholics, and by Catholics in high places, who assumed that the Church could only prosper through the use of ruse and policy and not by reliance upon the Will of God. He felt himself dreadfully alone. 'Oh, how forlorn and dreary has been my course since I have become a Catholic,' he wrote in his journal on January 21, 1863. 'Here has been the contrast—as a Protestant I felt my religion dreary but not my life—but as a Catholic my life dreary but not my religion.'

It was at this darkest moment of Newman's desolation that the popular English novelist and clergyman, Charles Kingsley, sat down to write a review of volumes VII and VIII of the *History of England* of his brother-in-law, Anthony Froude, in Macmillan's Magazine. The volumes were concerned with the Reformation years and Kingsley took the opportunity, as he usually did, to explain that Roman clerics were and had always been a tricky and treacherous lot. There was no reason why Newman's name should have come into the review at all. But Kingsley happened to write in a chance throw-away line, 'Truth for its own sake has never been a virtue with the Roman Clergy,' and then added, 'Father Newman informs us that it need not and on the whole ought not to be.'[1] Kingsley did not sign his name to this review. It appeared only with the initials C.K. and it was only by chance that Newman ever saw it. He only saw it because an anonymous correspondent sent him a copy. Newman had had to bear so much abuse over the years that he did not as a general rule, any more than other men who have been through such controversies, reply to attacks on him. But there was of course a particularly wounding threat in this attack. For the accusation was not so much that Newman was himself a liar—an accusation which he might have borne with contempt—but that he spoke for the Catholic Church when he proclaimed truth to be unnecessary. As a loyal Catholic, Newman naturally enough felt it far

[1] For all this story see the introduction to the *Apologia*.

more seriously incumbent on him to refute attacks upon the Church than to refute attacks upon himself.

But, apart from that, here was of course a situation which Kingsley doubtless did not at all understand. He knew nothing of the internal troubles of the Church in England. He thought of the Catholic Church as a monolithic body whose members all spoke with one voice, and that it was sufficient to show that one priest had said something and you had proved that they all said it. The truth of course was almost the exact opposite. Newman had bitter enemies in the Church at that time. There were plenty who were anxious to get him condemned. There were plenty who would be all too ready to believe that Newman with his tortuous mind had said that Catholics were free to tell lies, or something to that effect, and who would be only too glad to use the fact as ammunition to persuade Rome that Newman was a man so dangerous and irresponsible that he could not be left safely to speak at large. Therefore it was especially necessary for Newman, once it had been brought to his attention, to get this misstatement corrected. He had at first no expectation that the correction would lead to any major controversy. It did not occur to him that C.K. stood for Charles Kingsley. He had no notion who was the writer of the review, never thought that it was a matter of importance and was not bothered to inquire. All that he imagined was that it was necessary to call the attention of Mr. Macmillan to the misrepresentation, and that Mr. Macmillan, as a gentleman, would apologise and withdraw, and that would be the end of the matter. It was only when Mr. Macmillan in his reply did not make a full and satisfactory withdrawal but made the mistake of entering into argument about Catholic doctrines of equivocation, and professed surprise that Newman should have taken exception to the statement of a position which he still imagined to have been generally held by all Catholics, that Newman felt that the matter must be carried further.

Kingsley confessed his authorship and entered into the controversy. Newman very sensibly refused at this stage to be drawn into general arguments about Catholic beliefs or practices. His position was that Kingsley had made the definite statement, 'Father Newman informs us.' 'When,' asked Newman, 'had he informed them?' Naturally enough Kingsley could produce no such passage from any statement of Newman, but what was worse was that the only passage which he could produce which had the very faintest bearing on the point—

though it in no kind of way substantiated the accusation—was from a sermon which Newman had delivered in St. Mary's at Oxford, when he was still of course an Anglican. It was the prevarications of Macmillan and Kingsley which persuaded Newman that the public misunderstanding of his character was so deep that he could never hope for justice through a mere correction of a particular misstatement. There was nothing for it but that he should tell the world the full story of his life so that they might be able to understand why he was as he was and why he spoke as he spoke.

It is a curiosity of Newman's career that, while many—many quite unsympathetic to his opinions—would acclaim him as the greatest English prose writer of the century, yet he was never in any way a literary man who wrote only for a literary exercise. All his works were answers to some particular challenge of the moment, and might never have been written had not that challenge been delivered. This is most eminently so of the *Apologia*. He had never had any thought of writing an autobiography. We certainly owe the writing of it entirely to Charles Kingsley.

The *Apologia* is by general agreement one of the supreme spiritual autobiographies in Christian history. No purpose will be served by merely attempting to summarise its contents, for it is of course the main source for anything that is written about the life of Newman. It would be to as little purpose to repeat the deserved praises of its beauty, its flexibility and the vividness of its style. Anyone who has ever at all interested himself in the life of Newman will be familiar with the story of its compilation, remember how he wrote it standing at his desk, and with the tears rolling down his cheeks, how he wrote at breakneck speed, each sheet being sent off as soon as completed to the printer, so that the whole writing took only a matter of nine weeks. Our concern is not with eulogy but with the part that the *Apologia* played in revising and establishing the world's verdict on Newman. The general thesis— that at one bound it turned Newman from being a widely distrusted and unpopular character into one of the most revered figures of the age—is well enough known. Broadly speaking, it is largely true, but it is necessary to make four points.

First, it must be remembered that the *Apologia* is by definition a spiritual autobiography. The word 'spiritual' is the operative word. There is in this book none of the casual chatter about friends and relations and what is going on in the world which we are accustomed to look for in autobiographical writings. It is not that Newman was incapable of such gossip. Rose Macaulay is in error when in her *Letters to a Sister* she says that Newman was incapable of talking about anything but religion. The *Idea of a University* shows that he was more capable of entertaining, and valued more highly the entertainment of, general ideas than most men. Anecdotes about his making pictures of rabbits by the reflection of candle-light on the walls or his reading *Alice in Wonderland* with Dean Church's daughters show him very capable of a lighter—it may seem, even a childish—side. But such relaxations, however proper in themselves, were not in place in the *Apologia* which was concerned only with his religious opinions.

Second, the book is mainly concerned with his religious opinions up till 1845—up till the time that he became a Catholic. Its concern is to show the development of his ideas up till the time that he took that step. As to what his religious opinions had been during the period of what was all but twenty years between his reception and the publication of the *Apologia*, he was content to say: 'Since then [his reception] my religious opinions have had no development.'[1] In a way this was true enough. He had of course from the moment of his reception never hesitated or doubted in his loyalty to the Catholic Church and, in view of the gossiping stories that had been passing round about his scepticism or his return to the Church of England, it was natural that he should take the opportunity of rebutting them by such a curt sentence. If he had plunged into finely drawn dissertations about what he thought at this date and what he thought at that date, stupid people would have considered their suspicions justified. Still, as the stories of Edgbaston and Dublin, Brompton and Rome most amply show, it was far from true that he had had no religious history since his conversion, and that history, though it had in no kind of way shaken his fundamental faith, had taught him a great deal that he had not known nineteen years before about the method of approach to that belief.

Thirdly, we must always remember in all judgements about Newman his total failure to foresee his longevity. Just as at the time of his reception in 1845 he thought that he had come home to die; just as after the Achilli trial he thought that he was passing into the autumn of his days; so, when he wrote the *Apologia* at sixty-three, he imagined that he was writing the Finis to his life story. It never occurred to him that, far from having written his last work, he would in the evening of

[1] *Apologia*, p. 275, Part VII.

his days write further and write at any rate one of the most important books of the century. Today looking back a hundred years, we see Newman not primarily as the man who had picked his way out of the Anglican Church but much more the man who revised the whole method of apologetic of the Catholic Church. It is his development as a Catholic which is more important than his development as an Anglican.

The most important point is the fourth point. Just as it is true that, when we read history, we tend, if we do not watch ourselves, to assume that all history's characters knew from the first how long they would have to live—that Shelley knew that he would be drowned young, that Titian knew that he would be spared to go on painting into his nineties, that Napoleon, when he went to St. Helena, knew he had only six years to live—so we tend to assume that the results of conflicts and actions were foreseen and inevitable. So, knowing the name that Newman was to leave behind him, we tend to assume that the period of misunderstanding and contempt was bound of its nature to be ephemeral, that he had only to display the patience to bear it for a time and that when once he put pen to paper to explain himself in the *Apologia* that explanation was bound to be accepted with universal acclaim and apology to be showered upon him. It did not of course appear in the least like that to Newman when he began to write his *Apologia*. On the contrary, as he saw it, every enterprise of his over the last twenty years had ended invariably in failure, every attempt that he had made to explain himself had ended only in further misunderstandings, so that he could be excused if the mood in which he started to write was one of despondency and almost of despair.

Had it not been proved again and again to his experience that the suspicion of Rome entertained by educated mid-Victorian Englishmen was almost impossible of exaggeration? Did not the violence over the Ecclesiastical Titles Bill and the attacks on ecclesiastics who wore their habits in the streets prove that on this point the nation was almost insane? Had not all too many of the English who thought that he had been badly treated in the Achilli case, even while they had taken his side, taken it in grudging fashion—willing to grant that Achilli, since he too was after all a Catholic priest, was doubtless a rogue but thinking nevertheless that an ex-Oxford don should have found something better to do with his talents than indulge in such exercises of mud-slinging? And, among his own co-religionists, were there not many who because of his opposition to the Ultramontanes thought that he was a dangerous and unreliable man and that it was all too likely that he said what Kingsley accused him of having said—or at any rate something equally foolish and irresponsible? Was not Kingsley a widely popular novelist who owed his popularity exactly to the fact that he pandered completely to the prejudices of his day and told the Protestant English public that the hearty, unascetical, worldly life which they enjoyed living was a life highly approved of by the founder of the Christian religion? Newman knew that he could refute Kingsley's charges—that he could get the better of him in logic; but what hope had he that the British public would listen to him? Was it not far more probable that the *Apologia* would merely add one more to the dreary catalogue of misunderstandings with which his life had been filled?

Indeed, far from it being from the first inevitable and easy to foretell that the *Apologia* would be a triumphant success, it is rather a little difficult to see even in retrospect why it was so great a success—why the British public, which had been so unwilling to accept him in the past, was willing to accept him then. The *Apologia* brought Newman back into companionship with his old Tractarian friends who had not taken with him the step to Rome. They had been pained by some of his writings about Anglicans in his first years as a Catholic, by *Loss and Gain* and *Lectures on Anglican Difficulties*. But those days were now long past. In so far as they knew about his difficulties with more intransigent Catholics, they would have been less than human if those difficulties had not caused them to feel more kindly towards Newman. In writing the *Apologia* he was careful to write without personal offence and to consult those Anglican friends who had acted with him in the Oxford days. They gladly gave their assistance and the collaboration gave an opportunity to remake old broken friendships. Those Oxford High Churchmen had no cause at all to think kindly of the brutal John Bull-imperialistic version of Protestantism which Kingsley peddled and an exposure of him and his vulgarity was wholly welcome to them. 'He won by his kindness and fairness as he could never have conquered by attack,' wrote Keble of the *Apologia*. 'I see no end to the good which the whole Church, we may reasonably hope, may derive from such an example of love and candour under most trying circumstances.'

But the *Apologia* won applause among non-Catholic Englishmen far beyond the boundaries of the High Church. The reason, I think, was mainly decency. The oscillations of public opinion are notoriously unpredictable, but malice always has a term. Ordinary Englishmen were —perhaps had been for some time—a little ashamed of the way that the English nation was treating Newman. Differ from him as they might, no one could honestly believe that his was a shifty and dishonourable character, and still less could anyone hold such a belief after he had read the *Apologia* with the agony of a subtle soul desperately seeking for truth of salvation apparent on every page. After reading such a book every honest man saw the accusations of Kingsley standing evident in their vulgarity and indeed, while the controversy had begun through Kingsley's accusation against Newman of untruthfulness, the correspondence between them which was printed at the beginning showed that it was Newman who was answering frankly and without equivocation, it was Kingsley who was the equivocator, continually shifting his ground and lacking in the manliness to withdraw from positions which he could not substantiate.

The *Apologia*, then, won back for Newman his Anglican friends. It gained for him the position which he still holds among Anglicans as the first of English Catholics of modern times. But of course his Anglican friends, while they conceded his entire integrity, were by no means prepared to make such a concession about Catholics in general. A more common line was that of the man who was to become again at this time and to remain until their deaths the closest of his Anglican friends, Dean Church of St. Paul's. When the Church's authorities, argued Church, made inordinate and unjust attacks upon freedom, Newman of course spoke against such attacks. 'No one would have expected him to do otherwise.' But he was the only Catholic who spoke out. To Church, as to many other Englishmen, 'Newman was a name apart'—a man apart as uniquely great among Englishmen but also as the one Catholic of true integrity.

Among the Catholics the Old Catholics rejoiced at Newman's return to popularity. The controversies in which he was engaged were above their heads. They did not pretend to follow the arguments but they were glad at an abatement of hostility. But the Ultramontanes— almost all of them converts with Manning at their head—were by no means so pleased. We have already quoted an extract from Newman's journal of a date in 1867—two years after the *Apologia*—which shows how he still felt himself to be under their suspicion. To them Newman was a dangerous man, twisting, minimising and perverting the faith, which in their view he had never really acquired. The more popular he was the more dangerous he was. Before the *Apologia* they had been ready to write him off as an old man, whose day was done, and who no longer counted. After the *Apologia* they could no longer do that. They had to notice him. Some half-hearted attempts were made to win his favour. Monsignor Talbot obtained for him an invitation to preach at Rome and advised him that it would be greatly to his advantage to accept the invitation and to take the chance of putting himself into favour there. 'He had ceased writing and a good riddance. Why did he ever begin again?' was Talbot's real private opinion.[1] Intrigue and currying of favour were hateful to Newman—particularly when the suggestion of them came from one whom he looked on as an arch-enemy. He refused the invitation with brusque brutality. 'Birmingham people also have souls,' he wrote coldly.

That was the difficulty of Newman's position. The great majority of English Catholics in the 1860's, as of all Catholics at all times and in all countries, thought of course of their religion as a matter of going to Mass, of not eating meat on Friday and of attempting, with such success as might be, not to break the Commandments. Controversies about the development of doctrine or definitions of the exact nature of the Papal headship of the Church passed over their heads. Among such Catholics Newman was popular, but his trouble was that both in London and in Rome power was at that time in the hands of authorities who had a radically different conception from his of the nature of the Church's intellectual case. At Rome Pius IX had at about the same time that Newman was publishing his *Apologia* issued the *Syllabus Errorum*, in which he declared anathema on the notion that the Roman Pontiff could 'accommodate' himself to 'liberty, progress or modern civilisation.' Shortly before the appearance of the *Apologia* Pius IX had brusquely replied to the loyal message of address which the Munich Congress, summoned by Acton and Dollinger to consider means for renewing theology, had sent him, by writing to the Archbishop of Munich to forbid the Congress.[2] 'Is this the case of Galileo over again?' asked Newman.[3] 'The only policy for a Catholic is simply to be silent.'

[1] Words spoken by Talbot to St. John in Rome in May, 1867, and by him repeated to Newman.
[2] E. E. Y. Hales, *The Catholic Church in the Modern World*, Chapter 10, p. 138.
[3] *A Portrait Restored*, p. 40: 'The Apologia Revalued.'

Of course the importance of the *Apologia* has by no means been merely its immediate and short-term importance. It has proved to be one of the great and enduring books of the world. Coinciding in its issue with Pius IX's *Syllabus Errorum*, it has proved to be—what Newman never intended it to be—in a way the answer to the *Syllabus*. In contrast to Pius' denunciation of freedom or Gregory XVI's assertion that the belief in a free press was a 'madness' was Newman's frank appeal to free speech in the *Idea of a University* and the *Apologia*. When we read in our own time, in John XXIII's *Pacem in Terris*, the assertion that Man 'has a right to freedom in investigating the truth and— provided no harm is done to the moral order or the common good— to freedom of speech and publication;' we cannot doubt which influence has been the more potent over the modern Papacy. If at its issue the *Apologia* had its critics among Catholics as well as its eulogists, the criticism after the years was silenced when a new Pope succeeded to Pius and made clear to the world his approval of Newman by the Cardinal's hat. Not immediately, indeed, but gradually Newman was able to win for himself the position in men's minds as the unique spokesman of Catholicism at its best until his spirit was adopted by Pope John and his name specifically honoured by Pope Paul VI.

It is not of course that those who opposed him were stupid and evil men, but they were what Dr. Novak would have called 'non-historical Christians'—men who thought that in a changing world religion could be saved by the imposition merely of policies of authoritarianism and repression. Against that Newman saw that a new age required a wholly new method of apologetics—what Pope John was to call an *aggiorna-mento*—and required to rebuild the whole manner of Christian presentation to suit that challenge.

In London, Wiseman, his Vicar-general Manning, the Catholic papers such as the *Tablet* championed the Ultramontane case. There was always a generous lacing of personalities in all controversies between Victorian clergymen, and it must be frankly confessed that Newman contributed his share to such personalities. Yet fundamentally the battle between Newman and the other Catholic leaders was not at all about personalities. It was about the very fundamental question: what should be the attitude of the Church in the mid-nineteenth-century world?

9

Oxford and Infallibility

THERE ALWAYS HAS BEEN and still is and always will be argument about the Catholic policy towards education in a pluralistic society. How far is it desirable to bring up Catholic boys and girls in exclusively Catholic institutions, uncontaminated by the influence of the secular world around them? Is it better, since they will have to mix in that world eventually, to allow them, subject to proper safeguards, to do so in their years of education? It is a nicely balanced argument, and most people would probably agree that the answer largely depends on the nature of the society and on the individual pupil.

Few would deny today the need for that relaxation of rigidity for which Newman pleaded and for the creation of a variety of schools and colleges not all of the same pattern, and indeed there would probably be less certainty today even that a Catholic school was necessarily desirable for all pupils. Nothing indeed would be more likely to endanger a pupil's faith than to send him or her to a bad Catholic school so that, going out into the world, he discovers that he has been cheated with inadequate instructions and arguments that do not stand against refutation. The whole Catholic pattern up till Newman's time was drawn on the assumption that Catholics would continue throughout their whole life to move only in Catholic company—whether because they were citizens of a purely Catholic country or whether because, as in England, they belonged to a small minority which played no part in the general life of the nation.

Newman in his *Idea of a University* was the first writer to bid Catholics unequivocally to face the reality that that sort of society no longer existed and was certain never to exist again—that, when authority is shaping the education of Catholic youth, it must face the fact that sooner or later these youths must inevitably move out into, and take their place in, a non-Catholic world and that the purpose of education must therefore be not so much to preserve them from temptation as to equip them when the time comes to face it. When the declaration on Christian Education was being debated before the Vatican Council, it was at first proposed only to pay attention to the education in Catholic schools. Those who did not send their children to Catholic schools, it was thought, were sinning against the light and had only themselves to thank for what might happen to those children. This approach was abandoned as ungenerous and unrealistic, and the final version contains a passage calling for 'the collaboration between them [the Catholic schools] and other schools which the good of the whole community requires'. It indeed 'reminds Catholic parents of their duty to entrust their children, when and where they can, to Catholic schools', but at the same time is 'ready with special interest and help for the numerous children who are being taught in non-Catholic schools.'

In mid-Victorian England, as in the England of today, the hierarchy desired that as far as possible Catholic boys and girls should go to Catholic schools. If that was accepted then it was important to offer them a variety of Catholic schools from which to choose. With the hope of increasing this variety Newman had founded the Oratory school. The university policy was more doubtful. Up till the 1860's the question was not an open one, for, as had been said, England's two universities, Oxford and Cambridge, did not admit those who would not subscribe to the Thirty-nine Articles. The universities were closed to the Catholics by the universities' own action. In that decade that condition was rescinded and the universities now accepted Catholics. Should the Catholic authorities allow the Catholics to go to them?

The case with the universities was different from the case with schools. There were numerous schools scattered throughout the land. There was no great difficulty in adding one or two more. But throughout the centuries, while all the continental countries had a large number of universities, when even little Scotland with its tiny population had four, England alone had contented herself with two. In the nineteenth century the non-denominational London university was established. Newman had attempted to set up the Catholic university in Dublin. Manning was trying to establish his Catholic college in Bayswater, but the prestige of Oxford and Cambridge was such that no parent could be persuaded that to send a boy to one of these other institutions was not to submit him to a grave handicap. Nor were the Catholics numerous enough—as was to be amply proved in the Bayswater experiment—to staff a competent university. Therefore it was much more clearly true in the universities than it was in the schools that if Catholics were to be excluded from them they would be put at a disadvantage. Nevertheless it was the opinion of the Catholic authorities at this date that these universities were places of so deep-dyed a Protestant hue that it was a danger to any boy's Catholic faith that he should go to them. In paradoxical contrast to the present situation, Catholics in the earlier years of the last century were allowed to go to Trinity College, Dublin, at a time when they were not yet allowed to go to Oxford and Cambridge, and they were still forbidden by the Catholic authorities in England to go to the English universities for twenty years after they were allowed, in spite of a decree of *non-expedit* against any participation in the life of the new Italian state, to go to the irreligious universities in Italy.

Newman did not at this time dispute the prohibition, whatever the secret doubts, as we have seen, which he had begun to entertain after the Dublin fiasco. His difference from Wiseman and Manning was rather that, whereas they with the mentality of defence which was the Ultramontane fashion, argued that Oxford was invincibly Protestant and that the supreme need was to protect Catholics from contamination by its spirit, Newman with his kindly memories of the Oxford Movement and of the Oxford which 'made us Catholics' wished rather to soften Oxford's hostility to Catholicism and did not think that an impossible task. He had been offered a plot of land in Oxford between St. Giles and Walton Street. He wished to buy it and to build there an Oratory. He did not propose to go and live there himself. He understood that it would put too great a strain on the newly established friendship with his old Oxford companions if he should at once challenge them in person. But, if some good men could be established there, he thought that they might be able to soften Oxford's anti-Catholic prejudices and introduce a kindlier spirit. 'What I aim at,' he said,[1] 'is not immediate conversions but to influence, as far as an old man can, the tone of thought in the place with a view to a distant time when I shall no longer be here.' Ullathorne, his bishop, and the bishop in whose diocese Oxford lay, who had by that time quite got over his

[1] To Wetherell, Acton's associate on the *Rambler. Light in Winter*, p. 349: '1864-65—First Round in the Oxford Fight.'

former prejudices and was now Newman's friend, was an enthusiastic supporter.

But Wiseman, abetted by Manning, was an unflinching enemy. Ever since they had quarrelled over a misunderstanding about a dedication to Newman of Wiseman's panegyric on St. Philip Neri in 1856, Wiseman had been Newman's foe. He complained of Newman's 'insolence'. Patterson,[1] Wiseman's secretary, truly said Newman 'had the soul and manners of a king. He could rebuke . . . anyone—but to be insolent was not possible to him.' Yet Wiseman, by now an old and sick man and on his deathbed, aroused himself to what was for him extraordinary energy to combat Newman's plans. He behaved to Newman with great personal discourtesy. One day when Newman called on him by appointment at Archbishop's House, he barely spoke to him. He circulated a questionnaire about the Oxford project which Newman described as entirely question-begging. Newman said it was as if he had asked, 'Are you or are you not one of the wicked men who advocate Oxford education?' The fact was that, seeing that there was no other way in which they could get a proper university education, most of the other bishops, with Ullathorne at their head, thought it at least an open question whether it was not the lesser evil to let Catholics go to Oxford. In face of their opposition Wiseman did not feel able explicitly to forbid Catholics from going there but he did all that he could to dissuade them, and he feared and argued—as indeed was true enough—that if the Oratorians established themselves in Oxford, more Catholic parents would in fact send their sons there. Certainly if we accept the proposition that it was undesirable for Catholic under-graduates to go to Oxford it was reasonable to discourage Catholics of any condition from establishing themselves there.

In 1865 Wiseman died. Errington, a sensible, moderate-minded Old Catholic, had been his co-adjutor with right of succession. But Pius IX under strong Ultramontane pressure passed Errington over and appointed Manning as Archbishop in his place. The Ultramontanes like Ward were overjoyed. 'Henry Edward, by the grace of God and favour of the Apostolic See Archbishop of Westminster,' Ward cried, rushing round the room in high glee and knocking over all the furniture, when he heard the news. It meant of course that no sort of so-called liberalism of which Newman was suspect was to be tolerated by the Catholic hierarchy in England. Newman could expect no toleration of his

[1] Patterson to Neville. *Light in Winter*, p. 354: *ibid*.

Oxford plans, or of any other plans of such a sort. Manning was a diplomatist and Newman was no diplomatist. Manning never challenged an antagonist unless it was necessary. He began his reign by an appearance of conciliation towards Newman, writing to tell him that he would support the conferment on him of the titular bishopric which had been suggested for him when the Irish University plan was still alive. Newman a little foolishly and ungraciously replied by refusing to attend the official dinner with which Manning was welcomed at Westminster.

Just at this time when relations with his old Anglican friends were being renewed and improving, Pusey issued a book which he called his *Eirenicon*—a plea for better relations between Rome and the Church of England. It was, it must be confessed, a book somewhat oddly named, as it consisted predominantly of a list of the alleged gross errors of the Church of Rome, particularly condemning the exaggerations of mariolatry and the doctrine of papal infallibility. 'You discharge your olive branch as if from a catapult,' Newman teased Pusey.[1] and it may seem odd that at such a moment Newman should have thought it necessary to reply to his old friend. He did so for two reasons. He did so first because in the atmosphere of Ultramontane suspicion it was peculiarly important to show that friendly personal relations with Anglicans did not imply that he had come to accept their charges.

Secondly, he wanted to take the opportunity to show that exaggerated Ultramontane opinions which Pusey had imagined to be the dogmatic assertions of the Church of Rome were not of faith. Newman had by now come to the conclusion that it was his mission to restate the Catholic position which was so largely going by default owing to its misstatement by official Catholic apologists. It was a conclusion to which he had been driven by events quite contrary to his original desire or expectation. It would have been an insolently arrogant conclusion had he not been driven to it by events beyond his control and had not the outcome proved that he was so abundantly right. But it was a task that could only be accomplished by indirect manoeuvre. He could not directly attack the Ultramontane hierarchs. It was not to be expected that the performance of this second task would bring him the good will of Manning, and Manning in fact was very angry. 'Whether he knows it or not,' he wrote,[2] about Newman, 'he has

[1] *Light in Winter*, p. 373: '1866—Dancing on a Tightrope.'
[2] To Talbot. *Light in Winter*, p. 375: *ibid.*

become the centre of those who hold low views about the Holy See, are anti-Roman, cold and silent, to say no more, about the temporal power, national, English, critical of Catholic devotions and always on the lower side.'

Newman had at first been anxious to establish the Oxford Oratory. Now, finding the controversy that it aroused, he was much less keen. But it was now Ullathorne, his bishop, and in conflict with Manning, who urged him on to the task. On Palm Sunday, 1866, Ullathorne called and explicitly offered Newman the Oxford Oratory. What Ullathorne wanted now in Oxford was not so much an Oratory as a mission church. New Inn Hall Street was the site that was thought best suited for that. Newman was not keen but expressed his willingness to 'act according to the Holy Father's decision'. Pius, badgered from this side and from that, would not give a decision. Ullathorne, writing to support the case at Rome, muddled it by suggesting that Newman had proposed to establish a Catholic college at Oxford—which Newman had been careful never to do. Newman wrote in a private note,[1] 'I think bishops fancy that, just as justice does not exist between the Creator and His creatures, between man and the brute creation, so there is none between themselves and their subjects. So that they only look out to see how clergy and laity accept those acts of theirs which in one not a bishop would be unjust—e.g. whether the aggrieved accept them as an opportunity for gaining merit with humility, cheerfulness, submission.'

Manning wrote,[2] 'If Propaganda sanctions it I trust they will couple it with a renewed and stronger declaration against the Protestant universities. I think Propaganda can hardly know the effects of Dr. Newman's going to Oxford. The English national spirit is spreading among Catholics and we shall have dangers.' Cardinal Reisach was sent from Rome to inquire into and straighten out the difficulties. He saw everybody else in England but was careful not to see Newman. On Christmas Day, 1866, Ullathorne sent Newman what he called a copy of the letter from Propaganda granting permission for an Oratory at Oxford, but Newman was suspicious and he had reason to be. For he discovered later that Ullathorne had omitted from his copy a sentence of the original which forbade Newman himself from taking

[1] Sent to Hope-Scott. *Light in Winter*, p. 386: '1866—Oxford Oratory. Second Round.'
[2] To Talbot. June 26, 1866. *ibid*, p. 387.

up residence in Oxford. The *Westminster Gazette*, Manning's new paper, published the news with a paragraph saying that Newman 'had abandoned his plan of going to Oxford in deference to the opinion of a most eminent prelate.' Ullathorne protested to Manning. Manning wrote back to Ullathorne, repudiating the paragraph and saying that he hoped to come soon to Birmingham and see Newman. Newman, when Ullathorne passed on to him the message, replied,[1] 'I will say to your lordship frankly that I cannot trust the Archbishop. It seems to me that he never wishes to see a man except for his own ends.' Newman, knowing nothing of the sentence in Propaganda's rescript forbidding him to go to Oxford, thinking only that Propaganda had commanded him to establish an Oratory there, started to collect money, and met with surprising success. Manning was alarmed. He wrote to Talbot in Rome,[2] 'Dr. Newman has put out his circular for the Church in Oxford saying that it is with the approval of Propaganda. It will certainly be taken as approving the sending of Catholics to Oxford. There is not a word in the circular or in the bishop's letter to imply the reverse. . . . We are slipping sideways into the whole mischief.'

Barnabo from Rome wrote to accuse Newman of preparing boys at the Oratory school for Oxford where they would certainly lose their faith. Newman commented to his friend Hope-Scott that the only Oratory boy who had gone to Oxford, so far from having his faith there undermined, had distinguished himself by ducking a Tractarian in Mercury.

The most violent of the opponents of Newman and of Catholics at Oxford at that time was Father Vaughan, who by an odd chance was later as Cardinal Vaughan to reverse the rule and allow them to go there. 'Last night I was with Bo [Cardinal Barnabo]'; Vaughan wrote to Manning on March 29, 1867.[3] 'He had just heard from Newman. . . . "Is this the treatment," he said, "that I have a right to expect from your Eminence after twenty-two years of service to the Church?" . . . This is what comes of the Catholics of England, high and low, declaring to N. for the last twenty years that he is a new revelation, vouchsafed to them, a prophet and more than a prophet. He does not appear to have answered the charges of which B. has sent him a string, nor does

[1] *Light in Winter*, p. 391: '1867—He Will Break Me If He Can.'
[2] February 1, 1867.
[3] *Light in Winter*, p. 397: *ibid.*

B. now expect he will come to Rome. He amusingly repeated all he knew about him and described in an absurd way the heavy weight he always felt about his stomach whenever N. conversed with him. And he winds up by concluding that N. is disappointed in getting no mitre, that such is human nature, we must all look after ourselves, etc. N's anger, of which he is the object, has not much affected him. He considers it rather a feather in his cap, if I may say so.'

Vaughan quoted some second-hand gossip of another Father at Birmingham—he was not quite sure who—who was alleged to have said that the Oratory at Oxford was a first step to the permission for Catholic undergraduates to go there. 'If this be true,' he wrote,[1] 'and if they represent N. one could hardly feel a scruple at removing him from Oxford even with a pitchfork. Is it possible that he has been deceiving his bishop and acting surreptitiously?'

One E. R. Martin in the *Weekly Register* chimed in with[2], 'It is almost needless to say—for anyone who knows the prevailing spirit at Rome—that this distinguished man has no longer in Roman opinion the high place he once held. It could not be otherwise after the sermon on the Temporal Power, certain passages of the *Apologia* and the having allowed his great name to be linked with that of one of the bitterest haters of Rome in the dedication of Mr. Oxenham's translation of Dr. Dollinger's *First Ages of the Church.* . . . Good soldier of the faith as Dr. Newman has been and devoted Catholic as he still doubtless is . . . only an Ultramontane without a taint in his fidelity could enter such an arena as that of Oxford life with results to the advantage of the Faith in England.'

This was going too far. Two hundred distinguished Catholic laymen replied with a protest against such attacks. 'They may be of little importance in themselves,' they wrote[3] of those attacks, 'but we feel that every blow that touches you inflicts a wound upon the Catholic Church in this country.' Manning and Vaughan realised that Martin had gone too far and repudiated him but at the same time they did not abate in their private campaign. 'Dr. Newman is the most dangerous man in England,' Talbot was at this time writing to Manning,[4] 'and

[1] *Light in Winter*, p. 398.

[2] April 26, 1867, *ibid*, p. 399.

[3] *Weekly Register*. April 13, 1867. *Light in Winter*, p. 408: '1867—My Monkey is Up.'

[4] April 25, 1867, *ibid*, p. 408.

you will see that he will make use of the laity against Your Grace.'
'What is the province of the laity? To hunt, to shoot, to entertain.'
Vaughan from Rome reported to Manning that he had had an inter-
view with the Pope[1] in which he had told the Pope that 'N's presence
at Oxford has been publicly declared to be an encouragement to
Catholics to go thither; that he is the representative of the liberal and
national school of thought—and then, as the Holy Father said he had
written to express his willingness to obey, I referred to his unretracted
article in the *Rambler* about the *sensus fidelium* as a proof that he is not
a person to be relied upon. The Holy Father was very attentive but
said little; only this, that N. was very vain, that he had expressed his
readiness to obey the Pope; the extreme importance of prayer on this
occasion—which he dwelt upon very earnestly.' Newman was under
no illusions. He had by that time learnt of the secret instructions which
Ullathorne had concealed. He wrote to Monsell,[2] 'You may be sure
they are determined to put me down at all hazards—and if in no other
way by a charge of heresy. No matter if it is untenable, an inquiry may
be drawn out for a year or two when they think the chances are that I
shall be too old to undertake any new plan.' Again he wrote to
Ambrose St. John,[3] 'Now they have thrown off the mask and attack
not the school but me and my teaching. . . . How too can you trust
people, even though they are *blandi et suaves* when the secret instructions
to the bishop (which?) shows such blandness and sweetness are hollow.'

Newman had no wish to be disobedient but there is little doubt that
after the failure of his plan in Dublin and that of Manning in Bayswater
he did foresee that it was certain that sooner or later Catholics would
go to Oxford and Cambridge. In England there was no realistic alternative and even in such countries as the United States, where Catholic
Colleges were being built, he probably thought it likely enough that
with time sectarian bitterness would abate and that, when that happened, Catholics would increasingly go to the non-denominational
universities. He did not think it his business either to advocate or
prophesy any development in detail. His only concern was to plead
the cause of freedom and beg that authority should not unnecessarily
bang the door by premature dictatorial edicts. Let us see how things
develop and work fully in whatever institutions establish themselves,

[1] *Light in Winter*, p. 400.
[2] April 7, 1867, *ibid*, p. 400.
[3] *Light in Winter*, p. 403.

was his line, and this was of course precisely the line which the Council later followed in its Declarations on Christian Education and on the Formation of Priests. Where earlier rulings had been content to insist on parents sending their children to Catholic schools as of obligation and merely denounced as unacceptable any schools that were not Catholic, the Council paid indeed its tribute to Catholic schools and repeated that it was desirable to send children to them wherever there was no overriding obstacle to doing so; but at the same time it recognised the fact that a very large proportion of children do not go and cannot go to such schools and emphasised the importance of establishing good and friendly relations with these other non-Catholic schools, One can hardly imagine Manning at the First Vatican Council voting for such a decree. It was exactly in tune with Newman's mind to insist that the important task was gently to break down the prejudices of the Oxford mind rather than bluntly to denounce it.

The biographer of Newman, and indeed the biographer of Manning or of Ullathorne, is compelled to follow through in detail the unutterably tedious story of accusation and counter-accusation at Rome over this interminable Oxford intrigue. We are happily spared. No stories are less edifying and less interesting than those which are concerned with what a modern Cardinal has called 'episcopal in-fighting'. It is sufficient that in the end those forces which were determined to keep Newman out of Oxford were victorious. Ullathorne returned from Rome in August, 1867, and told Newman: 'I find that at Rome they consider the Oxford matter quite at an end.' Ullathorne had surrendered. 'He sincerely wishes to be kind to me, but to stand well with people at Rome supersedes in his mind every other wish,' wrote Newman; 'so he is a coward.' Newman, glad to be rid of it, abandoned the Oxford project. It added one more to the long list of enterprises which he had hoped to undertake and which had ended in frustration.

But in truth if we attempt to follow the story through the tortuous letters that passed between Newman and Manning, not only do we get ourselves involved in an intolerably tiresome inquiry, but we do an injustice to both parties. The battle was not really about personalities. It was about two radically contradictory conceptions of the nature of the Church. The battle of Oxford was one skirmish in that larger conflict.

It was self-evident to both parties to that conflict that unbelief was on the increase in every country in the first half of the century. The causes of this—Gallicanism before the Revolution and the secular influence of the Révolution, the purely political answer to it of the monarchs of the Holy Alliance—were clear enough. About the remedy there was difference. To the Ultramontanes the supreme task was to protect the faith of the faithful. Authority must protect them against the corruption of these new ideas by the fearless use of censorship and proscription. This mentality had ruled at the Vatican ever since the Popes had returned there at the fall of Napoleon. Pius IX had indeed had intentions of introducing liberal reforms when he had ascended the throne but the experiment in Roman liberalism had been utterly disastrous and he had returned from Gaeta more firmly determined to tread a path of reaction than even his predecessors had been. In 1865, the very year of Newman's *Apologia*, Pius had issued his *Syllabus Errorum*.

This formidable document posed grave problems to Catholics in such countries as Britain or the United States, where ideas of liberty and progress were commonly thought of as an essential part of the pattern of civilised living, and Dupanloup, the great bishop of Orleans,[1] attempted to save what he could from the wreck. He explained—very truly—that this document of the *Syllabus* must be read in its context. It did not consist of a series of absolute pronouncements *in vacuo*. It was rather a summary of a variety of acts of protest which Pius and his predecessors had uttered against specific evils over the past years. Its protests were in general against anti-clerical acts committed by the Spanish liberals in 1812 and the secularist Piedmontese when they seized the Marches and the Legations from the Pope in 1859 and dissolved the monasteries and convents there.

When the Pope condemned modern civilisation, argued Dupanloup, he was not condemning without distinction everything that was going on in the modern world. He was only condemning what the Piedmontese were doing under the pretended title of spreading modern civilisation. This was all very well and his statement earned for Dupanloup enormous and well-deserved gratitude from Catholics in America and Northern Europe who found that it removed a very large burden from their consciences. But it did not get Dupanloup many thanks in Rome, nor indeed was it to be expected that it would. For, though Dupanloup's explanation of the weight of the Pope's words might be theo-

[1] The leader of the Catholic party in France which advocated the acceptance of the Revolution.

logically correct, there was no denying that to use words that must be so widely misunderstood and that required so much explanation was almost criminally foolish and incompetent. If he did not intend to condemn the freedom of Catholics in America, a man of sense would have explained as much in the original document and not left it to another to make the explanation for him.

Dupanloup's exposition was welcome to many Catholics in England as in other countries. But unfortunately in England, while many Catholics had the natural desire that Catholic teaching should be made to appear as little contrary to common sense as possible, there was a body, small in numbers but intensely influential, who gloried in defying the opinion of the world. Ward, for instance, would have no explaining away of the language of the *Syllabus*. He argued in the *Dublin Review* that it was certainly an infallible document and would soon be plainly declared to be as much.

To set all doubts on this or any other similar matters at rest the Ultramontanes of this school of thought, with Manning at the head, wished for a clear dogmatic declaration of papal infallibility. It was through their influence of course that the Vatican Council was summoned for 1870 and met just at the time when the French defeat in the Franco-Prussian war led to the withdrawal of the French garrison from Rome and the seizure of the Patrimony of St. Peter by the Italian troops.

As for the Pope's temporal power, Newman explained his position on a number of occasions, and most notably in a sermon on *The Pope and the Revolution* which he delivered at the Birmingham Oratory on October 7, 1866. Naturally, he associated himself with all loyal Catholics and with very many who were not Catholics in condemning most strongly the personal discourtesy with which on a number of occasions Italian anti-clericals had treated Pius. But, as for whether under modern circumstances it was advantageous that the Pope should have any real temporal power, that was in his opinion a matter of expediency on which opinions might differ. He thought it a bad plan.

If others thought it a good plan, they were, according to Newman, entitled to their opinion, but, whether good or bad, it was certainly not a divine plan. Nobody could pretend that the temporal power was part of the commission which Christ had entrusted to Peter. If it had been conferred by the Emperor Constantine—which it clearly was not —what of it? The Emperor Constantine was not Almighty God. If, as appeared probable, the Pope was to be deprived of his temporal power in the near future, that would create a new situation to which the Church would have to adjust itself. The talk which Manning was putting about and which, to do him justice, he came to repent in his old age, that it was and would soon be declared an obligation of faith to believe in the necessity of the Pope's temporal power, was to Newman's mind nonsensical. After the Italian capture he wrote to Miss Holmes,[1] 'As to Rome I cannot regret what has happened. There is one thing worse than open infidelity and that is secret, and the state of Rome was such as to honeycomb the population of Italy with deep unbelief under the outward profession of Christianity.'

As for infallibility, there were only a few Catholics, such as Dollinger, who did not believe that, since the Church was infallible and since the Pope was the Head of the Church, therefore the Pope was in a certain sense infallible. The controversy was not so much whether the Pope was infallible as under what conditions he was infallible, and whether it was opportune to declare him so. Newman stood with a very large body of the most considerable figures in the Church of the day in thinking that it was inopportune. It had been suggested that he should go to the Council as one of the Pope's theologians. He owed this invitation to his old antagonist, Cardinal Cullen, who, though he had differed and still differed from Newman over clerical control of education, honourably refused to associate himself with any suggestion that Newman was a heretic. Bishop Brown, his old delator, who was an inopportunist about infallibility, also begged him to go. So did Dupanloup. So did Montalembert from his deathbed; but he declined the invitations. He had had enough of Rome and its corridors of power. 'As to bringing out my views,' he wrote, 'it is absurd.' Yet protests were essential. 'If there are no protests there will be no reaction.'

Even today many often speak as if the infallibility decree, the outcome of the Council, was a total victory for the Ultramontanes. This is far from being so. Extreme Ultramontanes hoped to see a very wide definition of papal infallibility. Ward, who revelled in shocking Protestant prejudices, said that he would like to see a Papal bull on his breakfast table every morning and would have every lightest word of the Pope accepted as infallible. Vaughan, then the editor of the *Tablet* and Manning's most faithful Achates, clamoured for the definition

[1] A cousin of Thackeray who came over to the Church at the same time as Newman.

because of its alleged practical advantages and attempted to prevent any discussion of the matter. 'Doubtful books will be condemned, rash speculations from science reduced to harmony with revealed truth,' he hoped.[1] The definition that was eventually accepted was by no means of that sort. It was very carefully moderate—much more nearly representative of Newman's mind than of that of Ward. 'The late definition,' wrote Newman, 'does not so much need to be undone as to be completed. It needs safeguards as to the Pope's possible acts—explanations as to the matter and extent of his powers. I know that a violent, reckless party, had it its will, would at this moment define that the Pope's powers need no safeguards, no explanations, but there is a limit to the triumph of the tyrannical. Let us be patient, let us have faith and a new Pope and reassembled Council may trim the boat.'[2]

It is of course true that, when this Second Council came, its purpose was not to attack bishops but rather to assert their collegiality, but of course such a declaration was in no way in contradiction with Newman's views—rather, if we remember his assertion of the apostolic succession, the reverse. Newman's objection was not to bishops as such but to particular bishops who in his view played false to their function by allowing themselves to become no more than the creatures of the Roman Curia; to Wiseman and Manning who played such a role out of sincere conviction, or to Ullathorne who played it through a mere lack of the courage to stand up against the pressure of a centralised bureaucracy. A truly independent hierarchy, a hierarchy speaking as Paul VI has promised us that it will speak through a truly independent synod, is just what Newman would have liked to see.

Yet Manning, though he had not won a total victory in Rome, still remained in power at Westminster. It was not of course that he was uncriticised among English Catholics. The great majority of English Catholics were simple people who did not follow the finer points at issue but who on the whole preferred Newman to Manning. Even among the bishops Manning was by no means universally popular. Bishop Goss of Liverpool,[3] for instance, objected to the Ultramontanes 'denouncing everybody as little less than heretics and infidels and as committing the unpardonable sin against the Holy Ghost whose decision and ruling they forestalled.' He objected to Manning: 'putting

---

[1] *Light in Winter*, p. 474: '1870—An Insolent and Aggressive Faction.'
[2] F. L. Cross, *John Henry Newman*, p. 170.
[3] *Light in Winter*, pp. 480–81: *ibid.*

himself so prominently forward as he does is both insolent and aggressive; neither his learning nor his standing among Catholics justify his assumption, and his testimony is opposed to the teaching of English Catholics.' 'Truth, simple English truth seems to have departed from the whole faction . . . nothing ever wounded the simplicity of my faith so much as the trickery with which I have become acquainted on my official intercourse with the Curia.'

Newman, not quite accurately, spoke of 'the three tailors of Tooley Street'—Manning, Ward and Talbot—who pretended to speak as if they were the people of England. He called the Ultramontanes 'an insolent and aggressive faction'. 'I never expected,' he said,[1] 'to see such a scandal in the Church. Such scandals, I know, have been before now, and in councils, but I thought we had too many vigilant and hostile eyes upon it, to allow even the most reckless, tyrannical and heartless ecclesiastics, so wounding, so piercing religious souls, so co-operating with those who wish the Church's downfall.' 'On account of things of this kind I view with equanimity the prospect of a thorough routing out of things at Rome—not till some great convulsion takes place (which may go on for years and years and when I can do neither good nor harm) and religion is felt to be in the midst of trials, red-tapism will go out of Rome, and a better spirit come in, and Cardinals and Archbishops will have some of the reality they had, amid many abuses, in the Middle Ages. At present things are as effete, though in a different way (thank God) as they were in the tenth century. We are sinking into a sort of Novatianism,[2] the heresy which the early Popes so strenuously resisted. Instead of aiming at being a world-wide power we are shrinking into ourselves, narrowing the lines of communion, trembling at freedom of thought and using the language of dismay and despair at the prospect before us, instead of with the high spirits of the warrior, going out conquering and to conquer.'

The obstinate fact remained that, though Manning might not be all England, he was Primate of England. Pius IX was still Pope of Rome. Newman was in the difficult position that he wanted to restate the Catholic position and it was a restatement of an authoritarian position to which all the existing authorities were unsympathetic. An opportunity, as it happened, came to him to improve relations with authority.

[1] Letter to Maskell. *Light in Winter*, p. 493: '1870—Viva il Papa Infallibile.'
[2] An exceptionally rigid type of early heresy, which taught that the Christian should withdraw himself from the world.

Newman had an independent but also an exact mind. Just as at the time of the restoration of the hierarchy, though he had disapproved of what had been done, he had been anxious to correct misapprehensions about it, so with the infallibility decree, though he did not like it, he would not allow it to be misrepresented. He was perhaps the more ready to correct misapprehensions as they gave him the opportunity to show that the decree did not say what a number of the Ultramontanes would have liked it to have said. Thus when on September 7, 1872, *The Times* in a leading article on the Papal approval of the St. Bartholomew's Day massacre, wrote that in future all Catholics would be bound to accept such papal actions as expressions of divine will, Newman was able effectively to rebuke *The Times* for its confusion of infallibility with impeccability.

Gladstone in his *Expostulation* expressed in substantially the same spirit his horrors of the absolute obedience which was now imposed upon Catholics. Newman was able to expose the confusion in a letter to the Duke of Norfolk. 'Certainly,' he was able to write, 'if I am obliged to bring religion into after-dinner toasts. . . . I shall drink—to the Pope if you please—still to conscience first and to the Pope afterwards.' *The Times* itself agreed that Newman had satisfactorily answered the charge. Gladstone behaved with extreme generosity. He wrote to Newman, 'You may from the newspapers of this morning perceive that yesterday was a busy day for me, for I had to fold my mantle and die.' (Gladstone had just fallen from office.) But he thanked Newman 'for the genial and gentle manner on which you have treated me and the evident unwillingness you have shown to fasten upon me censures which you not unnaturally think I deserve.' Even Manning at Rome explained to Cardinal Franchi that Newman's line of reply was one exactly suited to the English temperament.

10

The Grammar of Assent

AT THE TIME of the controversy with Kingsley Newman had found that it was impossible to clear up the misunderstandings by the mere answer of particular accusations and had thought that there was no alternative but to give a total statement of his whole position. He had done so in the *Apologia* and done so with conspicuous success. But the *Apologia* had left one gigantic gap in his apologetic case still to be filled. In his early chapters Newman had shown why he believed in God. In his later chapters he had shown why the Church which Christ had founded was at Rome rather than in the Church of England. But there was a large gap between believing in God and believing in the Divinity of Christ. Critics could fairly claim that in the *Apologia* Newman had failed to bridge that gap. Of course, as has been said, no sane critic suggested that Newman did not himself sincerely believe in the Divinity of Christ. Reference has already been made to the famous description of one of Newman's sermons in St. Mary's which has been left to us by James Anthony Froude.[1]

'Newman had described closely some of the incidents of Our Lord's Passion; he then paused. For a few moments there was a breathless silence. Then in a low clear voice of which the faintest vibration was audible in the farthest corner of St. Mary's, he said, "Now I bid you recollect that He to whom these things were done was Almighty God." It was as if an electric stroke had gone through the church, as if every person present understood for the first time the meaning of what he had all his life been saying.' That was the tribute of one who was by that time quite unsympathetic to Newman's opinions and there would be no difficulty in collecting a thousand other passages from his sermons which bear witness to the sincerity of Newman's faith. Even those who

[1] *Short Studies*, IV 286: 'The Oxford Counter Reformation.'

accused him of scepticism were not so foolish as to assert that he was a conscious fraud, going through a patter of mumbo-jumbo in which he did not believe. Their accusation was rather that an essentially sceptical intellect could find no solid ground for belief and at the same time could not face the terrors of sheer nihilism; and so, doubtless deceiving itself, it accepted a faith which its principles gave it no right to accept. It was because this was said that it was essential, if he was going to criticise the traditional apologetics, that Newman should provide an apologetic of his own—should bridge that gap—should show for what reason a man had a right to believe in Christ.

In those years Newman had written what was to prove his most popular poem, the *Dream of Gerontius*. Perhaps the merits of the *Dream of Gerontius* as a poem are sometimes exaggerated; (should we much remember it if it were not for Elgar? Newman never took his own poetry very seriously). At any rate the poem did not get this particular argument very much further. It showed indeed that Newman himself believed in Christ and in a future life and in purgatory, but it did nothing to demonstrate that his beliefs were correct.

All Newman's books were, as we have said, books of occasion. It was to show that his criticism of traditional apologetics did not lead to scepticism that Newman now wrote his *Grammar of Assent*. The Oxford Movement had never been a ritualistic movement. The ritualistic developments of later Anglo-Catholicism had never had any place among the early Tractarians. Nor had Newman in his Catholic days any special interest in ritual. He has made no contribution to the later liturgical reforms in the Church. If anything, his bias would have been against the vernacular. His interest was in apologetics. It was to that that he turned his mind. His first task was to clear up a confusion about the word 'reason', a confusion for which quite frankly he was himself in a measure responsible. Newman sometimes speaks very highly and sometimes very scathingly of reason. The truth was that he used the word in two quite different senses. What he condemned was the man who, having accepted the authority of Christ and the Church, then proceeded to criticise particular doctrines that Christ and the Church taught. Though he in places denounces this process as 'reason', his objection to it really is that it is 'unreason'. If there is a voice of God it is absurd to question it. Thus he had written in his *Essays Critical and Historical*.[1]

[1] pp. 31-32: 'On the Introduction of Rationalistic Principles into Revealed Religion.'

'As regards Revealed Truth, it is not Rationalism to set about to ascertain by the exercise of reason what things are attainable by reason and what are not; nor, in the absence of an express Revelation, to inquire into the truths of religion as they come to us by nature; nor to determine what proofs are necessary for the acceptance of a Revelation, if it be given; nor to reject a Revelation on the plea of insufficient proof; nor after recognising it as divine to investigate the meaning of its declarations and to interpret its language; nor to use its doctrines, as far as they can be fairly used, in inquiring into its divinity; nor to compare and connect them with our previous knowledge with a view to making them parts of a whole; nor to bring them into dependence on each other, to trace their mutual relations and to pursue them to their legitimate issues. This is not Rationalism; but it is Rationalism to accept the Revelation and then to explain it away; to speak of it as the Word of God and to treat it as the word of man; to refuse to let it speak for itself; to claim to be told the why and the how of God's dealings with us, as therein described, and to assign to Him a motive and scope of our own; to stumble at the partial knowledge which He may give us of them; to put aside what is obscure, as if it had not been said at all; to accept one half of what has been told us and not the other half; to assume that the contents of Revelation are also its proof; to frame some gratuitous hypothesis about them, to trim, clip and pare away and twist them in order to bring them into conformity with the idea to which we have subjected them.'

Thus, though reason has no business to question the conclusions of authority once authority is accepted, it is of course reason which tells us whether the claims of authority are valid—whether we ought to accept them. Therefore its function is all important. But reason in this sense, he argues, is a much wider instrument than is often thought. Reason is not simply concerned with abstract and bloodless syllogisms. The conclusions to which such syllogisms lead depend on the premises from which they proceed. One can demonstrate whatever one cares to demonstrate according to the premise which one chooses to assume and nobody changes his faith as a result of such a demonstration unless he wants to change it. Newman, as he said, wished always 'to go by reason, not by feeling' but 'it is the concrete being that reasons . . . the whole man moves; paper logic is but the record of it.'[1] To Newman, as to Bergson, merely logical tests are valuable only as the

[1] *A Portrait Restored*, p. 48: 'The Apologia Revalued.'

166

check on the demand of the whole personality—of the Elan Vital.

When we say that a thing is proved we must mean that it is impossible to think it otherwise, and on that test the common arguments for the existence of God as repeated in the seminaries were clearly not proved. For they clearly were not universally accepted. 'Everyone spontaneously embraces the doctrine of the existence of God,' he said in his *Discourses to Mixed Congregations*,[1] 'as a first principle and a necessary assumption. It is not so much proved to him as borne in upon his mind irresistibly as a truth which it does not occur to him nor is it possible for him to doubt, so various and so abundant is the witness for it contained in the experience and the conscience of everyone. He cannot unravel the process or put his finger on the independent arguments which conspire together to create in him the certainty which he feels; but certain of it he is . . . at the same time he certainly would find if he was in a condition to pursue the subject himself that unbelievers had the advantage of him so far as this—that there were a number of objections to the doctrine which he could not satisfy, questions which he could neither conceive nor explain; he would perceive that the body of proof itself might be more perfect and complete than it is; he would not find indeed anything to invalidate that proof but many things which might embarrass him in discussion or afford a plausible, though not a real, excuse for doubting about it.' It was in this sense—in his own sense of the word 'reason', substantially in Pascal's sense—that Newman was able to accept the First Vatican Council's pronouncement that 'God, the beginning and end of all things, can certainly be known from created things by the natural light of human reason.' 'The practical safeguard against atheism,' he had said many years before in one of the University Sermons, 'in the case of scientific inquirers is the inward need and desire, the inward experience, of that Power existing in the mind antecedent and independent of their examination of His material world.'

It was not so much a matter whether the traditional proofs for the existence of God ought to be accepted as that in fact they were not universally accepted. Competent and honourable men did not find them cogent. That being so, it was a waste of time to go on repeating to the world what the world did not accept. It was necessary to find some common ground on which all mankind must stand, and Newman, like Kant, placed much more reliance for his belief in God on the

[1] pp. 261-2: 'Mysteries of Nature and Grace.'

argument from conscience than on the traditional arguments. The importance of the *Grammar of Assent* lay in its frank recognition that a new world required a new method of apologetics. St. Thomas had written for a world that generally accepted the Catholic case and required only reasons for justifying it in doing so. St. Thomas professed to appeal to reason for his demonstration of the existence of God, but there is little practical advantage in saying that a proposition is reasonable if it is not widely accepted as such. The schoolmaster can correct his pupil who in his sum has written down five as the product of two and two and simply tell him that he is wrong. Since Kant's time it was to no purpose to point out to those who rejected St. Thomas' proofs that these proofs were irrefutable, for there was at least competent opinion that was prepared to challenge them. Newman's ambition was to find a new method of apologetic that would command a more general assent.

In face of the dangers of the times Pius X was to react against the criticisms of St. Thomas and in his condemnation of Modernism to command all seminaries to base their teaching on St. Thomas. When the first draft of the Constitution on Divine Revelation was laid before the Second Vatican Council it was strenuously criticised for putting its points in too arid and scholastic a language. The draft was withdrawn on Pope John's orders and the final draft, which recognised the authority both of Scripture and of Tradition was more in line with modern methods of speech and indeed had much more resemblance to the declaration of the Protestant Faith and Order Conference at Montreal than to anything that came out of the First Vatican Council. It recognised, quoting the phrase of Newman, that revelation, far from being an inert block delivered once and for all and then left lying on the table, 'develops in the Church with the assistance of the Holy Spirit.' If mankind was to be persuaded, methods of repression could not be successful in the long run. The Decree on the Formation of Priests asserted that all schools of philosophic thought must be fairly considered in the seminary training each on its merits, and Thomism was no longer to be accorded a unique status. As Cardinal Gracias bore witness, Newman's influence was one of the first that had led to this change.

But how could one bridge the gigantic gap between the existence of God and the Divinity of Christ? A gigantic gap it certainly was. However extraordinary we may decide that the historical evidence shows

Christ to be, can it of its nature be sufficient to sustain the claim which is so much more extraordinary, which is made for Him?

Newman's first concern was to demolish the notion that this universe made sense by itself and that therefore the Incarnation, if true, was, as it were, an unnecessary addition to its history. On the contrary, he argued, this universe was of its nature uncompleted and required something from beyond itself if it was to make sense. The greatest of pre-Christian thinkers—Plato, Isaiah, Virgil—he argued, had all recognised as much—had seen and demanded that something more must be coming. Unaided man was faced by two irreconcilable propositions. On the one hand happiness must be his end. On the other hand he had this obstinate, irremovable feeling within him that there was such a thing as good and bad, that honour was a reality, that he was under obligation to pursue the good and to avoid the bad, and yet, as far as this world went, virtue often in no sort of way led to happiness. Therefore there must be some further existence in which the process was equated.

The humanist sought to build a morality that was purely of this world, but the obstinate difficulty about such a morality was the inescapable fact of death. The most important experience of a human being is death and humanism had nothing to tell us about it. We die and, if death is the end of all, what does it matter if we have observed the rules of morality or not? What does it matter how this world which we are so soon to leave is faring? In any event the gap between him to whom death is extinction, or at least the future so utterly unknowable that it is foolish to base our principles of conduct upon hopes concerning it, and the Christian to whom this world is a testing ground for the ultimate reality is necessarily immense.

'What shall be said,' he had written in the *Apologia*,[1] 'to this heart-piercing reason-bewildering fact [that in this world virtue and happiness were so often not equated]? I can only answer that either there is no Creator or this living society of men is in a true sense discarded from His presence. . . . If there be a God, since there is a God, the human race is implicated in some terrible aboriginal calamity. It is out of joint with the purposes of its Creator.' Therefore, unless we are to believe that all our intimations of the possibility of companionship with God are without meaning and we are finally and utterly and absolutely

[1] p. 243, Part VI.

discarded, as he argued in his *Discourses to Mixed Congregations*,[1] 'the very fact I say, that there is a Creator and a hidden one, powerfully bears you on and sets you down at the very threshold of revelation and leaves you there looking up earnestly for Divine tokens that a revelation has been made.'

'A religious man,' he had said in one of his *Sermons on Various Occasions*,[2] 'who has not the blessing of the infallible teaching of revelation is led to look out for it for the very reason that he is religious. He has something but not all; and if he did not desire more it would be a proof that he had not used, that he had not profited by, what he had. Hence he will be on the look-out. Such is the definition, I may say, of every religious man who had not the knowledge of Christ; he is on the look-out. As the Jewish believers were on the look-out for a Messias who they knew was to come, so at all times and under all dispensations and in all sects there are those who know there is a truth, who know that they do not possess it except in a very low measure, who desire to know more, who know that He alone who has taught them knows what they know, can teach them more, who hope that He will teach them more, and so are on the look-out for His teaching.'

He is on the look-out for the reassurance of revelation because the alternative is despair. 'Man rises to fall,' says Newman[3] of man in his merely natural life, 'he tends to dissolution from the moment he begins to be; he lives on indeed in his own children, he lives on in his own name, he lives not on in his own person. He is, as regards the manifestations of his nature here below, as a bubble that breaks and as water poured out upon the earth. He was young, he is old, he is never young again. This is the lament over him, poured forth in verse and in prose, by Christian and by heathen. The greatest work of God's hands under the sun, he, in all the manifestations of his complex being, is born only to die.'

Therefore reason encourages the man without revelation to look for a revelation, and the greatest of the pre-Christians did in fact look for some such further event. But how then are we to prove that the Christian revelation was the true revelation? Why should Christianity be more true than all other religions—the Mahommedan or the Hindu? The claims of any other religion to be the true revelation he dismisses

[1] p. 278, Part VII.
[2] p. 67.
[3] *The Second Spring.*

in the *Grammar of Assent* somewhat brusquely. 'There is,' he writes,[1] 'only one religion in the world which tends to fulfil the aspirations, needs and foreshadowings of natural faith and devotion. . . . It alone has a definite message to all mankind. As far as I know, the religion of Mahomet has brought in to the world no new doctrine whatever except indeed that of its own divine origin and that character of its teaching is too exact a reflection of the race, time, place and climate in which it arose to admit of its becoming universal. The same dependence on external circumstances is characteristic, as far as I know, of the religions of the Far East.'

Therefore man asked for a revelation and Christianity alone was capable of satisfying that demand. It was unique. But obviously such reasoning, however cogent we may admit it to be, could not of itself prove that the Christian revelation was true. The argument might indeed turn exactly the opposite way. It might be that because Man was so avidly looking for a revelation therefore he accepted with insufficient testing the claims of the Christian revelation. Before we have a right to accept the Christian claims we must consider them on their own intrinsic merits. Might not truth lie rather in the Jewish hope than in the Christian confidence? All that he was prepared to assert at that stage of the argument was that 'either Christianity is from God or a revelation has not yet been given to us.'

Apologists have of course directed our attention to the actual strength on analysis of the Gospel claims—in particular of the claims for the Resurrection. Doubtless Newman would not have denied the strength of such arguments but he did not greatly rely on them. The Vatican Council in its document on Divine Revelation was careful to assert that both Scripture and Tradition were sources of revelation but they were not two separate and independent authorities. There was interplay between the one and the other. Who was it but the Church that decided what books were to form the canon of Scripture? How very meagre would be our knowledge of Our Lord's life if we knew of Him only the events recorded in four short Gospels, three of them largely repetitive of one another—and no more?

Newman did not admit that the Gospels were the only court of appeal. Whether or not the New Testament told us the truth about Christ, at least it could not be denied that it told us what the early Christians believed to be the truth about Christ. To Newman the most

[1] *Grammar of Assent*, p. 430: 'Revealed Religion.'

powerful arguments seemed to be those derived from the story of the early Christians and the rise of the Church in the first generations of the Christian era. It was a record of martyrdom. Now martyrdom does not indeed prove a man right. History has plenty of instances in every age of men who have been willing to die for the most fantastic faiths. But it does prove a man to be sincere. Why should a man die for a cause that he did not in the least believe? Before the test of martyrdom it was doubtless true that many Christians abandoned their faith. What was there surprising in that? The remarkable fact was not that some reneged but that so many did not renege. Newman quoted evidence to prove—what few would be under any temptation to deny—that St. Paul, St. Peter and St. John all firmly believed in the Divinity of Christ. He showed that the early Christians believed in it and that those who were men of fortitude were willing to die for it. The remarkable historical fact, of which there can be no denial, was that this small band of undistinguished Christians, preaching a Gospel that seemed at first sight fantastic, should in so short a time have been able to challenge and impose themselves on the Roman world. He was impressed not so much by the picture of Christ that a man might derive from the unaided study of the Gospels as by the dominating image of Christ that was so evidently possessed by the early Christians. What was the explanation of their success and of this impression?

He considers the suggestions put forward by Gibbon and dismisses them as insufficient.[1] Gibbon has accounted for the Christian rise by five reasons: by the zeal of the Christian inherited from the Jews, by their doctrine of a future state, by their claim to miraculous power, by their virtues and by their ecclesiastical organisation. But how much further do these reasons by themselves get us? The zeal of the Christians? But why were they zealous? Surely only because they so firmly believed. Was their belief true or false? Their doctrine of a future state? The Orient was full of tales of a future life. The Christians differed from other Orientals not in telling such tales but in advancing a solid reason why they were to be believed. Their claim to miraculous power? Again the Orient was full of people who made such claims. Could they produce reasons why their claims were to be accepted? Their virtues? But, if virtuous, why were they virtuous? Indeed many of Gibbon's pages are devoted to arguing that they were not so very virtuous. Their ecclesiastical organisation? But, if they were tightly organised, they

[1] *Grammar of Assent*, p. 430; *ibid.*

were only so organised in order to defend themselves against the attacks of their enemies.

Why were they so attacked? Indeed Christianity's critics are for ever arguing that the first Christians were simple-minded congregationalists and that the organisation of the Church was a later growth and a later corruption. The rigid organisation of the Church, argued Newman, was indeed a response of self-protection against persecution. No doubt it was necessary for Christians to organise if they hoped to survive against such threats. But why should they wish their religion to survive at all? Why should they not simply have abandoned it when the profession of it became dangerous and gaily have consented to throw their incense before Caesar? That is clearly what they would have done had they not passionately believed in the truth of what they professed. Gibbon's explanation was no explanation at all. Were the Christian professions true?

What did the early Christians claim? Basically they claimed two things. First they claimed that Christ was God and pointed to the historical fact of the Resurrection as their proof. Secondly, they claimed that Man was called to a duty of universal love—to love his neighbour as himself. This, argued Newman, perhaps not quite fairly to the greatest Hebrew prophets like Micah, was a wholly new demand. These demands were wholly novel, as was the proclamation of a religion offered not to one nation but to all mankind. Whence had these teachings come? The early Christians believed that they had come from the teachings of Christ. Certainly we find the record of such teachings ascribed to Christ in the New Testament. The Gospels are there. If the sceptics tell us that their evidence is not sufficient to command acceptance, then we are forced to the conclusion that, if not the record of truth, they are the invention of some very extraordinary composers. Who were these four strange crook-novelists who, in this thesis, must have invented the story of Jesus Christ? Newman quoted the sayings of Rousseau, that, if the Gospels were invented, 'L'inventeur en serait plus étonnant que le héros.'[1] He found that argument convincing.

Newman's overt acceptance of the challenge of Gibbon may not today sound very original. We are today all too well accustomed in every day's newspaper to writers and thinkers who challenge the

[1] The inventor would be more amazing than the protagonist. *Discussions and Arguments*, p. 366: 'An Internal Argument for Christianity.'

Christian claims. Such challenges were less common a hundred years ago. There were plenty of people then who disbelieved but it was much more common for them to keep their disbelief to themselves. It was more the custom when speaking or writing in public to write or speak as if the Christian story, though it might have little relevance to the problems of the day, was nevertheless in itself certainly true, and thus by verbally accepting the story these pretended believers, who were in reality sceptics, escaped the task of answering the challenge, 'If Christianity is not true, what then did happen at the time of its origin?' Even today there are all too many who evade the challenge. Gibbon, the first, as Newman said, of English ecclesiastical historians, had at least faced the challenge. Newman set himself to show that he had faced it unsatisfactorily.

No one had better reason than Newman to know that the mere profession of Christianity did not automatically ensure a character of virtue. In the *Grammar of Assent* he noted the strange warning of Christ that we must not expect His followers to be very good. Man had his double nature. He was as he was in practice. But he also had the consciousness of what he ought to be. God existed and yet God was hidden from us. We did not see him face to face. We knew that it was a failure of our own which prevented us from seeing him face to face. The truth of the Christian claim, he thought, was proved not by the fact that men obeyed it but by the fact that, presented with it, they recognised it as something that they ought to obey—that they would be only fully themselves when they lived according to the law of love and that they were less than fully themselves so long as they lived in accordance with a lower code. 'We needs must love the highest when we see it.' It was for that life that man was made, whatever he might make of his own life in practice.

Newman did not pretend that any single argument, taken by itself, was sufficient to furnish an absolutely compulsive case for the Divinity of Christ. The fact that so many men—some of them good and some of them learned—after examining the case felt themselves unable to accept it was proof that the argument was not in itself compulsive. He saw no purpose in putting forward one single syllogistic proposition and announcing that it was compulsive when in fact many people were not convinced by it. The mind in his view did not work in that way. We reached conclusions not as a result of one single proposition but as a result of a coincidence of probabilities which, taken cumulatively, eventually compel a certainty. Thus Newman had never been to America. Show him an atlas on which America was marked and it might be mistaken. Produce to him a witness who asserted that he had been to America, and who knows but that he might be a liar? Nevertheless, although he had never been to America, the accumulation of evidence in favour of there being such a place as America was such that it was to play with words for Newman merely to say that it was probable that such a place existed. He knew that such a place existed.

So he had already written years before in his *Via Media* and quoted in his *Development of Doctrine* that 'for Revelation and indeed for belief in the existence of the Creator we have but probability to show at most.' Yet, as he wrote[1] in his *Grammar of Assent*, quoting his favourite, Bishop Butler, 'Probable proofs by being added not only increase the evidence but multiply it. Nor should I dissuade anyone from setting down what he thought made for the contrary side. . . . The truth of our religion, like the truth of common matters, is to be judged by all the evidence taken together. And unless the whole series of things which may be alleged in this argument and every particular thing in it can reasonably be supposed to have been by accident (for here the stress of the argument for Christianity lies) then is the truth of it proved.' Thus he wrote in his *Apologia*,[2] to justify his acceptance of the Catholic Church, that before his acceptance 'I believed in a God on a ground of probability, I believed in Christianity on a probability and I believed in Catholicism on a probability and all three were about the same kind of probability, a cumulative, transcendent probability but still probability; in as much as he who made us has so willed that in mathematics indeed we arrive at certitude by rigid demonstration but in religious enquiry we arrive at certitude by accumulated probabilities.'

There is not only a difference between demonstration and probability. There is also a difference between real and notional assent. We may be told, accept on authority, in a manner believe, something whose reality has never properly impinged itself upon us. Or we may take a proposition into ourselves, make it a real part of our being. Newman in the *Grammar of Assent*[3] takes the example of a passage of Sophocles

[1] p. 319: 'Informal Inference.'
[2] p. 248: Part VI.
[3] p. 75: 'Real Assent.'

or Virgil. A schoolboy reads it—a passage he supposes, 'describing the birth of some chance morning at an Ionian festival or among the Sabine hills.' He reads it but it makes no great impression on him. It is to him 'a mere rhetorical commonplace'. Then in later life he comes back to such passages with full understanding. They 'pierce him as if he had never known them before.'

The Gospel was to him therefore both poetry and history. He appealed to Pascal and quoted from him.[1] 'Consider the establishment of the Christian religion. Here is a religion contrary to our nature, which established itself in men's minds with so much mildness as to use no external force; with so much energy that no tortures could silence its martyrs and confessors; and consider the holiness, devotion, humility of its true disciples; its sacred books, their superhuman grandeur, their admirable simplicity. Consider the character of its Founder; His associates and disciples, unlettered men, yet possessed of wisdom sufficient to confound the ablest philosopher; the astonishing succession of prophets who heralded Him; the state at this day of the Jewish people who rejected Him and His religion; its perpetuity and its holiness; that light which its doctrines shed upon the contrarieties of our nature—after considering these things let any man judge, if it be possible to doubt about it being the only true one.'

Newman summarises the argument as he himself saw it in his *Grammar of Assent*.[2] 'A Deliverer of the human race through the Jewish nation had been promised from time immemorial. The day came when He was to appear and He was eagerly expected; moreover One actually did make His appearance at that time in Palestine and claimed to be He. He left the earth without apparently doing much for the object of His coming. But when He was gone His disciples took upon themselves to go forth to preach to all parts of the earth with the object of preaching Him and collecting converts in His name. After a little while they are found wonderfully to have succeeded. Large bodies of men in various places are to be seen professing to be His disciples; owning Him as their King and continually swelling in number and penetrating into the populations of the Roman Empire; at length they convert the Empire itself. All this is historical fact.

'Now we want to know the farther historical fact, viz., the cause of their conversion; in other words what were the topics of that preaching

[1] p. 308: 'Revealed Religion.'
[2] p. 464: *ibid*.

which was so effective? If we believe what is told us by the preachers and their converts the answer is plain. They "preached Christ", they called upon men to believe, hope and place their affections in that Deliverer, who had come and gone; and the moral instrument by which they persuaded them to do so was a description of the life, character, mission and the power of that Deliverer, a promise of His invisible presence and protection here and of the vision and fruition of Him hereafter. From first to last to Christians as to Abraham, He Himself is the centre and fullness of the dispensation. They, as Abraham, "see His day and are glad" . . . How without the hand of God could a new idea, one and the same, enter at once into myriads of men, women and children of all ranks, especially the lower, and have power to wean them from their indulgences and sins and to nerve them against the most cruel tortures and to last in vigour as a sustaining influence for seven or eight generations, till it founded an extended polity, broke the obstinacy of the strongest and wisest government which the world has ever seen, and forced its way from its first caves and catacombs to the fullness of imperial power?'

There have been those who have maintained that this acceptance on a balance of probabilities is something very different from what the orthodox Christian normally means by faith. Newman frankly confessed as much. 'In determining as above,' he wrote in the *Grammar of Assent*, 'the main features of Natural Religion and distinguishing it from the religion of philosophy or civilisation, I may be accused of having taken a course of my own, for which I have no sufficient warrant. Such an accusation does not give me much concern. Everyone who thinks on these subjects takes a course of his own.'[1] He confessed that there was a challenge that he was under obligation to answer. He had already written some time before in his *Discussions and Arguments*,[2] 'It is the very characteristic of the profession of faith made by numbers of educated Protestants, and it is the utmost extent to which they are able to go in believing, to hold out not that Christian doctrine is certainly true but that it has such a semblance of truth, it has such considerable marks of probability upon it, that it is their duty to accept and act upon it, as if it were true beyond all question or doubt; and they justify themselves, and with much reason, by the authority of Bishop Butler. Undoubtedly a religious man will be led to go as far as this, if he can-

[1] *Grammar of Assent*, p. 404: *ibid.*
[2] pp. 391–392: 'An Internal Argument for Christianity.'

not go further, but, unless he can go further, he is no catechumen of the Catholic Church.' But how exactly did Newman's position differ from that of these seekers after truth or from the Probabilism of Georg Hermes which had been condemned by the Catholic authorities earlier in the century? It must be confessed that there are passages in Newman some of which we have quoted which leave it by no means clear.

Faith is, in his conception, in no way in contradiction to reason. Faith, he had quoted from Huet in the *Development of Doctrine*,[1] 'confirms our staggering reason,' and so in his *Grammar of Assent*[2] he reproduces and quotes again the arguments which he had used back in 1841 against the notions of Sir Robert Peel and Lord Brougham that man could be saved by Mechanics' Institutes and education alone. He wrote there: 'First comes knowledge, then a view, then reasoning and then belief. That is why science has so little of a religious tendency; deductions have no power of persuasion. The heart is commonly reached not through the reason but through the imagination, by means of direct impressions, by the testimony of facts and events, by history, by description. Persons influence us, voices melt us, looks subdue us, deeds inflame us. Many a man will live and die upon a dogma; no man will be a martyr for a conclusion. . . . I have no confidence then in philosophers who cannot help being religious and are Christians by implication. They sit at home and reach forward to distances which astonish us; but they hit without grasping and are sometimes as confident about shadows as about realities. . . . Logic makes but a sorry rhetoric with the multitude; first shoot round corners and you may not despair of converting by a syllogism. . . . Logicians are more set upon concluding rightly than right conclusions. . . . To most men argument makes the point in hand more doubtful and consequently less impressive. . . . Life is for action. If we insist on proofs for everything we shall never come to action; to act you must assume and that assumption is faith. . . . Now I wish to state all this as a matter of fact, to be judged by the candid testimony of any persons whatever. Why we are so constituted that faith, not knowledge or argument, is our principle of action, is a question with which I have nothing to do; but I think it is a fact and, if it be such, we must resign ourselves to it as best we may.'

[1] *Development of Doctrine*, p. 168: 'Genuine Developments Contrasted with Corruptions.'

[2] p. 92: 'Real Assents in Contrast to Notional Assents and Inferences.'

We conclude by the balancing of probabilities, but, having concluded, we can accept on faith and act by it. We do not need to be constantly reopening the question.

The Vatican Council was, of course, not concerned to demonstrate the existence of God or the divinity of Christ or the validity of the claims of the Church. It assumed these articles and was concerned only to show what conduct was required by their acceptance. To that extent the *Grammar of Assent*, which was rather concerned to show the reasons for belief, could not provide as it were ammunition for the Council in the way that other books such as the *Essay on Development* or *On Consulting the Faithful on Matters of Doctrine* were able to do. But it has had a greater effect than they on the general mind of the age. These other works were debates about the constitution of the Church. To one who did not grant the claims of Christ at all they were irrelevant. But the Council had in its decree on the seminaries admitted that the Thomist system was no longer to be the only one tolerated. Where Professor Gilson, at the height of the Thomist tide, had prophesied that Duns Scotus would soon be condemned, Pope Paul in recognising his centenary recognised him as an essential aid to the ecumenical dialogue between Catholics and Anglicans.

It is in the decrees on Catholic Education both in schools and in seminaries and in Schema XIII on the Church in the Modern World that the influence of the *Grammar of Assent* has been most visible, just as the influence of the *Essay on Development* has been most visible in the general decree on the Constitution of the Church. The fashion of Catholic education up till Newman's time had been to build its curricula on an assumption that Catholicism was true and merely to teach, as facts to be accepted and memorised, the doctrines of the Church. Those who did not accept the Church's authority were simply to be condemned as in error. Such tactics only made sense, if they made sense at all, in a society where Catholics lived in isolation, never destined throughout life to make any serious contacts with non-Catholics. If they were to go out, as the modern Catholic must inevitably go out, into a society in which they had to work side by side with non-Catholics, they were necessarily compelled to develop a double mind—applying the normal canons of evidence and calculation to the affairs of everyday life and closing their minds with a snap on the few matters on which there was real dogmatic Catholic teaching. Faith was unlikely to survive in an atmosphere of such ambivalence, nor were competent expositors of it to the secular world likely to emerge from a seminary in which they had been kept in total ignorance of the workings of that world. The *Grammar of Assent* was the first great attempt to give a defence of Christian faith in a language that allowed, recognised and answered the lack of faith of the modern world.

The *Grammar of Assent* derives from Pope Paul's judgement an increased significance because in it Newman, rejecting the purely intellectualist approach to the problem of God, talks a language much more like that of Duns Scotus than that of St. Thomas. It is also much more like that of the modern analyst and existentialist and we can see that growth of tolerance reflected in the present language of the Church. Where the early nineteenth-century Popes had been only concerned to denounce, the modern documents are concerned to explain and to understand. Contrast for instance Pius IX's full-blooded denunciation of all enemies of the Church with the careful and reasoned attempt to discover what had led atheists to become atheists of John XXIII in *Mater et Magistra* or in the Schema XIII of the Church in the World Today; contrast Gregory XVI's denunciation of freedom of opinion as 'insanity' with John XXIII's assertion of its rights in *Pacem in Terris;* compare the *Syllabus Errorum*'s advocacy of a literal interpretation of the Scriptures with the assertion of a duty of hermeneutic exposition of them in Pius XII's *Divino Afflante Spiritu;* or the earlier Pope's denunciation of liberalism, progress and democracy with the Council's assertion of the autonomous rights of science and its endorsement of democracy in its judgement that 'admirable is the practice of those nations in which the greater number of citizens take part with true liberty in political life.'

The older Popes often write as if they were only interested in the well-being of Catholics. Such an accusation could even be sometimes sustained against Pius XII. John XXIII always wrote as if he was interested in the well-being of all mankind. Schema XIII, instead of challenging the world with a full-blooded statement of the absolute and demonstrable proof of the existence of God, opens out with the mild, very existential, very Newmanesque statement, 'Man will be always interested in religion,' and argues from this fact of experience. There is an almost total contrast between the language of the Vatican of a hundred years ago and that of Pope John and the present Pope and the major fact in Catholic history that stands between those days and this—the major cause of the change of language—has been the writing of Newman.

Newman disliked what he himself called 'cut-and-dried logic'. His appeals were personal appeals to the 'whole man'. He was not naturally at home with the mediaeval scholastics, who wrote in an age where the existence of God could be taken for granted, but with Pascal who was acutely conscious of the fundamental challenge. He was more at home with Bishop Butler and Hume than with Catholic philosophical authors and among his contemporaries, as Professor Cameron has suggested in his essay on *The Logic of the Heart* in his *Night Battle*, with such writers as Kierkegaard or Dostoievski and, I would have added, Browning. In opposition to those who fitted words of rigid meaning into their syllogisms he asked: 'After all, what is language but an artificial system adapted for particular purposes which have been determined by our wants?' 'Half the controversies in the world,' he said,[1] 'are verbal ones and, could they be brought to a plain issue, they would be brought to a prompt termination.' 'Even the words of inspired Scripture [are] imperfect and defective.' For man, when he speaks of ultimate matters is striving to express something that is beyond the capacity of language to express.

> 'Our reach must exceed our grasp.
> Else what's a heaven for?'

Who may have the better in these debates in the long run this is no place to inquire, but it is clear that Newman, by insisting that the difference so very largely turns on what is the meaning of the words which we use, was talking language much more easily intelligible to the disciples of Wittgenstein and the modern analysts than was the language of St. Thomas. Whereas the Thomist and the analyst are moving on parallel lines which can never meet, Newman is very much more clearly talking their language—not indeed agreeing with them in their conclusions but using language which can very often be turned against them on their own principles. Different as were his conclusions, his method of approach was, as Professor Cameron, I think, rightly argues, very largely derived from Hume—'this acute, though most low-minded of speculators', as he calls him—and this is important since the theory of knowledge or lack of knowledge of the modern logical positivists is also so largely Hume, dressed out in a new language.

Newman agreed very largely with the pragmatists that action is the only real test of belief. 'Action,' he argued, 'is the criterion of true faith.'

[1] University Sermons, p. 192: 'Faith and Reason.'

He had little regard for the enunciation of abstract intellectual propositions which have no influence over conduct. He agreed that knowledge comes from experience. But he argued that experience of external objects was very doubtful, our experience of the reality of conscience much more certain. He agreed that everything was very largely a matter of words but thought that, if men professed atheism, they generally did so because they did not understand the meaning of the words that they used. It was impossible to frame a language that did not by its implications concede the case for God. How could we talk without continually using the word 'ought'? It might be true that it was meaningless to profess belief in what was not verifiable. But what was more clearly verifiable than the existence of faith—than the feeling that there was a mystery beyond the world of every day of which we could not certainly know the details? All art derived from that feeling —from the attempt to express the inexpressible—and the existence of art was more certain than the existence of chairs and tables. Belief in Faith is no abstract belief. Experience only seems to reject religion because the analysts give to experience their own definition which really begs the question. Religious utterances have, as Professor Cameron puts it, 'their own logical grammar'. To believe, Newman thought along with Kierkegaard and the existentialists, is to commit oneself. All this does not necessarily mean that Newman was on every point always right, and there may come a day when the world has moved on again and when his language has become as irrelevant as that of the schoolmen but certainly for the moment his work is essential for any dialogue with the modern world, for it was he more than any other that talked its language.

The *Apologia* has of course had many more readers than the *Grammar of Assent*. That is doubtless because of its narrative character. Which is the better book it is to no purpose to decide, but in a way the argument of the *Grammar* is of a more general interest than the argument of the *Apologia*. The latter argument is mainly concerned whether truth lies with Rome or with the Church of England—a comparatively narrow argument to a generation whose main concern is whether truth can be found at all. The *Grammar*, though it is a loyally Catholic book, is yet a book which expounds to the reader the general reasons for belief. There is little in it that could not be read as easily by a non-Catholic as by a Catholic. Newman was of course greatly concerned by the growth of atheism and disbelief and thought it necessary to write against the conventional apologetics of the day because he thought that they were wholly insufficient to check this growth. It was improbable that an attempt to prevent Catholics in a pluralist society from reading and hearing the irreligious ideas that were current around the world would be successful. Were they immediately successful in protecting a Catholic against contamination they could hardly hope to produce a Catholicism that was not merely infantile. As Newman put it,[1] 'Our theological philosophers are like old nurses who wrap the unhappy infant in swaddling band or boards—and put a lot of blankets over him and shut the windows that not a breath of air may come to his skin—as if he were not healthy enough to bear wind and water in due measure. They move in a groove and will not tolerate any one who does not move in the same.'

It was Newman's ambition to produce an adult Catholicism. But what exactly did he mean when he spoke of the growth of atheism and when he said, 'Ours has a darkness different in kind from any that has been before,' or, 'Christianity has never yet had experience of a world simply irreligious'? Here again—as in his use of the word 'reason'—he was perhaps at fault in using a word in a slightly unfamiliar sense. Newman did not mean that the majority of people in his day, any more indeed than the majority of people today, were professed, defiant, proclaimed atheists. Such a being is obviously a comparative rarity and he pays a sort of tribute to the religion which he is defying by talking so much about it. Whether a man professed himself an atheist—or whether he said that for all that he knew there might be a God who had set the ball rolling but who certainly could not or would not now interfere with its circulation—was to him a matter of indifference. Agnostics and deists and even men who called themselves Christians—some, as we have seen, in the Vatican itself—Newman included in his definition of atheist. A religious man was in his belief a man who believed that God interfered in the affairs of men. An irreligious man—an atheist—was one who believed that He did not interfere.

Later, towards the end of his life, in the next decade, all England was greatly excited over the Bradlaugh case. Should Bradlaugh, a professed atheist, be allowed to take his seat in the House of Commons? The greater number of clerics, including Manning and most of the Catholic bishops, thought that he should not be allowed. Newman took the

[1] In August, 1869, in a letter to Henry Wilberforce. See *Light in Winter*, p. 488: '1870—Viva il Papa Infallibile.'

line that the distinction between Bradlaugh and the average Englishman of the day was a distinction without a difference and that it was absurd to make a fuss over the matter. 'What the social and political world means by the name God,' he wrote,[1] 'is too often not the Christian God, the Jewish or the Mohammedan—not a personal God but an unknown God; as little what Christians mean by God as the Fate, Chance or *Anima Mundi* of a Greek philosopher. Hence it as little concerns religion whether Mr. Bradlaugh swears by no God with the Government or swears by an Impersonal, or Material, or Abstract and Ideal something or other which is all that is secured to us by the Opposition.' The Catholics, having just recently won their own political emancipation, were, he thought, ill advised to use their freedom to deny emancipation to others. They would be better advised to occupy themselves in converting themselves to their own religion of which so many of them were sadly in need.

It requires indeed a great strength of imagination, however much formal logic may demonstrate that an unlimited Being would necessarily do so, really to believe that the Creator of the Universe can care about the fate of an individual man any more than we can care about the fate of a single ant which we may see running out of its heap. Why should He? Yet such a belief is clearly the demand of Christianity. But it is a demand of which many Catholics, oscillating between deism and superstition, are not in fact capable. Newman had years ago noted in his *Parochial Sermons* that the way was of its nature narrow and the full truth something which one could only expect to find in a very few. 'There are seasons,' he said,[2] 'when a sudden enthusiasm arises in favour of the truth. . . . Yet such a popularity of the truth is but sudden, comes at once and goes at once, has no regular growth, no abiding stay. . . . Truth indeed has that power in it that it forces man to profess it in words; but when they go on to act instead of obeying it they substitute some idol in the place of it. On these accounts when there is much talk of religion in a country and much congratulation that there is a general concern for it, a cautious mind will feel anxious lest some counterfeit be in fact honoured instead of it; lest it be the dream of man rather than the verities of God's word which has become popular and lest the received form have no more truth in it than is just necessary to recommend it to the reason and conscience—lest in short it be Satan trans-

[1] Bradlaugh Case, Chapter 20, p. 229.
[2] *Parochial Sermons*, I. 62: 'Secret Faults.'

formed into an angel of light rather than the Light itself which is attracting followers.'

At the time when he wrote the *Idea of a University* Newman had taken the view that in all periods of history a real, as opposed to a proclaimed, disbelief in religion was quite common. In the Middle Ages, he thought, plenty of people did not really believe but the result of social pressure was that they cloaked their disbelief and remained nominally within the fold. It was better, he argued, in his day when those who ceased to believe frankly confessed their disbelief. But in later life he came to change this view and to think that many who believed themselves to be Christians even in his own day were in fact not really so.

Newman, born with the turn of the century, was by the 1870's an old man and in his own opinion a very old man. As we have seen, he had for many years been in a continual state of amazement at the discovery that he was still alive. After the publication of the *Grammar of Assent*, it never occurred to him that he had any future before him. All seemed to have ended in a not very satisfactory draw. He had his devoted friends—both inside and outside the Church. For them he was grateful. He had his quiet, unhurried life at Edgbaston. He had suc-ceeded in building up for himself such a position that there was no longer any great probability that any of his works would be actually condemned. Yet the mind of the Church both at Rome and at West-minster seemed to be entirely opposed to his way of thinking. The personal indignities to which the genial old Pius IX had been sub-mitted by his enemies had been so gross that no Catholic of loyal chivalry was willing in these closing years of his life to raise a word in criticism of him. At the same time he was manifestly not intellectually competent to manage the affairs of the Church. All as a result fell into a doldrum of inaction. Newman's works in this doldrum age would be allowed to lie about unhindered. But he could not hope that they would have much influence on the course of things.

In 1877 Trinity College made him an honorary Fellow and he returned to his old College with its snapdragon on the wall to receive his honour and to dine at the High Table. To him, to whom memories of the past always meant so much, it was indeed a moving occasion. It proved that the bitterness of the past was forgotten, but it was not an evidence that he was likely to wield a great power in the future. Rather, if anything, the reverse. The old fighter was being honoured because no one had any longer any reason to fear his blows. Then in 1878 Pius IX's long reign at last came to an end and Leo XIII succeeded him on the throne. Leo did not ascend the throne with any dramatic repudiation of his predecessor's policies. That is not the Roman way. In some respects indeed he continued those policies. He would have no dealings with the new Italian State. The Italian Catholics were to be neither electors nor elected at the Italian polls. He remained obstinately a prisoner in the Vatican. But his mind was a world away from the mind of Pius. It was not in Leo's view the task of a Catholic to hide himself away from the life of an evil and godless world. The Catholic must play his part in and transform that life. The industrial system had grown up in countries that were not Catholic. The Church had up till that date had nothing to say about the social problems which industrialism was creating.

Leo decided to end that—decided that the Church must proclaim her social remedies. In this task he found among English Catholics more support from Manning than from Newman, for these were problems nearer to Manning's interest. But it was also necessary that the Church should show itself in the intellectual sphere able to speak and to understand the language of the modern world. A restatement of the Catholic position—a new philosophical approach, a new approach to Scripture —was necessary and how better could a Pope give evidence that a wind of change was blowing that by lifting the cloud that hung over Newman and bestowing on him the most signal mark of Papal honour?

Students of Lytton Strachey and those who have followed—perhaps critically—in his footsteps are familiar with the controversies about how Manning did or did not attempt to prevent the Pope from offering Newman the Hat. Again these are controversies for the biographers in which we need not involve ourselves. The essential point is that, whatever the methods that he may have used, Manning had a perfectly honourable reason of principle for not wishing that Newman should be distinguished. He and Manning stood for two radically different conceptions of Catholicism. Up till Pius IX's death Manning could flatter himself that his view was the Establishment view and that the most that Newman could expect was to be tolerated. Newman's elevation was a sign that new views were now in favour at Rome and that the road of the future was to be the road of persuasion and not of coercion.

Newman was seventy-eight when he was made a Cardinal in 1879 and was eighty-nine when he died in 1890. It was not then to be expected that his years of cardinalate should be years of great activity. Their importance was rather to Newman as a symbol of recognition and honour and to England and the world as a sign that new brooms were sweeping at the Vatican. Manning had no ambition to be cast as a John the Baptist to such a Messiah and he was not well pleased. But Newman even as a Cardinal and even in his eighties was not idle.

Two years before he had been created Cardinal he had issued with a special preface a new edition of his *Via Media* of forty years before. In that book, written of course in his Anglican days, he had, as will be remembered, commended the Church of England as a wise middle way between the excesses of Rome on the one hand and of Non-conformity on the other. His beliefs had so completely changed since he wrote that book that its reissue might at first sight seem to be little more than an exercise of literary curiosity. It was not so at all. Although by these later years he was by no means any longer able to see in the Church of England his *Via Media*, he still held as firmly as in youth to the Aristotelian maxim that truth was always to be found in the mean. The one test of truth was general consent and where there were differences truth was to be found in that belief which stood in the middle between and in some measure embraced the extremes to both sides of it. For practical purposes it was necessary to adopt a policy which divides society as little as possible. Extreme policies may be advocated on platforms or in pulpits. Only central policies are practicable.

So just as in youth he had hoped to find this *Via Media* in the Church of England, now in old age he advocated a *Via Media* within the Catholic Church. On the one hand the rights of liberty must be invoked against the extravagances of the Ultramontanes with their excessive authoritarianism and with their demands for submisson to teachings that were quite unsupported by the Church. On the other hand he must protest against the excesses of licence and the new Modernism which was repudiating doctrines that quite clearly had the Church's authority —which was rejecting the whole historical basis of Christianity. He took the occasion of his Cardinalitial address to repudiate such doctrines and to express his abhorrence of the double-thinker who pretended to accept the authority of the Church and then refused its teachings.

In 1884 he published in the *Nineteenth Century* an article on *The Inspiration of Scripture*, in which he argued against the absurdity of a theory which ascribed to the Scriptures a verbal inerrancy and which required the reader to accept the accuracy of every incidental statement in the Bible on history or science. This was a view that had been widely held in Protestant circles in Newman's youth—indeed had at that time been held by Newman himself who in a famous passage had explained how we know that there was in early times a universal flood because Scripture told us of it. Indeed as late as 1852 he had written,[1] 'revealed religion furnishes facts to other sciences which those sciences, left to themselves, would never reach. Thus in the science of history the preservation of our race in Noah's Ark is an historical fact which history never would arrive at without revelation.' In those days most Catholics had taken an attitude towards Scripture not so very different from that of the Protestants. In view of the verbal contradictions of certain verses in Scripture with certain other verses it is not very easy to see how any person who had ever read the Bible could have taken that view of it. Yet a totally authoritarian religion is able to make contradictory affirmations and survive them by the easy device of repressing those who attempt to point out the contradictions, and it was such a spirit and such policies which reigned in the Catholic Church up till the death of Pius IX.

With Leo XIII a new spirit came in on scriptural interpretation as on other matters. In *Providentissimus Deus* Pope Leo was to give expression to this new teaching which Newman had already expounded in his essay in the *Nineteenth Century*. The Bible was, he argued, the inspired work of God in the sense that it gave both in the Old and in the New Testament a truthful account of the workings of God in this world. But it was not a manual of history or of science. Whether the story of Creation as given in *Genesis* was factually accurate as a scientific account was as it might be. Whether every anecdote recorded was a verbatim report, whether the order of events was always precisely as recorded was as it might be. We must apply the ordinary scholar's tests to decide on the authorship or the dates of the various books and so on. Indeed the Bible itself was but the title deed of the Church. There was little relevance in appealing to the Bible against the Church because it was the Church itself which decided which books should be admitted to constitute the Bible. Therefore the fundamental documents were the Creeds. Where the Bible was concerned with the narration of events with which the Creeds were not concerned, their assertions were indeed

[1] Inge, *Outspoken Essays*, p. 195.

of importance but not of absolutely final importance. Did Christ walk on the water? How did He turn the water into wine? There is perhaps no great reason why things should not here have happened just as the Gospels said, but, if some new discovery should show that they happened otherwise, it would not bring the Christian religion to an end. But on the historical events vouched for by the Creeds—in particular, that is to say, on the historical truth of the Resurrection—the Christian religion stood or fell.

Therefore, Newman, while arguing in favour of a degree of freedom of interpretation, was careful at the same time to show his middle way —was careful to show the limits beyond which freedom of interpretation could not be carried by a man who wished still to be called a Christian. He held his middle course between the Ultramontanes on the one hand and the Modernists on the other.

II

Newman and the Modernists

NEWMAN HIMSELF died in 1890 and the Pope who had honoured him survived him for thirteen years and died in 1903. During those last years of Newman's and Leo's lives the new Modernism—which at first was called concessionism—was beginning to show itself and both Leo and Newman were careful to define their positions towards it. But it was only in the next reign, that of St. Pius X, that the clear battle was finally joined. The reign of Pius X, which ran from the beginning of the century until the outbreak of the First World War, was dominated by his campaign against Modernism. Modernism was unsparingly condemned first by the Decree of the Holy Inquisition *Lamentabili Sane Exitu* of July 3, 1907, and secondly by the Pope's own encyclical, *Pascendi Dominici Gregis*, of September 8 of that same year. The story is only of importance to the student of Newman in so far as the claim was sometimes made, at times by some of the Modernists in their own justification, at times by conservative critics anxious to warn the faithful against too great confidence in Newman, that the Modernist theories were in some ways a derivative from the theories of Newman.

Thus Father Tyrrell, the leading English Modernist, argued that Newman's acquittal by Rome was only equivocal. 'Evidently Rome lays great stress,' he wrote,[1] 'on this Newman question and they must not be allowed to throw dust in the public eyes. Notice how the *Observatore*[2] cuts down Gasquet's assurances that "no theory, no idea, no opinion" of Newman's had been touched; how it cuts out the *Essay* from the Catholic writings—though it was the process that made him

[1] Lewis May, *Father Tyrrell and the Modernist Movement*, p. 249: 'Some Letters and a Comparison.'

[2] *Sic.* It should of course be *Osservatore.* Tyrrell knew very little about the Continent.

(and others in his wake) a Catholic—and yet how it has to leave in the hopelessly anti-scholastic *Grammar of Assent*. I should be inclined to say, "Very well. The Pope says we can accept the *Grammar of Assent* and Newman's attitude to scholasticism. With that I withdraw all I said against the encyclical; but at the same time I confess that it is an utterly unintelligible and misleading document."' Tyrrell argued that Newman was only not condemned by name because Leo XIII had made him a Cardinal and a Vatican tradition forbids a Pope from overtly challenging his predecessor. Newman's thinking, argued Tyrrell, was in fact condemned. At any rate it is certainly true that Newman who, after his dark night of the soul under Pius IX, had enjoyed the full warmth of sunshine under Leo XIII, a little receded in reputation under Pius X.

In order to judge, it is first necessary to understand broadly what Modernism was. The explanation of it, if it is to be brief, is not altogether simple. Modernism was never a creed with one simple coherent corpus of doctrine. When Pius X condemned it, a number of the Modernists replied, as a number of Americans had replied when Leo XIII had condemned Americanism, that the Pope was condemning an abstraction. They did not doubt, they argued, that the doctrines were worthy of condemnation. But who held them? They denied that they, or anybody else, held the whole corpus of doctrine that were there condemned. And there was, it must be confessed, some cogency in their reply. One thinker made one assertion and another made another, and the summary of them was a little unfairly lumped together as Modernism. But though, if we were engaged on a detailed study of Modernism on its own merits, it would be necessary carefully to distinguish the different assertions of different thinkers, a broad summary is sufficient for our present purposes.

Modernism, then, in broad can be said to have launched three separate attacks. It attacked the historical reliability of the Gospels—and in particular their accounts of the life of Christ. It attacked the traditional Catholic view of philosophy; and it attacked the traditional view of the nature of the Church.[1]

Take first the criticism of the New Testament expressed by the most notable of the Modernist critics, the Abbé Loisy. According to Loisy the Gospels are for Christians no more than what the Pentateuch is for Jews—a patchwork of history and legend. Mark, he maintained, shows a Jesus who follows a progressive development. St. Peter at Caesarea

[1] See Inge's *Outspoken Essay on Roman Catholic Modernism.*

Philippi was the first to infer Jesus' Messiahship. Jesus himself never declared it until His trial before the Sanhedrin. Matthew and Luke on the other hand saw Jesus as the Son of God from the very beginning of His ministry. John went further yet. He set forth in his opening words a theological claim to a divinity for Jesus that was before time and quite irrespective of His earthly birth, and proclaimed His recognition as God on His very first public appearance by John the Baptist. There was, Loisy thought, hardly a pretence of historical accuracy in John's account. 'The Christ of the Synoptics,' he writes, 'is historical but He is not God. The Johannine Christ is divine but is not historical.' Even of the synoptic evangelists Mark was an unknown non-Jewish Christian who wrote some time after the destruction of Jerusalem in 70 A.D. and wished to give a picture of Christ conformable with the Hellenic-Christian tradition in which he lived. Matthew was written by a non-Palestinian Jew at the beginning of the second century. It is the work of an ecclesiastic anxious to give authority to support the claims which ecclesiastics had by then come to make for themselves. All the stories, about, for instance, Jesus' miraculous birth are to be totally dismissed; '*Rien n'est plus arbitraire comme exégèse ni plus faible comme narrative fictive.*'[1] Luke was a much better story-teller than Matthew but, thought Loisy, '*Il paraît cependant impossible de leur reconnaître une plus grande valeur de fond.*'[2] The Fourth Gospel was wholly without historical value.

The true life of Jesus, according to Loisy's chapter, *La Carrière de Jésus*, in his *Evangiles Synoptiques* was something as follows. Jesus was born at Nazareth about four years before the Christian era. None of his family accepted His claims during his lifetime. He became a disciple of John the Baptist. When John was thrown into prison Jesus attempted to take his place as leader. He claimed to be the Messiah and promised the immediate coming of 'the Kingdom of God' on earth. He attracted some followers—mostly among the *déclassés*—but aroused the hostility both of the Pharisees and of Herod. At last Jesus in company with His disciples decided to go up to Jerusalem and there proclaim himself Messiah. His disciples on the way lost their nerve but Jesus calmed them with promises of the high posts that were awaiting them after victory. At first He met with some success, succeeding for instance in clearing the Temple, but the forces against Him were such that eventual defeat

---

[1] Nothing is more arbitrary as exegesis, nor more feeble as fiction.
[2] It seems impossible, however, to allow them a greater essential value.

was inevitable. 'The situation' wrote Loisy. 'could only end in a miracle or a catastrophe, and it was the catastrophe which happened.' He was arrested and crucified. His disciples fled in panic. His body was thrown into some common trench, but His disciples, after recovering from their stunned panic, imagined and persuaded themselves that they had seen the Risen Lord. 'The supernatural life of Christ in the faithful and in the Church,' wrote the Italian Modernists in their *Programme of Modernism*, 'has been clothed in a historical form which has given birth to what we might somewhat loosely call the Christ of legend.'

In fact the Modernist formula was to deny the possibilty of any miraculous event which they found asserted in the Gospels and to rewrite the story according to their own ingenuity in a non-miraculous form. '*L'historien*,' wrote Loisy, '*n'a pas à s'inspirer de l'agnosticisme pour écarter Dieu de l'histoire; il ne l'y rencontre jamais.*'[1] But it was manifestly no objective study of historical evidences which caused the Modernist to reject the miraculous claims of the Gospels. He rejected them not on an historical but on a metaphysical principle. He determined before he came to the study of the history that a miracle was an impossibility and therefore on that *a priori* principle rejected every miracle that he found there asserted. Newman showed as an example the principle upon which Hume confessedly formed his opinions about miracles. 'What have we to oppose, 'wrote Hume,[2] 'to such a cloud of witnesses but the absolute impossibility or miraculous nature of the events which they relate? And this surely in the eyes of all reasonable people will alone be regarded as a sufficient refutation.' It was a curious position for one who proclaimed himself a professor of scepticism and of the impossibility of dogmatic knowledge, and the position of the Modernisers was on this point essentially the same as that of Hume.

'He introduces into us,' wrote Laberthonnière of Christ in *Le Réalisme Chrétien et l'Idéalisme Grec*, 'the principles of that which ought to be. That which He reveals He makes in revealing it'. Christ is a power or force rather than a fact. This might be a description of the Holy Spirit. It is not easy to see how it can be a description of Jesus Christ.

'As faith may be viewed as opposed to Reason,' Newman had stated before in a University Sermon, 'in the popular sense of the latter word, it must not be overlooked that Unbelief is opposed to Reason also.

[1] The historian has no need to draw inspiration from Agnosticism in order to dislodge God from history: he never encounters him there.

[2] *University Sermons*, p. 223: 'Love, the Safeguard of Faith against Superstition.'

Unbelief, indeed, considers itself especially rational, or critical of evidence, but it criticises the evidence of religion only because it does not like it and really goes upon presumptions and prejudices as much as Faith does, only presumptions of an opposite nature. . . . It considers a religious system so improbable that it will not listen to the evidence of it; or, if it listens, it employs itself in doing what a believer could do, if he chose, quite as well; what he is quite as well aware can be done; viz, in showing that the evidence might be more complete and unexceptionable than it is. On this account it is that unbelievers call themselves rational; not because they decide by evidence but because, after they had made their decision, they merely occupy themselves in sifting it'.

> 'All we have gained then by our unbelief
> Is a life of doubt diversified by faith
> For one of faith diversified by doubt.
> We called the chess board white—we call it black,'

he might have quoted from Bishop Blougram.

As for what happened, the probability was, the Modernists argue, that the reality was something like what the Abbé Loisy suggested. For according to Father Tyrrell the pretence that we could reach absolute certainty about past history was a fraud. We never knew enough to be sure, and in fact we always believed what we wished to believe and then afterwards used our reasons as weapons to defend the position which we had chosen to take up. 'The great mass of our beliefs,' Tyrrell wrote, 'are reversible and depend for their stability on the action or permission of the will.' The question, 'What really happened?' was a question according to him that was both unanswerable and unimportant. The historical story was, he said, only what he called 'the frame-stuff' of the ideas. We must, said Le Roy, 'interpret dogmas in the language of practical action.' The *lex credendi* was in fact and ought to be the *lex orandi*. The validity of a dogma depended not on its objective truth but on 'its prayer value'. In fact we believed that which helped us. If a belief helped us to be good we might as well, like William James and the pragmatists, say that it was true. It was as near to being true as a man—being of his nature incapable of truth—could hope to get. We live of our nature by hopes and aspirations.

The comment on all this is obvious. All of us who think at all are aware of the staggering nature of the Christian claim. Whichever the side of the fence we come down on, we can understand those who decide that they cannot accept the evidence for its gigantic claims, and, if they reject the claims, then, challenged by the question 'What did happen?' they will inevitably give some answer along the sort of lines that Loisy offered. If told that some element of this explanation is improbable, they will reply, 'At any rate it is less improbable than the orthodox Christian story.' We are well aware that there are such people, respect them and are not surprised at them. But, we naturally ask of the Modernists, 'If you cannot believe more of the Christian story than that, why do you want to go on calling yourselves Christians and even performing at Christian altars rites which on your own showing are a meaningless mumbo-jumbo?' It is idle to say, like the pragmatists, that we continue to perform the rites because the rites work. They only work because those who assist in them believe in their validity. It is hardly to be believed that a Mass which to all its assistants was a hollow mockery would for long continue to have much effect on their lives. Prayers surely have their value because those who pray them at least believe that they are addressed to Someone real. Even the psychologist, who denies the validity of religious beliefs, would agree that to have effect those who utter the prayers must at least believe the prayers to be valid. The question, then, that we are inclined to ask is not so much whether the Modernists were Christians in the sense in which that term had ever been used as 'Why, when they were so obviously not Christians, were they so anxious to be called Christians?'

There is clearly no answer in objective reason. It was for reasons of personal relations that they wished to escape condemnation. They were almost all of them either French or Italian priests. Doubtless none of them, when they were ordained, held their Modernist opinions. They had moved into these opinions in the course of their priesthoods. They had friends. They were attached to institutions. They had become accustomed to the habits of Catholic life. They had their Catholic relations. It is—to many people at any rate—very difficult to break with the habits and company of a religion in which a man has been brought up, even when he has ceased perfectly to believe it. The great majority of the Modernists were, as I have said, from Catholic countries and with generations of Catholic ancestry behind them—from France or Italy. There was only one English-speaking Modernist of the first importance. He—Father Tyrrell—was of quite a different background. He was by origin an Irish Protestant, himself a convert. He had no Catholic relations who would be saddened by an apostasy, and it is not perhaps quite so easy to see why when he became, as his autobiography shows that he did become, wholly disillusioned with the Society of Jesus to which he had taken his vows, he did not quite easily and gladly abandon his membership of the Catholic Church. He had indeed always a contempt for Protestantism and can have been under no temptation to return to the religion of his cradle, but it is not very easy to see why he was not content, like so many others of his day, to become an unattached Free Thinker. But most of us are not quite fixed and certain in our beliefs and unbeliefs. We half-believe and half-disbelieve—accept at moments and reject at moments—and Tyrrell could never quite free himself from a hankering after those Sacraments in which he so frequently expressed his lack of belief—at least in the sense in which any traditional Catholic had ever believed in them.

Yet it is not here our concern to attempt to estimate the motives or characters of the leading Modernists. All that it is necessary to assert is that it was not surprising that Pope Pius X should have found it necessary to condemn these teachings. He did so in no uncertain terms. In *Pascendi Gregis* he asserted[1] that

1. The scholastic philosophy is to form the basis of all sacred studies.
2. There is to be strict censorship of the opinions of the professors and directors in the seminaries. The regular course in scholastic philosophy is to be required of all candidates for the doctorate of theology or canon law.
3. The bishops are to assist the work of the censor by prohibiting the reading in seminaries of any Modernist literature which, owing to the quantity published, may have escaped the attention of Rome.
4. The bishops must appoint censors in their dioceses to examine all books and periodicals. Their signed *nihil obstat* must precede the granting of an episcopal *imprimatur*.
5. Vigilance committees are to be set up in each diocese to collect any evidence of Modernist writing or teaching and are to meet every second month and deliberate secretly.
6. These committees are to keep their eyes especially open for Modernist treatment of social questions and social institutions.
7. Bishops are to report to Rome every three years, and under oath, on the doctrines current amongst their clergy.

The tone of this document is certainly harsh. But it was until recent

[1] E. E. Y. Hales, *The Catholic Church in the Modern World*, Chapter XV.

times always the custom of Popes—rightly or wrongly—to speak in uncompromising language. It was thought a requisite of their authority and dignity that they should do so. It was not until John XXIII that a new habit of kindly moderation of language was introduced. Had Pius X merely quoted specific passages in the writings of Loisy and Tyrrell and the rest and passed his condemnation on them, there would have been hardly any room for serious controversy. It was the generalised and unspecified nature of his condemnation that aroused criticism. If there is a revealed religion then it must of its nature have revealed some concrete doctrine, and, if there is a divinely founded Church, then it is reasonable that its *magisterium* should firmly correct any who assert as Catholic doctrine something that is not in fact Catholic doctrine. But the dogmas of the Church are few and truth for the most part can only be attained in a system of free speculation, each man learning from the criticisms of another. Truth, as Newman had written in the *Idea of a University*, can only be attained by 'many minds working together.' The fault of Pius X was that he sought to extend the few points upon which ruling was necessary so as to establish a general supervision of all thinking. In such an atmosphere neither thinking nor Catholic life could survive. There was a disease, but the disease, dangerous as it was, was less dangerous than the remedy of it.

The Modernist leaders were, prior to their condemnation, teachers in seminaries and writers. Their influence was pervasive. Pupils and students read their works and were influenced by them. Had the Pope condemned the specific errors of particular writers the condemnation might have been effective. A blanket condemnation of 'Modernist literature' without any exact definition what Modernism was—generalised threats of 'strict censorship' and 'vigilance committees', the search for Modernism in social institutions, the order to bishops to report to Rome—smacked all too much of the methods of Dostoievski's Grand Inquisitor and suggested all too ominously the subsequent methods of brain washing and the Russian *cheka*. Leo XIII had wisely recommended a study of scholastic philosophy as an antidote to a régime of repression where no philosophy was studied at all. Pius X sought to turn scholastic philosophy into a new authoritarianism, and, not content to recommend its study as a mental discipline, to impose it as a military rule and to make it 'form the basis of all sacred studies.' It was particularly unfortunate that Pius should have included in his condemnation of Modernism a condemnation of 'Modernist treatment of social questions and social institutions'. The Pope explained that he meant by that that Christian Democrats were 'strictly bound to dependence on ecclesiastical authority by complete submission to the bishops and their representatives.'

Such a policy, if pursued, would inevitably mean that no Catholic politician could hope to exercise any influence in a modern State, since it is clear that the bishops have not, and those who are sensible among them do not claim to have, any special competence to advise on parliamentary tactics, and their interference would inevitably create such prejudice against Catholic politicians as to make it certain that legislation would in fact be much more anti-Catholic than would otherwise have been the case. Leo XIII had been careful to express his social programme in language as generally acceptable to all men of good will, as little dependent on appeal to Catholic authority as possible. That was the necessary policy if it was to have any effect. Pius X reversed that policy. Pope Pius' ruling is also almost directly the opposite of that which has been happily laid down by the Second Vatican Council in its insistence on the apostolate of the laity. It was a misfortune, as has been said, that Murri, one of the leading Italian Christian Democrats, was also a Modernist and it was this which persuaded the Pope in confusion to strike at the one movement while he was striking at the other.

How did Newman come into all this? Newman, as we have seen, stood for a middle way. Opposed to the Ultramontane authoritarianism, he thought that reason should be used in order to reach the decision that the Church's authority should be accepted, but he was vigorously opposed to the so-called 'rationalism' which, having accepted the Church, would then turn upon it and question the details of its teaching. He would not have been inordinately horrified at Free Thinkers who denied the Christian story and the Church's claims; he was well aware that such men were common in the world of his day. But naturally enough he would have had no patience with men who claimed to remain within the Church and at the same time to reject the whole traditional story of Christ's life. Left to himself, he would have occupied his middle position and struck out impartially against those who made in the name of authority claims to which authority gave them no right and those who denied the proper rights of authority. In the time of Pius IX and Manning it was not easy to get that central position accepted. In the time of Leo XIII it was accepted. In the time of Pius X as a cloak of suspicion was cast over all speculation it became once more difficult to get it accepted. In the world of secret 'vigilance committees' the Catholic could no longer know where he stood. Secret meetings, delations one could not tell by whom, condemnations one could not tell for what, became the odious order of the day. The corruption of the character of those who were called upon to exercise authority in such a manner by far outweighed any good that might have been done by the suppression of error. It was impossible to pretend that the Catholic had any longer a right to be free.

The Modernists wished—indeed their very name told us that they were doing so—to preach doctrines different from those that had been taught in the past. They declared war on the static Catholics who had no ambition except to repeat what had been said by earlier generations. It was not surprising then perhaps that they should appeal to the example of Newman in support of what they were doing. For Newman, after all his troubles, had ended up a Cardinal and if they could show that they were merely saying what Newman had said, their condemnation would be difficult. And had not Newman defied the apostles of static dogma by asserting that doctrine must of its nature develop?

But there were of course in reality a number of differences between Newman's theory of the development of doctrine and the Modernists' assertion of novel doctrines. The Modernists contradicted previous doctrine. Where the teachers of earlier generations had said that Jesus Christ was the only 'Son of God, born of the Virgin Mary, who rose again the third day from the dead' the Modernists simply denied that these things were so or had ever happened. Newman when he preached a developing doctrine did not of course for a moment preach a novelty of doctrine. All Christian truth was to him implicit in the original teaching of Christ. From the first, Christians had been taught and had believed that Christ was both God and Man. It was only when Christians disputed among one another what these assertions meant that the Holy Ghost through the mouth of the Church defined their meaning. Did the fact that Christ was begotten mean that He was created? No, it did not. Had He two natures or one nature? Two wills or one will?

Secondly, Newman never claimed any right to teach the Church. He propounded a theory which professed to explain how the Church came to teach what it did teach. But the explanation, though important, was only of secondary importance. What was of primary importance was the teaching, and to Newman the notion that a man should repudiate the historical claims of the Gospel story and still call himself a Christian would have been simply unthinkable. The matter, Newman and the disciples of Newman would have argued, could only have ever appeared to be in dispute because the mind of the Vatican under Pius X thought of truth, as it were, on the Right. Truth was to such men authoritarian and therefore an assertion of liberty was temerarious. The doctrines of the Left were to be condemned root and branch, but even the doctrines of the Centre, though perhaps not absolutely heretical and absolutely to be condemned, were nevertheless suspect as tending to lead men to the Left—as a step in the wrong direction. Newman of course challenged that whole method of analysis, and his challenge, if perhaps out of favour in the Rome of Pius X, is most certainly wholly in favour in the Rome of John XXIII and Paul VI. To Newman truth was not on the Right with a moderate deviation from it in the Centre and an extreme deviation on the Left. Truth was in the Centre, from which both Right and Left were deviations—the Left in the direction of too little authority and the Right in the direction of too much.

The assertion that Newman was in any way responsible for the excesses of the Modernists is certainly untenable. In a letter[1] to Bishop O'Dwyer of Limerick Pius X gave it a direct repudiation. 'Be assured,' he wrote, 'that We strongly approve of your pamphlet proving that the works of Cardinal Newman—far from being at variance with Our encyclical—are actually in close agreement with it. . . . For even though in the works written before his conversion to the Catholic faith one might find statements which bear a certain likeness to some Modernist formulae, you rightly deny that they in any way support them. . . . But, as for the many and important books he composed as a Catholic, it is hardly necessary to repel the charges of affinity with the Modernist heresy. . . . Indeed though things might be found which appear different from the usual theological mode of expression, nothing can be found which would arouse any suspicion of his faith. . . . an excellent and most learned man. . . . You have done what you could among your own people and especially the English, to prevent those who have been abusing his name from deceiving the unlearned.'

Newman's theory of the doctrine of development is unassailable. In his theory he suggested a way of explaining and defending what was in fact the doctrine of the Church. The Modernists suggested a way of explaining away the doctrine of the Church—of suggesting that some-

[1] *Acta Sanctae Sedis*, 1908, XLI, p. 200.

thing different had happened from what the Church asserted. It needs no saying that that was a task from which Newman would have recoiled with horror. The weakness of the Modernists' case is revealed by its very title. Most men, said Dr. Johnson, 'have no reason for their opinions save fashion,' but this, though it is perhaps true, is not a creditable truth. In shaping a practical policy it is sensible to pay attention to the fashions of the day, for people will obey without compulsion the instructions which they expect. A wise statesman will, unless there is overwhelming reason to the contrary, preserve a monarchy in a land that has a tradition of monarchy—not because monarchy is in itself superior to a republic but because the people of that particular nation are accustomed to it. So, too, in religion it is reasonable in drafting rules of discipline to pay attention to the habits of the day. But it is absurd to look to fashion as a guide to opinions on doctrine or on the nature of God.

On the contrary the wise man will consider the fashionable opinions of his day, weed out those that are merely ephemeral from those that are inherited from the traditions of the ages, accord to the latter a real title of general consent and found his doctrines on them, but expect the former, as they have come with the day, to perish with the day. *Securus iudicat orbis terrarum* means not only that the general opinion of the world can sit in judgement on the eccentric inhabitants of one particular locality but, even more, that the general opinion of the generations can sit in judgement on the eccentrics of one particular age. It took a very little time for Modernism to show itself to be no more than it claimed to be—the fashion of a very rapidly passing age. It soon ceased to be even modern and by the years after the First World War Monsignor Knox was able to laugh at the Modernists by showing that they had none in their ranks who were less than sixty years of age. Of Newman on the other hand it could be argued that in the end and after much difficulty he created a fashion. It could not possibly be argued that he only adopted one. On the contrary when he first spoke his words were found novel and surprising and shocking. They have only later become fashionable because they have been found to be convincing.

Newman's critics profess to find evidence of his incipient Modernism not only in his theory of development but also in his *Grammar of Assent*. Now it is certainly true that the traditional Thomist apologetic began by giving its allegedly absolute proofs of the existence of God and, having, to its own satisfaction, established God's existence, went on to discuss Man's relationship to God. When Newman first visited Rome as a Catholic in the late 1840's he was, it will be remembered, mainly struck by the ignorance there of Thomist thought and it is certainly true that at that time Roman thought had sunk to a very low intellectual level, and its professors based their positions on a stock of text-book answers rather than on any solid understanding of the Thomist or of any other intellectual position.

But with the death of Pius IX and the accession of Leo XIII there had been a great renaissance in Catholic intellectual life. That Leo XIII did not himself think of Newman's writings with which he was well acquainted as dangerous or heretical is sufficiently proved by the honour that he paid to him. Yet there was no question that Leo, calling for a revival of Catholic philosophy, did very definitely assert that the new philosophy should be based on the principles of St. Thomas Aquinas. Now Newman, though he never overtly challenged St. Thomas, did certainly approach the fundamental problem of the existence of God along different lines. We may according to our choice say that he wrote as he did about St. Thomas simply to guard himself or we may think that he did so out of genuine humility. Whichever the interpretation, he had written in the *Apologia*,[1] 'I am speaking for myself only; and I am far from denying the real force of the arguments in proof of a God drawn from the general facts of human society, but these do not warm me or enlighten me; they do not take away the winter of my desolation or make the buds unfold and the leaves grow within me and my moral being rejoice.' For himself, 'were it not for this voice [the voice of conscience] speaking so clearly in my conscience and my heart I should be an atheist or a pantheist or a polytheist when I looked into the world.'

The difficulty, as indeed St. Thomas himself recognised, with the argument of First Cause is that, if the chain has to end somewhere with a *causa causans* and if in any event things go out into mystery, there is no reason why the universe should not have existed from eternity as freely as that it should have been created by God. It is true that we cannot wholly comprehend what the first proposition means, but then can we wholly comprehend what the second means? Of course if there was a beginning there must be a God, but why should there be a beginning? What does a time before there was time mean? To Newman

[1] *Apologia*, p. 278: Part VII.

the notion of deducing the existence of God from the existence of an external universe appeared to be a deduction of the sure from the unsure. To him the 'two luminous beings'—himself and God—were the two certain realities. All else was but a matter of probability. To him the existence of conscience within was far more certain than the existence of external reality and it was not possible to owe unless the debt was owed to Someone. To whom could it be owed except to God? and he therefore, like Immanuel Kant or Wordsworth, derived his certainty of the existence of God from his certainty of the existence of conscience within him. His was what was called a 'personalist' rather than an 'intellectualist' basis.

It is true of course that Father Tyrrell did use some language that has a certain appearance of similarity to this. He spoke of a Vital Immanence of God in Man, a Divine Permanence of God. But, whereas there was at any rate reason to think that with Loisy the 'divine spark within' was a substitute for a God beyond mankind, with Newman the divine spark was an evidence of God's existence. 'What is to prevent such experiences being found in any religion?' asked Pius X in his encyclical, condemning such personalist views as 'delirium', 'insanity', 'audacious sacrilege', a 'monstrosity'. They in fact differ very little from the views which are to-day recommended to all the faithful as almost of obligation in the Vatican Council's decrees on Religious Liberty, on non-Catholic and on non-Christian religions.

There were of course certain difficulties in St. Thomas' position, as indeed there are difficulties in any attempt to give a coherent solution to the ultimate mysteries. Does this prove, it may be asked, that there is a God transcendent to the universe—its Creator? May it not be merely that there is some mystical connection between the individual and the sum of things which makes it impossible for him to be content unless he in some way co-operates with its purposes? And, if the objector asks, 'What exactly does that mean?' or 'How can it be?' it may as reasonably be asked, 'What exactly does it mean to say that there is a God Who created the universe?' By any road we are forced back at last to an incomprehensible mystery and a form of words which of its nature only very inadequately expresses the truth.

All this did not greatly matter in the free society which it was the ambition of Leo to create. Leo was anxious only to recommend the study of the works of St. Thomas and no sensible man could doubt that St. Thomas' works deserved recommendation on their own merits and required recommendation in the de-intellectualised Rome which Pius IX had bequeathed to him. Leo was not so much concerned that clerics should read St. Thomas Aquinas in preference to other philosophers. He was rather concerned that they should read St. Thomas Aquinas in preference to reading nothing at all. In Leo's Rome there would certainly have been ample room for Thomism and Newmanism—and for frank and free debate between them from which both sides would doubtless benefit. Pius X's Rome was a different place. In Pius' Rome Thomas Aquinas was to be used not as a stimulant to thought but as an inquisitor—as a part of the revealed truth—as a test of orthodoxy from whom the Catholic student could only differ at peril. 'The scholastic philosophy,' said St. Pius, 'is to form the basis of all sacred studies.' And 'vigilance committees', which are to 'deliberate secretly' are to be set up in each diocese to collect any evidence of Modernist writing or teaching.' 'Bishops are to report to Rome every three years, and under oath, on the doctrines current amongst their clergy.'

Few will today deny that, grave as were the dangers of Modernism, they were, as we have said, small in comparison with the dangers of the methods that were taken against it, and of course, as is the happy habit of Rome, the extravagances of these demands have in fact been allowed quietly to sink into abeyance. The secret vigilance committees no longer meet. Teaching clerics are still required to take the anti-Modernist oath but they no more attend to its details than Anglican ordinands attend to the details of the Thirty-nine Articles. Of course the full gamut of the policy would have been as intolerable to Newman as to any other man of free mind, and he was fortunate to have been dead before the coming of what one of the most distinguished of modern theologians has called 'the reign of terror'.

As to the theory of development it is, as I have said, as a theory unassailable. There only begin to be difficulties when we come to ask if the theory wholly accounts for the facts. It is indeed plausible enough to argue that all the definitions of the early centuries arose out of controversies that had arisen within the Church. Men argued with one another what exactly was meant by the doctrine of the Divinity of Christ which all accepted. To still controversy the Church spoke and defined what was the doctrine. The controversy which led to the definition of the Papal infallibility in 1870 was, it might be argued, essentially of the same nature. Everyone had agreed since the early centuries that the Church had authority to teach and that the Pope was the Head of the Church. If so, what did authority to teach mean? Did it not of its nature mean infallibility? How can a teacher have authority if he may be wrong? And if the Church has infallibility, does not that mean that the Pope had under certain circumstances infallibility? And, if so, under what circumstances? Newman was of course, as we have seen, one of those who, while he did not doubt that the Pope had a certain infallibility, thought it better not to define the doctrine. But, wherever prudence might lie, it could not be denied that the papal controversy had about it the traditional pattern in that here was a generally received doctrine about whose implication there was difference of opinion and therefore it was well within the tradition of Catholic development that there should be a definition.

But Newman was unhappy about the definition and the manner of definition because he was concerned that some of those who called for it were anxious for a definition not merely in order that a disputed point might be made clear. They clamoured for the definition not because it was true but because it was 'a comfort for faith'. We have quoted Vaughan's dangerous argument in this sense. To Newman such a reason, coming as at that time it did, from the extreme Ultramontanes, was an illegitimate reason, and indeed bore a certain resemblance to the reasons for faith to be later advanced by the Ultramontanes' enemies, the Modernists. Truth to Newman had its own unshaken rights. There was only one possible justification for declaring a doctrine to be true, and that was that you believed it to be true.

However, though Newman was one of those who believed the declaration of papal infallibility to be inopportune, he had no doubt that it was true and no hesitation about accepting it as true when it was proclaimed. The other definition of those years—that of the Immaculate Conception—was of a somewhat different nature. Newman rejected unanswerably any misconception which imagined that the doctrine of the Immaculate Conception was something newly invented by Pius IX or imposed by him upon the Church. He showed that the doctrine had the tradition of centuries behind it and that, once granted the primal mystery of the Incarnation, there was no inherent improbability in its truth. 'It is,' he wrote in the *Apologia*,[1] 'a simple fact to say that Catholics have not come to believe it because it is defined but that it was defined because they believed it. . . . It was in consequence of the unanimous petition, presented from all parts of the Church to

[1] p. 288: Part VII.

the Holy See, on behalf of an *ex-cathedra* declaration that the doctrine was apostolic, that it was declared so to be.'

But whether it was opportune to declare it a dogma, to require belief in it, was of course quite another question. On that Newman never expressed his opinion. The fact that the Church had a right to define did not of course in itself prove that the definition was opportune.

12

Newman and the Aggiornamento

WHILE THE CENTRAL DOCTRINE of the Church is of course preserved unchanged over the generations, yet Pope varies greatly from Pope in his ideas of policy and his methods of approach. It is perhaps an unnecessary obstacle to the understanding of Vatican policy that, even when a Pope recommends a radically different tactic from that of a predecessor, it is never the custom for him to say so in so many words. Every Pope always speaks with the profoundest respect of his predecessors. It is for the student to discover the difference between them as best he may. Thus under Pius IX and his immediate predecessors the Papacy had almost gloried in its retreat into the catacombs. If it was told that an age was growing up to whom the Christian message would seem an irrelevance, its reaction was that that was an evidence of the folly and worthlessness of the age. If it was told that the new industrialism was creating grave social problems, its reaction was that there was no industrialism in the Papal States—that few of the workers in, and fewer still of the owners of, factories were Catholics and that therefore these problems were of little Catholic interest. Under Leo XIII, who had been almost the Leader of the Opposition in Rome during the closing years of Pius IX's reign, there was a great reaction. Leo conceived it as one of his main tasks to give to the world the Catholic teaching on the social problems of the age and did so in his *Rerum Novarum*. But these were not problems in which Newman took any special interest. Under Pius X the Papacy slipped back again. Social policies were reduced to minor proportions. The Pope was more concerned that those who interested themselves in them should not say anything heretical than that they should say anything sensible or should make any contribution to their solution. The reign was dominated by the theological battle against Modernism.

Yet the years of Pius' pontificate were the years during which the dark clouds of the coming European war were visibly gathering, and the Pope naturally watched their gathering with horror and despair. The times were, however, very different from the mediaeval days when a Pope like Innocent III could aspire to rule as arbitrator between the Christian princes and to impose peace upon them. Since the growth of the absolute national state in the seventeenth century, the Popes could no longer hope to impose their wills upon secular rulers. Pius VI made his protest against the French Revolutionaries and Pius VII made his protest against Napoleon, Pius IX against the Piedmontese when they attacked the Papal States. But they were no longer able in any way to aspire to mediate in the conflicts between secular rulers. Even Leo XIII, while he saw the importance of giving the Catholic teaching on social questions if the Church was to re-establish her teaching as relevant to the modern world, does not seem to have thought that it was possible or perhaps desirable for the Church to say anything on international politics. It is true that he allowed himself to be drafted by Bismarck into acting as arbitrator between Germany and Spain over the Caroline Islands. But this was a very minor gesture. In general he did not greatly preach a Catholic internationalism. Indeed as part of the settlement of the dispute with Bismarck over the Kulturkampf, he brought pressure to bear to induce the deputies of the German Catholic Centre party against their better judgement to vote for the German Government's enlarged military programme.

Leo XIII ascended the Papal throne in 1878 and died in 1903. During his reign it was perhaps possible to hope that the secular statesmen of Europe would by their own wisdom succeed in avoiding a major catastrophe. Pius X's reign from 1903 to 1914 was from this point of view more ominous and one in which it was less possible to be hopeful. Pius' last action was to reject the Austrian Emperor's request that he bless the Austrian declaration of war. He announced that his task was to bless peace rather than war and within a week he was dead. The Pope of the war years was Benedict XV and it was by war's awful problems that his pontificate was dominated. Whatever the case for the Pope's abstention from intervention so long as the secular Powers gave some appearance of an ability to arrange matters for themselves, it would have been absurd that a Pope should complacently allow European civilisation to destroy itself in fratricidal conflict and should find no word of Christian protest to utter against such a crime.

He protested against the system that had allowed such a situation to arise. He repealed the order of *Non Expedit* which up till then had barred the Catholic from Italian politics. Whatever the violations of freedom to which the unbridled economic competition against which Leo had protested may have given birth, they were as nothing to the violation of freedom by a regular system of military conscription even in time of peace, which had in the years since 1870 been adopted by every Continental European country. Benedict issued his protest against this system. He saw clearly the folly of the ambition of the two groups of European Powers to fight one another to a standstill. Victory in long-drawn-out quarrels goes always not to the one protagonist or the other but to a *tertius gaudens*, and he saw that the result of a long-drawn-out battle between the two European groups would not be the victory of the one group or the other but the overthrow of Europe's centuries-old hegemony. He saw the importance, if it were possible, of bringing the conflict to an end and in 1916 he made suggestions to the two groups that they should call their fighting off and make peace on a formula of No Annexations and No Indemnities. His suggestion of course met with no success. All that happened was that he was reviled by each side for being a pawn of the other, though few today would be found who would not regret that attention was not paid to his wisdom rather than to the follies of the secular statesmen. But our concern is with Newman.

Newman, as has been said, never particularly concerned himself with the social problems of which Leo spoke so much, but he was almost alone among the Catholic leaders of the nineteenth century to concern himself with the morality of war. When the Crimean War broke out, Newman applied his mind to its challenge, and decided that it could not be called a just war. He therefore opposed it. He developed his thesis under the title of *Catholicus* in a series of letters to the *Catholic Standard*, entitled 'Who's To Blame?'. He had already in some public lectures, given in Liverpool, examined the history of the Turks and reached the conclusion that their record was not one in support of which it was justifiable to send men to fight in a war. The letters are interesting as giving one of the few expositions of Newman's purely political opinions. He argued that free Parliamentary institutions were best suited for a nation in peace but were not competent for war. This, however, was not a disadvantage as it ought to have the consequence of making such a country reluctant to go to war. He had a great admiration for John Bright in whose constituency the Birmingham Oratory was

situated and rebuked Simpson of the *Rambler* when he spoke harshly of
him. 'He is our member,' he wrote,[1] 'and it is not so often that you get
so honest a man. And I should not like to commit myself to opposition
to him'. It was, Newman argued, a great advantage to have a strong
and united nation, as he believed that Britain had, like the Athens of
classical times, and not the least of such advantages was that it was then
not necessary to have a strong government—a thing which was undesirable. It was only when the nation was divided that the State had
to pursue policies of violent repression in order to save society from
disorder.

Newman argued that the Napoleonic wars and the victories of the
Duke of Wellington had been misfortunes for England. They had given
a prestige to military victory which did not suit the British character
and which was certainly opposed to all Christian teaching. He denounced the pagan jingoism which was carrying the nation into an
unnecessary war in the Crimea. He was shocked by the support of it by
a professing Christian like Charles Kingsley and doubly shocked when
Kingsley, in order to show that he did not believe that the average
English, as opposed to Irish, Catholic was any longer disloyal, pointed
—probably justly enough—to the number of English Catholics who
had fallen in the war. The pretence that this was in some ways a
Catholic war because it had nominally broken out over a conflict
between Greek and Latin monks and because Napoleon III, at that
time still the defender of the Pope in Rome, posed as a pretended
defender of the Catholic cause Newman dismissed in appalled silence.
England, he thought, was a country that had been able to preserve
freedom because she had been careful to avoid war. If she allowed
herself to become an imperialist nation she would inevitably lose her
freedom.

It is not very clear where he imagined that he found this peace-loving
period in English history, but at least that was how he argued. He argued
the more vigorously because he himself he confessed, felt the attraction
of the soldier's life. Reading the Duke of Wellington's dispatches, he
confessed, made him 'burn to be a soldier'. But such an attraction was, he
thought, a dangerous attraction. Power corrupted. 'May I,' he wrote,[2]
'never be a Minister of State or a Field Marshal!' It may have been
simply because he underrated the dangers when catastrophe was avoided. Yet he was no opponent of a moderate display of braggadocio

[1] May 25, 1859, *Light in Winter*, p. 196.   [2] '*Who's To Blame?*'

provided that it did not end in war. He was not, like so many of his friends, committed to Gladstonian liberalism. Twenty years after the Crimea, at the time of the Congress of Berlin, he supported Disraeli and was mocked at by his friend, Dean Church,[1] for doing so.

'As to Disraeli's fireworks,' Newman wrote to Blatchford, 'I confess I am much dazzled with it and wish it well. It is a grand idea, that of hugging from love the Turk to death instead of the Russian bear, which, as a poem of romance, finds a weak part in my imagination. And then it opens such a view of England, great in the deeds of her forefathers, showing that they are not degenerate sons but rising with the occasion to the fulfilment of the *"tu ne cede malis sed contra audentior ito."*[2] And then it is so laughably clever a move in a grave diplomatic congress— and then it opens up such wonderful views of the future that I am over- come by it.' Church mocked: 'How curious that he should be dazzled and what a curious bit of English feeling. . . . I should think that N. was almost the unique cross between a true Briton of the proud school of Chatham and Burke and the enthusiastic, devout, fervid Roman Catholic.' Many will feel that Church had the better of it and that the Newman of the Crimea had a sounder case than the Newman of the Congress of Berlin. Yet of course it must be remembered, when we appraise Newman's verdict on Disraeli that Disraeli had not led us into war. He had brought back from Berlin—according at least to his own boast—'Peace with honour'.

Yet, whatever his views on war, naturally Newman did not foresee a cataclysmal war which would threaten the whole fabric of civilisation. He still lived in an age which took the achievement of civilisation for granted—as something finally attained which no wickedness or folly could ever again shake. He did not foresee the sort of threat with which Benedict found himself faced. Still less did he foresee the development of modern weapons of such power as to make it almost impossible, according to the opinions of Pius XII[3] and John XXIII,[4] that war in modern conditions will be contained within the boundaries permitted by Catholic traditions. It is on other fields than this that we must look for the special significance of Newman in the modern world.

[1] B. A. Smith, *Dean Church*, Chapter X, p. 292.
[2] Yield not to evil, but proceed boldly against it.
[3] Address to 8th Congress of the World's Medical Association, September 30, 1954.
[4] *Pacem in Terris.*

Dean Inge, in his not unsympathetic study of Newman in his essays on *Newman* and on *Roman Catholic Modernism*, prophesies that the future of the Catholic Church will almost certainly lie with the Catholicism of Manning rather than with the Catholicism of Newman. The Modernists in the pretended name of scholarship had demanded a rejection of the traditional Christian story far more radical than, in Inge's opinion, any sane scholarship could justify. He did not quarrel with Pius X for condemning Loisy and Tyrrell. Still, in the Dean's opinion, the Church was being driven by an inner law of its own nature to an ever more rigid repression of all freedom of thought. There was no real place within its ranks for such men as Newman who continued to claim a right to think for themselves. Inevitably with the coming years, thought Inge, men of independent mind would leave, or be expelled by, the Church. It would survive only as a shrinking, defensive body. The cultural life of the world would treat it increasingly as an irrelevance to all its serious problems.

Dean Inge wrote his essays in 1908—in the very centre of the reign of Pius X and of his campaign against Modernism. His prophecies did not at that time appear improbable. In the years between the wars and throughout the pontificates of Pius XI and Pius XII the vigour of repression abated, but yet it was not possible confidently to say whether on balance things were moving in the direction of greater repression or greater freedom. During these two reigns one can fairly say that Newman's reputation was such that he was no longer under taint of suspicion for heresy or Modernism. The Societies and institutions that adopted his name increased all over the world. Newman was in many ways in his personal habits the most insular of men. In his *Parochial Sermons* when he wants to find a secular parallel to the awful loneliness of a damned soul if it should be summoned to heaven, he can think of nothing better than that of having to live among foreigners. 'How miserable,' he says,[1] 'for example, would it be to have to live in a foreign land among a people whose faces we never saw before and whose language we could not learn.' Yet by a curious paradox his fame, owing to the writings of such men as Bremond and Przywara—even though Bremond's interpretations were by no means universally accepted—was growing more rapidly on the Continent than in England. In America his name was a title name even if his name was perhaps better known than his works.

[1] *Parochial Sermons*, I. 6.

But he had not yet attained the position which he was to attain under John XXIII and Paul VI as a unique forerunner of things to come. 'The cloud is lifted from me for ever,' Newman had said when he received the news of Leo's conferment on him of the Cardinal's hat. Thenceforward his had been beyond serious challenge an honoured name in the Catholic records. But it was only with John XXIII that the spirit of Newman was adopted in an explicit and special sense as the spirit which more than any other was to direct the future of the Church. The votes of the Vatican Council have signified the acceptance by the overwhelming majority of the bishops of the Newmanite interpretation of Christianity. How far votes will be reflected in actions remains to be seen.

The view that there was a total volte-face of Papal policy when John XXIII succeeded Pius XII is of course an absurdity. In much of his policy—in his liturgical reforms, in his encouragement of biblical studies and in a way even in his ecumenical contacts—John, as he himself was the first to confess, was following in the footsteps of Pius. There were indeed some matters upon which Pius was more progressive than John. Yet it is an equal absurdity which pretends that Pope John was merely a good old man, thumbing the pious pages of Father Faber. John's great achievement was that he broke a sound barrier. He was not the first Pope to love all mankind. But he was the first Pope to convince all mankind that he loved it. He won the affection of men and women of every race and creed in a degree to which few, if any, in history have ever won it. Doing so, he created a great opportunity not only for the Church but also for the Christian spirit, of which it is still to be seen whether we shall be able to take advantage.

Pope John's call for *aggiornamento* did not in any way put him into opposition to his immediate predecessors but it did mean that his whole conception of the Church was a conception radically different from that of either Pius IX or Pius X, even though Leo XIII and Benedict XV would neither of them have found it unsympathetic. Whereas the earlier Piuses thought of the Church as an institution on the defensive and of Catholics as people whose faith was to be protected against a wicked and godless world, John thought of Christ as the bringer of universal love, as the God who had died for all men and whose divine message must be carried to all men. This meant that, looking back over a hundred years, John's mind was much closer to the liberal Catholic thinkers of the nineteenth century, whom Pius IX so severely snubbed, than it was to Pius himself. It cannot seriously be denied that this was so, uncertain as it may still be where the final victory will lie, and of course it meant that John was much more sympathetic, as Leo had been more sympathetic, to Newman than were Pius IX or Pius X. But, it may fairly be asked, is there any justification for giving to Newman a unique position among the nineteenth-century thinkers as a dominating influence over the Second Vatican Council? Was not the spirit of Dupanloup and Montalembert, Ketteler and Moriarty also there present? If Lammenais and Dollinger towards the end of their lives fell into defiance of the Church were there not lessons to be learned from their earlier years?

It would seem today a paradox were one to agree with Dean Inge's opinion that the future of the Church was likely to lie with Manning rather than with Newman. Whether Manning was too authoritarian even for his day or whether it was desirable that there should be a period of authority in order to redress a balance and to make Catholicism strong and known we need not discuss here. But no one would, I fancy, today deny that Manning was at the best a man for a period while Newman saw into the generations of the future and spoke for an age that was yet to come, indeed 'a man for all seasons'. But that means that Newman was never a mere party-leader. He is not even a party leader today. His influence is not confined to the progressive majority in the Council. The conservative minority and those who with the Pope have been working to prevent divisions in the Church have equally been able to find their inspiration from his work. It would be a great mistake if, to apply the present phraseology, we sought to label Manning as a conservative and Newman as a progressive. In this, as in all things, Newman's way was always the middle way. In the present controversies the progressives no doubt have the better of the argument but it is necessary to appreciate the fear of honest conservatives who think that there is a danger that in the passions of *aggiornamento* the progressives will abandon the whole claim of the Church to be the uniquely divine institution and see it as merely one among a number of religious bodies. If there be such a fear and if there be on occasion reason for such a fear, it goes without saying that there is no difficulty in finding passage after passage in Newman which insists on the necessity for the Church to assert without qualification her divine nature. Between the two extremes stands Newman, asserting alike the just rights of authority and the supremacy of reason, in his wider sense of the word.

The justification for claiming that Newman had a unique influence over the deliberations of the Council is derived from the Fathers' own confessions. It was Cardinal Gracias from India who told the Council[1] in its debates on collegiality that Newman's *Essay on the Development of Christian Doctrine* was the test whereby the Council ought to proceed. Above all it was Pope Paul VI[2] who, at the celebration of the Beatification of Dominic Barberi, gave his especial tribute to Newman. He spoke of Newman as 'the promoter and representative of the Oxford Movement, which raised so many religious questions and excited such great spiritual energies. . . . who, in full consciousness of his mission— "I have a work to do"—and guided solely by love of the truth and fidelity to Christ, traced an itinerary the most toilsome but also the greatest, the most meaningful, the most conclusive that human thought ever travelled during the last century, indeed one might say during the modern era, to arrive at the fullness of wisdom and of peace.'

If we accept it that the Pope was here choosing his words with meticulous care—which it is only reasonable to suppose that he was on such an occasion as this—then this was a very extraordinary tribute. Newman's itinerary was 'the most toilsome but also the greatest, the most meaningful, the most conclusive, that human thought ever travelled during the modern era.' Could words be stronger? The superlatives seem to mark him out as of a different class from that of any of those who worked with him. He was guided 'solely by love of the truth' at a time when, as we have seen, others—some in the Ultramontane camp and some in the Modernist—were clamouring for or against new assertions of authority on the ground that such assertions would or would not prove advantageous. Do not the Pope's words justify us in saying that, whatever virtues we may justly find in other characters, Newman's influence over the Council was unique? Newman had, it will be remembered, from the very moment of the decision of the First Council, foreseen and prophesied the inevitability of a second Council. Who else had shown such prophetic wisdom? It was Pope John who fulfilled Newman's prophecy.

Why was Newman's influence unique? We can say with Cardinal Gracias that his *Essay on Development*, at its first issue somewhat suspect, has now been almost officially adopted as the doctrine of the Church. We could say almost the same of the *Grammar of Assent*. He pleaded,

---

[1] Michael Novak, *The Open Church*, p. 111.

[2] Herder, *Correspondenz*, January 1964.

and almost got himself condemned, for his championship of the apostolate of the laity which now is officially proclaimed. Catholic policy is increasingly stamped by his ideas on education. He championed what are today the accepted rights of the scholar in biblical interpretation. He found, in short, the Church at one of the lowest moments of its history a servile society and turned it into a free society. It would be hard to find any other character in the Church's history who has so totally transformed the nature of Catholic apologetics.

Mr Coulson[1] is amply justified in claiming that he did this fundamentally because he was the first of ecumenists. He of course believed that it was the duty of a Christian to preach the good news to all people, but he did not mean by that that success could be measured by crude statistics of immediate conversions—nor did conversions come, nor was Christ most worthily served, primarily by preaching to other people. What was primarily desirable was that the Catholic should be worthy of Christ. The consequences of that worthiness lay with God rather than with Man. 'To me,' he wrote,[2] 'conversions were not the first thing, but the edification of Catholics.' A true conversion must necessarily be a slow business, a gradual turning of the whole personality. Quick conversions and mass conversions were to be suspect. Organisation was necessary but the obsession with it was dangerous. 'We want seminaries far more than sees,' he wrote. 'We want education, view, combination, organisation—above all view. It is cruel that so many able men are doing so little.'[3]

Newman, when first he became a Catholic, thought it his duty to show why he had left the position which he had previously held. It was doubly his duty to do this when in his dark hours some gossiping tongues were putting it about that he was repenting of his change, and in those earlier years he on occasions—as in the Lectures on Anglican Difficulties or in Loss and Gain—rebutted Anglican arguments with a force of satirical ridicule which some of his admirers cannot help but a little regret. In the later years of his life after the Apologia and after his renewal of his Anglican friendships he had neither need nor wish to write thus.

It was between 1868 and 1881 that Newman supervised the re-

[1] *Theology and the University.*

[2] Journal. January 21, 1863. *Autobiographical Writings*, p. 258.

[3] Letter on the Restoration of the Hierarchy. See J. Coulson, *Newman: A Portrait Restored*, p. 15.

publication of his works, including his Anglican works, in a uniform edition. The suggestion of the republication of these Anglican sermons came from Copeland, his old curate at Littlemore, still an Anglican clergyman. The purpose of them was, as Copeland put it in his *Selections of Parochial and Plain Sermons*, 'the promotion of mutual sympathy between estranged communions and alienated hearts.' 'The division of the Churches,' said Newman himself, in Sermon Ten on *Subjects of the Day*, 'is the corruption of hearts.' He had said his say on the points on which the denominations differed. But no one had better reason than he to know of the volume of sincere Christian faith that there was among many who were not Catholics, and of the harm and unnecessary obstacle to unity created by many Catholics who ignored this sincerity. Device and policy were both hateful things—hateful when employed in any cause—diabolical when employed, as they sometimes were, in the supposed cause of religion. Our obligation was to truth. It was for God to settle what consequences might follow from the telling of it. 'My view,' wrote Newman to Copeland, 'has ever been to answer and not to suppress what is erroneous—merely as a matter of expedience for the cause of truth, at least at this day. It seems to me a bad policy to suppress. Truth has a power of its own, which makes its way; it is stronger than error.'

Yet the path of truth was a difficult path. A simpleton imagined that getting better was a straightforward business and that the saint was in every way a more attractive man than the unsaintly, and the man on the road to it more attractive than he who was not attempting the journey. It was not so. Every rung of the ladder to heaven had its own especial temptations. 'No paradox,' he had once written[1] to Dalgairns, 'is truer than this, that the higher we are in holiness the more we are in danger of going wrong. I have been accustomed to compare the ascent to perfection to the mounting of a higher ladder. As the climber gets higher the ladder dances under him—behold the state of the soul mounting towards heaven. I thus account for the wonderful falls of holy men —the utter shipwreck of ascetics—the heresies of grave and learned teachers—the delusions in which Satan enwraps souls which he cannot on the whole separate from God. This is why saints are so few—they drop off as they get more likely to be saints.'

To Newman's mind Christ founded a Church. There was and there must be a machinery of authority. How else could we be protected from

[1] *Newman: A Portrait Restored*, p. 21.

error? The machinery must be respected, but Newman never made the mistake of thinking that it was the machinery to which his devotion was owed. In his early years as a Catholic when he was still engaged on the Dublin University project he had indeed thought[1] that 'over and above the attribute of infallibility which attached to the doctrinal decisions of the Holy See, a gift of sagacity had in every age characterised its occupants. Further experience of Pius IX made this sentiment. . . very considerably weakened as far as the present Pope is concerned.' English Catholicism, he wrote in 1863 to Miss Bowles, was under a quasi-military power. In contrast, the Middle Ages seemed to him to 'have a manliness and boldness of which now there is so great a lack.' Yet whatever the truth about these matters they were secondary. Popes and Bishops and ecclesiastics were necessary. Decentralisation, which is now so much in the air, was in Newman's opinion desirable. Far too much authority was concentrated in Rome and the unwieldy bureaucracy creaked in its machinery.

Yet the issue was not as simple as some of the reformers today believe it to be. It is easy enough to point to examples where justice has been denied or too much delayed because of overcentralisation. But there have also been examples both in the past and in the present where it has been a great blessedness for the Church that there existed a strong independent voice at Rome which could speak without fear of persecutors or local influences. The faithful in countries of persecution can be thankful that there is the voice at Rome which can still speak when the local prelates are either silenced, or have their words twisted or are unable to speak except under duress. When the cause of decentralisation was too unguardedly pressed at the Vatican Council, it was the Ukrainian Archbishop Slipyi, only released a few weeks before from a Siberian prison camp, who pleaded for the preservation of a strong authority at Rome. The progressives have too easily forgotten the days of the First World War. In that war the local bishops of all the belligerent countries with few, if any exceptions, fell timid victims to the nationalistic cause of their particular nation. Each became little more than its nation's flagwagger. It was the voice of Pope Benedict, and his almost alone, which saved the honour of the Church and spoke gravely with a truly Christian voice to the City and the World.

Yet, however such things may be, religion was not about Popes and bishops and ecclesiastics, necessary as they might be. Religion was

[1] *Autobiographical Writings*. Memorandum. The Catholic University, p. 320.

about Christ, and in devotion to Christ Newman found himself able to join hands with those of other denominations from whom he was in other ways divided, each recognising the personal insufficiency of their men of authority, whether their orders were valid or invalid. The last tribute and the clearest analysis of Newman's mind came from the most intimate of his Anglican friends, Dean Church, in his obituary notice in the *Guardian*. It is a tribute the more valuable because it came from one who on a nice balance of judgement took the opposite side to that of Newman—one who remained to the end within the Church of England and was at the time of this writing its most distinguished son. After speaking with sorrow of the time of estrangement immediately after Newman's conversion Church wrote,[1]

'As time went over him in his new position two things made themselves felt. One was that though there was a New Testament life lived in the Roman Church with conspicuous truth and reality, yet the Roman Church, like the English, was administered and governed by men—men with passions and faults, men of mixed characters—who had, like their English contemporaries and rivals, ends and rules of action not exactly like those of the New Testament. The Roman Church had to accept, as much as the English, the modern conditions of social and political life, however different in outward look from those of the Sermon on the Mount. The other was the increasing sense that the civilisation of the West was as a whole, and notwithstanding grievous drawbacks, part of God's providential government, a noble and beneficent thing, ministering graciously to man's peace and order, which Christians ought to recognise as a blessing of their times, such as their fathers had not, for which they ought to be thankful and which, if they were wise, they would put to what, in his phrase was an "apostolical" use.'

Church would not for a moment listen to any suggestion that Newman at any time after his conversion had even for a moment wavered in his loyalty to the Church of his adoption.[2] 'The force,' he wrote, 'with which these two things made themselves felt as age came on—the disappointments attending his service to the Church and the grandeur of the physical and social order of the world and its divine sanction in spite of all that is evil and all that is short-lived—produced a softening in his ways of thought and speech. Never for a moment did

[1] *Occasional Papers*, Vol. II, p. 472: 'Via Media.'
[2] *Ibid.*

his loyalty and obedience to his Church, even when most tried, waver and falter. The thing is inconceivable to anyone who ever knew him, and the mere suggestion would be enough to make him blaze forth in all his old fierceness and power. But, perfectly satisfied of his position, and with his duties clearly defined, he could allow large and increasing play, in the leisure of his advancing age, to his natural sympathies and to the effect of the wonderful spectacle of the world around him. He was after all an Englishman; and with all his quickness to detect and denounce what was selfish and poor in English ideas and action and with all the strength of his deep antipathies, his chief interests were for things English.'

But England was not Christendom. Where was the Christian life to be found?

'Form after form was tried by him, the Christianity of Evangelicalism, the Christianity of Whately, the Christianity of Hawkins, the Christianity of Keble and Pusey; it was all very well but it was not the Christianity of the New Testament and of the first ages. He wrote *The Church of the Fathers* to show that they were not merely evidences of religion but really living men; that they could and did live as they taught, and what was there like the New Testament or even the first ages now? Alas, there was nothing completely like them; but of all unlike things, the Church of England with its "smug parsons" and pony carriages for their wives and daughters, seemed to him the most unlike; more unlike than the great unreformed Roman Church with its strange, unscriptural doctrines and its undeniable crimes and its alliance, wherever it could, with the world. But at least the Roman Church had not only preserved, but maintained at full strength through the centuries to our day two things of which the New Testament was full and which are characteristic of it—devotion and self-sacrifice. The crowds at a pilgrimage, a shrine or a "pardon" were much more like the multitudes who followed Our Lord about the hills of Galilee—like them probably in their imperfect faith which we call superstition—than anything that could be seen in the English Church even if the Salvation Army were one of its instruments.'

One does not, it must be confessed, naturally think of Newman as a man who would have been at his ease sharing the loaves and fishes of the five thousand or even indeed on a pilgrimage to Lourdes. Pope John XXIII would, one might think, have moved about more comfortably in such a company. One pictures Newman more easily in a study or a library or at the most in a pulpit. Wherever the fault may have been, his personal relations were not always without difficulty, but when we think of the scholar, when we think of the controversialist, when we think of the sensitive man so often involved in personal difficulties, we must not forget at the same time the recognition which those who knew him invariably gave to his unique charm and capacity for friendship—and that in an age in which it was strangely rare for one clergyman to speak with charity of another clergyman. Ward, who was far from uncritical in his admiration, confessed that there was no man whom he had ever met who carried with him the charm that Newman carried, and Newman, in his later years at any rate, distributed his friendship not by denomination but by love. It was his personality which was his uniquely ecumenical gift. As Dean Church wrote in a notice of the *Apologia*, 'Surely never did any man break so utterly with a Church, who left so many sympathies behind him or took so many with him, who continued to feel so kindly and with such large-hearted justice to those from whom his changed position separated him in this world for ever.'[1]

[1] *Occasional Papers*, Vol. II, p. 386.

Bibliographical Note

The literature on Newman is so voluminous that no purpose could be served by attempting a complete bibliography. It will be sufficient to mention a few books most likely to be of use to a reader interested in these studies.

The first ambition of such a student will be naturally to read Newman himself. In *Newman: A Portrait Restored* by Coulson and Alchin (Sheed and Ward, Stagbook, 1965), Mr. Coulson has included a Guide to Newman's Works, which were all published in uniform editions between 1868 and 1881. The first authoritative *biography* of him was written by Wilfrid Ward and appeared in 1912. Long before that, almost immediately after his death, there had appeared the strange memoirs of his brother, highly critical of the Cardinal's character, entitled *Contributions to the Early History of Cardinal Newman*, and at about the same time the *Life* by R. H. Hutton was published. *Newman's Letters and Correspondence*, edited by Anne Mozley, appeared in 1890. They are somewhat edited in a Victorian fashion and all of the Cardinal's many references to his bowels are excised. From the Anglican point of view, the most important nineteenth-century work is Dean Church's *The Oxford Movement*. There are, of course, in the Victorian fashion, full-length biographies of all those, Catholic or Anglican, with whom Newman has dealings of importance.

Newman's Autobiographical Writings, edited by Father Tristram with additional notes by Father Dessain, appeared in 1956 (Harrap). Father Fergal McGrath's *Newman's University: Idea and Reality* was published in 1951 (Longmans). Maisie Ward's *Young Mr Newman* was published in 1952 (Sheed and Ward), and Sean O'Faolain's *Newman's Way* in 1952 (Longmans).

Foreign literature on Newman is also voluminous. Bremond's *Newman*, Przywara's *Newman's Synthesis* (in six volumes in German but reduced to one in the abridged English edition, Sheed and Ward, 1930), and Father Bouyer's *Newman, His Life and Spirituality* (Burns & Oates, 1958) should be mentioned. So should *Newman: A Portrait Restored* by Coulson and Alchin (above referred to) and the essay on Newman's Idea of an Educated Laity by Mr. Coulson in *Theology and the University* (Darton, Longman and Todd, 1964).

But amid a voluminous literature which is today steadily pouring out, the two major debts of every lover of Newman are certainly owed to Miss Meriol Trevor for her definitive two-volume Life: *The Pillar of the Cloud* and *Light in Winter* (Macmillan) and to Father Dessain, whose unflagging industry is still engaged on completing his total collection of *Newman's Letters* (Nelson). Father Dessain's own biography of Newman, *John Henry Newman* (Nelson) has already appeared. I am indebted to Miss Trevor for her generous permission to let me use her work as a quarry for Newman quotations.

A full bibliography of works on papal policy from Pius IX to the present day would, again, in itself require a volume. The best author to whom to send a reader for a summary is Mr. E. E. Y. Hales with his *The Catholic Church and the Modern World* and *Pope John and his Revolution* (both Eyre and Spottiswoode). Father Tyrrell's works should be studied to see the argument from the Modernist side, and along with them, Lewis May's *Father Tyrrell and the Modernist Movement* (Eyre and Spottiswoode) and the essays on Newman and on the Roman Catholic Modernists in Dean Inge's *Outspoken Essays* (Longmans).

The time is too close for definitive works about the recent Vatican Council. But a number of studies have appeared in English as in other languages—the English ones mainly from America. One may mention Xavier Rynne's three volumes, Robert Kaiser's *Inside the Council* (Burns & Oates), Michael Novak's *The Open Church* (Darton, Longman and Todd, 1964), R. McAfee Brown's *John XXIII*, Father Purdy's *The Church on the Move* (Hollis & Carter, 1966). Of these, Professor Novak's book is perhaps the most valuable for these particular studies. The full text of the Council's decrees has been published by Messrs Chapman and full running commentaries on its proceedings appeared month by month throughout its progress in Herder *Correspondenz*. These reports are particularly valuable for the references made by the Pope, Cardinal Gracias and others to Newman.

C.H.

Index

Index